The Jewish Inn in Polish Culture

This book is a publication of

Indiana University Press
Office of Scholarly Publishing
Herman B Wells Library 350
1320 East 10th Street
Bloomington, Indiana 47405 USA
iupress.org

First Printing 2025

A version of chapter 6 was published as "Weathering the Crisis" in *The Light of Learning* by Glenn Dynner [New York: Oxford University Press, 2024] and is reprinted with permission. An earlier version of chapter 10 was published as "Ciulim lelowski jako lokalne dziedzictwo jedzeniowe" in *Lelowianie, Polacy, Żydzi. Szkice etnograficzne o konstruowaniu lokalnego dziedzictwa* by Magdalena Zatorska [Warsaw: Wydawnictwo Uniwersytetu Warszawskiego, 2018] and is used with permission.

Cataloging information is available from the Library of Congress.

ISBN 978-0-253-07292-4 (hardcover)
ISBN 978-0-253-07293-1 (paperback)
ISBN 978-0-253-07294-8 (epub)
ISBN 978-0-253-07295-5 (pdf)

CONTENTS

PREFACE: AN INVITATION TO THE JEWISH INN

Bożena Shallcross

To begin with an ending, one of the last literary mentions of a visit to an authentic Jewish inn was penned by Alfred Döblin in his *Journey to Poland*.[1] The year was 1924, and the inn was in Gura Kalwarja (Pol. Góra Kalwaria, Yid. Ger), a town that was a location of the Gerrer Hasidim and their famous rebbe—the main reason for the prominent German-Jewish writer's visit. The rebbe's presence there was also the source of the inn's business, as Hasidic men stayed there during their pilgrimage to receive the rebbe's blessing.[2] Döblin's short visit was but a glimpse of this old cultural formation that—in its numerous iterations and shapes—was soon to disappear along with the entire Jewish world in Eastern Europe. The Ger innkeeper opened the door. His wife and daughter scrutinized the guests with their gaze. They served only cold food and no alcohol—these delinquencies signaled the ongoing decline of such sites of hospitality. The guests nonetheless did not express disappointment.

Alter Kacyzne, the Polish-Jewish photographer known for his ethnographic inclination, offered a more sympathetic glimpse at a Jewish inn's interiority during the 1920s (fig. 0.1). His camera captured a rare ethnographic moment as it embraced an old innkeeper and his wife seated in a room crowded with simple furniture. The presence of innkeepers' wives seldom interrupted the patriarchal iconography of the inn, in both its photographic and pictorial versions. Kacyzne's shot is even more intriguing because the couple avoids the conventional, straight gaze toward the camera.

Figure 0.1 "Jewish Innkeeper and His Wife," Suchostaw, Tarnopol province. Photo by Alter Kacyzne, 1920s. YIVO, RG 1270 f. 615. Reproduced by permission of YIVO Institute for Jewish Research.

She attempts a smile; he slightly leans toward her while looking at her. Their body language bespeaks a long-gone intimacy in which a strong togetherness in poverty persists. Their large, worn hands—actors of the hospitable everyday—foreground the inn's narrative of labor.

The Polish ethnographer Zygmunt Gloger considered hospitality as the inn's most important (business) function, but the inn was a much more complex site that, out of necessity, had to play several simultaneous functions.[3] Ancient tradition, respected across continents and ages, required that travelers, local or not, be given assistance while on the road—a certain form of altruism that ultimately benefited both sides. Hospitality was not just an inherited old concept but a historical process revived through nuanced exchanges and negotiations between host and guest that resulted in the innkeeper's and his customers' (dis)satisfaction. Economic competition and antisemitic bias often deformed its business component as well as polarized anxieties of hospitality. These aspects of hospitality extended beyond the complementary roles of guest and host in the historical formation of the Jewish inn, for the inn's business almost always involved one more actor: a gentile landowner who leased the inn to a Jewish lessee and host.

The walls of a generic inn provided a sanctuary for hosts and customers alike to engage in a variety of activities that were sometimes at odds with one another: rest, vivid conversations, eating, business dealings, and entertainment; for the latter, music, dance, and drinking were indispensable. Unostentatious, wooden, and shabby, the Jewish inn was easily overlooked or avoided by seekers of high-quality comfort or sophisticated pastimes. Yet even today the phenomenon of the inn marks a remarkable affective reflection and symbolization. Therefore, the present volume identifies the inn as an important symbolic incubator of Jewish cultural possibilities and probes its changing artistic potential across ages, through varying genres, media, and analytical approaches. The Jewish inn opens the reader to the vernacular as well as the void and absence. The suggestion of absence is not simply due to the genocidal destruction during World War II, but also to the psychic and imaginary absence that characterizes the Jewish inn's first, foundational iterations.

The authors of the volume are interested in a specific instantiation of the inn as the place of the Other, in the *żydowska karczma* (Jewish inn), and not in the inns that belonged to local parish priests or other owners. As a public space of consumption and entertainment, the inn was both a place of transit, a temporary shelter for travelers, and a site of respite from daily toils for locals. Over time, it transformed into a multifunctional core of the village life that answered all practical needs. Hirsz Abramowicz eloquently and tenderly described Jewish inns as sites of the everyday, emphasizing their manifold uses that went beyond their main operation. For all practical purposes, they functioned as shops and repair shops, where "one could buy a box of matches, cigarettes or cheap tobacco, a glass of beer or *kvas*. Also available were tar or grease for wheels, leather straps, nails, etc. . . . At the inn, one could care of whatever might occur on the roads: a broken axle, hub or linchpin, or a torn yoke thong."[4] From the innkeeper's point of view, it was a place of labor, habitation, and business whose concrete everydayness he shared with his family and customers (gentry or peasants) in need of a space suitable for diverse business dealings and amusements. These functions intersected with a scarcity of comfort; travelogues and memoirs written across ages detail lack of privacy and excessive noise as constant themes of complaint. Such nuisances were due to the building's simple structural layout, where the few bedrooms for travelers were next to one large common room in which other guests enjoyed loud conversation

Figure 0.2 "The Court Inn," Bukowiec, Lower Silesia. Photo, 1952. Politechnika Wrocławska, DUN1/NS/39/2179. Lower Silesian Digital Library. https://dbc.wroc.pl/publication/56538. Image courtesy of Biblioteka Politechniki Wrocławskiej.

and entertainment, including important events like weddings, which often took place in inns. Occasionally, even courts were located or held sessions there; one such court inn still stands in Bukowiec (see fig. 0.2).

The multifunctionality of such establishments is captured in the abundant Polish terminology. Words such as *wyszynk* or *szynk* (Yid. *shenk*) highlight their alcohol-serving function, while the word *zajazd* emphasizes their purpose as lodgings. Other terms, such as *oberża*, *austeria*, and *karczma* (Yid. *kretchme*), are used interchangeably, referencing both functions. We selected "inn"—the English word that encompasses both purposes—for our title, but allowed for the use of other related terms, such as "tavern," to capture this semantic interchangeability.

Recognizable as a distinctive type of vernacular architecture, the inn stood out as a salient part of the cultural landscapes of what are today Polish, Lithuanian, Belarusian, Ukrainian, and, to a lesser extent, Russian lands. Various historical sources (documents, paintings, drawings, photography, several literary genres including letters) indicate that the typical inn had an arcaded facade buttressed by pillars or columns supporting a low hip roof made of wooden shingles or simply thatched. One-story structures

Stara karczma polska podług szkicu malarza Orłowskiego z r. 1817.

Figure 0.3 "The Polish Inn." Drawing by Aleksander Orłowski, from Zygmunt Gloger, *Budownictwo drzewne i wyroby z drzewa w dawnej Polsce* (Warsaw: Wł. Łazarski, 1909), vol. 2: 88. Public domain.

prevailed. In his handbook, Gloger differentiated between two common designs of inn buildings;[5] one type had a *T*-shaped floorplan in which the so-called *stan* (Pol. couch-house and stable) was situated perpendicularly to the part of the building designated for people, with the entrance in its midsection, as illustrated in the drawing attributed to Aleksander Orłowski (fig. 0.3).[6]

The second type of inn had an elongated rectangular shape with the stan in one of its ends, as shown in the postcard of the Bukowiec court inn (fig. 0.2), with the facade situated along the road. The double entrance to the couch-house can be seen on the far right.

Gloger also provided a historical-ethnographic and de-essentializing depiction of the inn as built by Polish carpenters, leased by a Jewish innkeeper, and owned by a local nobleman. In this interpretation, the inn was a special and often contested meeting ground of classes and a center of the economic and social order of feudal, prepartitioned, and partitioned Poland.

Such themes are closely connected to the practical status of the innkeeper; his representation as a host, a Jew, and a businessman, however entrenched, was often transcended by his image as a willing disseminator of culture. Especially the main nineteenth-century narratives about the Jewish innkeeper and his identity—produced by writers, poets, and social critics—invoked by his radical transformation from the local businessman to the patriarchal and patriotic figure associated with the grand narrative of Polish freedom. After the November Uprising, the innkeeper was transformed—much in accordance with the Romantic poet Adam Mickiewicz's extensive vision of Jankiel the innkeeper's role—into a noble supporter of the Polish political agenda in his roles as an emissary, a soldier, a disseminator of political news and censored ephemeral prints, and even a dulcimer virtuoso. In his monograph about the Jewish taverns, the historian Glenn Dynner also notes cases that support the image of an innkeeper as a champion of the Polish cause. On the other hand, he writes that a radically different figure of the Jewish innkeeper emerged during the January Uprising as some Jews took the Russian side.[7] This phenomenon, known as the innkeepers' "divided loyalty" toward both Poles and Russians as two antagonists in the wider political game, opens a less complimentary view of the innkeepers and the places they ran.[8] An unflattering perception of the Jewish inn as chaotic and poorly maintained, even "dirty," appears in the writings of Józef Ignacy Kraszewski, Eliza Orzeszkowa, and Bolesław Prus—the prominent Polish authors who engaged, along with the critic Aleksander Świętochowski, in thoughtful reassessment of the Polish-Jewish community. This trope refocuses our attention to the question of biases deeply entrenched in the Polish imaginary, specifically the stereotype of a Jewish innkeeper as a usurer who was also responsible for the Polish peasantry's alcoholism. Ironically, this stereotype endured despite the eventual abolition of the Polish landlords' liquor monopoly known as *propinacja* and the inn's slow decline that ensued in the second half of the nineteenth century.[9] Such a negative image of an innkeeper is invoked, for example, in the vivid exchanges between a peasant, a priest, and an innkeeper in Stanisław Wyspiański's drama *The Wedding* (*Wesele*, 1901).

The inn continued its decline in the early twentieth century lingering on the economic and topographic peripheries. During World War II, as a result of antisemitic and genocidal Nazi policies, the inn vanished as a Jewish space. The postwar era, when the historical Jewish presence in Polish lands was all but silenced by the government of the Polish People's Republic,[10] was not conducive to the exploration of the symbolic potentiality of the Jewish tavern.[11] The revival of interest in the inn's symbolic potential occurred only after 1989, mainly due to the systemic change that allowed an emergence of privately owned enterprises. The post-Communist relaxation of the discourse between Jews and gentiles opened new perspectives on the history of Polish Jewry, along with full acknowledgment of the tragic loss of the Jewish community. In the context of this post-Communist reality, occasionally named the Jewish Revival, the cultural heritage of Polish Jews plays a more prominent role, and yet today's Jewish inn appears to be an often-superficial copy of this lost cultural capital. To put it simply, in postmodern Polish culture, the Jewish inn retained its place in the cultural imaginary as a richly symbolized product, albeit a shadow of absence and void catered for and sustained by tourism. If one were to look for confirmation that the historical and cultural formation known as the Jewish inn exists today in historically Polish lands, one would find little concrete material evidence. There are but a handful extant inns in today's Poland—in Jeleśnia, Sucha Beskidzka, Bukowiec, Lublin, and Sławków—which date to the eighteenth century.

In this context, more recent, advertised as Jewish, to mention only the Tejsza Inn in Tykocin, belong to the procession of simulacra invoked postnostalgically in tourism, space, and cuisine, where they function as venues for profit, which, after all, always incentivized the inns' existence. For more idealistic observers, the existence of the Jewish inns of today hints at the possibility of renewal, however minuscule and imperfect, of the Jewish world. Thus, the re-creation of the Jewish inn is in principle metonymic, for it stands for the vanished larger whole. I would recall Kazimierz, a quintessentially historical Jewish neighborhood in Kraków, that represents the successful commercialization of this picturesque space due to an increased appreciation of the site's historical value, its aura, and the numerous cultural initiatives taking place there.[12] These various gestures and efforts at restoring Jewish life as symbolized by the inn reveal both the duality of the inn as a cultural phantom limb and its hybridization as a shareable gentile-Jewish space.

The Ariel restaurant, located in a historical rabbinic house on Szeroka Street in the center of Kazimierz, is a successful venue for intercultural meetings, mostly among tourists attracted by its quaint interior and architecture, the Jewish cuisine, and klezmer music, despite its eclectic tastes and aspects. It is but a reconciliatory vestige of the once-thriving life in Kazimierz. There are more such Jewish sites in Kazimierz that represent the inn's multipurpose space broadened to a wider platform, such as the popular Kraków Festival of Jewish Culture. Sociocultural anthropologist Erica T. Lehrer views the festival as illustrative of the changing dialogue between Jews and gentiles from the nostalgic themes to the more creative redefining of Jewish folk music and cuisine as an international, performative, multilingual phenomenon of aficionados from Israel, Poland, the United States, and the Jewish diaspora around the world.[13]

Is the return of the Jewish inn in Polish consumerist society only another iteration of the old and the same, or rather, an emergence of something new? Since its restoration is but a poor reflection of its past life, some pose the essential question whether a true renewal would require a Jewish tavernkeeper to be there, fully present and in charge. Alas, his human presence and business acumen are lacking; for a more realistic answer one should look beyond the regime of absolute authenticity and essentialization. It is too early to say to what extent these processes indicate a fluent formation of a new hybrid identity project.

This preface is but a brief context for this volume whose main objective is to present a new and critical understanding of the Jewish inn in its symbiotic complexity and historical development. Usually absorbed by the studies of the shtetl, in this volume the inn is given separate attention marked by multidisciplinary approaches. The present deliberations, divested from shtetl culture and structured as a constellation of several conceptual chains, probe such strategies as vernacular architecture and its representation. They map the significance and interrelationship between music, dance, literature, and other arts in the spatial arrangement of the inn; the innkeeper's intricate background of diverse social interactions, including the rising presence of women within the inn's family structure; the redistribution of its functions and services in interwar and postwar Poland; and current postnostalgic efforts in reviving it as a niche commercial enterprise or a symbolic platform for building and selling Jewish culture.

These conceptual chains form a transdisciplinary revision of the discourse centered around the Jewish inn and present the inn's cultural fecundity as this volume's creative contribution to Polish-Jewish studies. Our principal discovery was the realization that from the inn's inaugural representations it was already a construct underscored by phantasmatic moments that grew to be more prominent in Mickiewicz's foundational image of the Jewish inn in the Polish national epic *Pan Tadeusz* and, later in the same century, to eventually attain near erasure as the inn was appropriated by the city. The emergence of the inn as a highly significant cultural theme is foregrounded in part 1. Halina Goldberg vividly reconstructs the appearance of the inn in the first Polish ballet of national significance entitled *A Wedding in Ojców* and the subsequent trajectory of its rewriting and restaging along with the attending antisemitic stereotypes. Her analysis is in conversation with Bożena Shallcross's discussion of the spatial arrangement of the tavern in Adam Mickiewicz's *Pan Tadeusz*. Shallcross demonstrates that it was Adam Mickiewicz who shifted the inn to the realm of phantasm through both his loose adherence to mimetics and his heterochronic treatment of the inn's architecture, as well as through the highly idealized character Jankiel, the innkeeper.

In part two, Judith Kalik painstakingly reconstructs the geographic distribution of inns and competition for lease contracts, indicating the importance of Hasidism in the changing cultural landscape. In part 3, Benjamin Vogel's discussion of Jewish musicians' presence in the life of the inn and his exploration of the tools of their profession is based on iconographic materials, which include a novel reading of Cyprian K. Norwid's sketch of the Mickiewiczian character Jankiel. Beth Holmgren examines the mobility of the shtetl karczma and its gradual absorption into urban spaces. Swallowed by the city, the inn transformed into myriad courtyards, cafés, and hotels scattered all over Warsaw and other urban locations. In major Polish cities during the second half of the nineteenth century, the inn was also absorbed by the entertainment industry in culturally specific sites such as city tenement courtyards.

In part 4, Glenn Dynner's archival discovery brings into focus the innkeeper's daughter and reveals her choices and dilemmas as accessible through her autobiographical writing. The political implications for young Polish-Jewish women who occupied an in-between position in society are also deftly interwoven in the structure of Stanisław Wyspiański's masterpiece *The Wedding* and its construal of Rachela, an innkeeper's daughter whose speculative aesthetic predilections and inner dilemmas are analyzed in this volume by Eliza Rose. In doing so, both chapters suggest new avenues in studies of sophisticated female subjectivities resisting the traditional male-dominated world of the inn.

It was World War II that dealt the final blow to the inn's existence as a distinct cultural formation. The inn's ontology metamorphosed into postwar spectral archaeology and architecture, engaging—as part 5 of this volume shows—not only with the grammar of vestiges and silences but also with representations of the lost inn. The sense of loss that resulted from its demise is demonstrated in Alexander Lindskog's reading of Julian Stryjkowski's novel *Austeria*, which gestures to the Holocaust experience and the void it caused. Iwona Kurz discusses the critical reception of the same novel's cinematic adaptation by the filmmaker Jerzy Kawalerowicz, which captures the first day of World War I and the emergence of the inn as a space of bygone togetherness. In part 6, Magdalena Zatorska argues that Jewish culinary tradition proved to be a fertile ground that brought about a new dish called *ciulim*—a reinvention of the traditional Jewish Sabbath dish (Pol. *czulent*, Yid. cholent) by a small local community of Polish Christian women in the village of Lelów in southern Poland. Sławomir Sikora depicts a postnostalgic scenario that discerns the potentiality of performative revival of the inn and similar venues through various hybrid formations appearing not just in Poland but across Central Europe and calls for a reconceptualization of authenticity in a contemporary reimagining of the inn.

Mapping the demise of the inn and its long reinvention through tourism and collective memory is less of a discursive challenge than would be definitively establishing the exact moment of the Jewish inn's origin. The latter seems a mirage, an academic phantasm, as the inn—being a contemporary site that aspires to cultural hybridity—does not give any evidence that would allow such a strict approach. Therefore, this volume offers not a triumphant storyline but a narrative punctuated by dramatic turns, illusions, and discoveries that shed new light on the cultural potentialities of the Jewish inn.

Notes

1. "We talk to people, enter a Yiddish tavern. An old tavern keeper lets us in. Inside, we are inspected by his stooped wife and his daughter." Alfred Döblin, *Journey to Poland*, ed. Heinz Graber, trans. Joachim Neugroschel (London: I. B. Tauris, 1991), 78.

2. The German-Jewish writer and his guide went there to meet the Grand Rabbi Avraham Mordechai Alter (1866–1948), the fourth Gerrer Rebbe, a spiritual leader of the Ger Hasidic group in prewar Poland numbering over one hundred thousand members.

3. Zygmunt Gloger, *Budownictwo drzewne i wyroby z drzewa w dawnej Polsce*, vol. 2 (Warsaw: Wł. Łazarski, 1909), 84–91.

4. Hirsz Abramowicz, *Profiles of a Lost World: Memoirs of East European Jewish Life before World War II*, ed. Dina Abramowicz and Jeffrey Shandler, trans. Eva Zeitlin Dobkin (Detroit: Wayne State University Press, 1999), 60.

5. Gloger, *Budownictwo*, 84–91.

6. Aleksander Orłowski (1777–1832) was a Polish painter and draftsman active in the Russian Empire.

7. Glenn Dynner, *Yankel's Tavern: Jews, Liquor, & Life in the Kingdom of Poland* (Oxford: Oxford University Press, 2013). Dynner masterfully demonstrates the complexity of Jewish solidarity; see the chapter "Soldiers, Smugglers, and Spies: Jewish Tavernkeepers during the Polish Uprisings of 1830 and 1863," 103–30.

8. "Divided loyalty" is an operative term used by Israel Bartal and Magdalena Opalski in their monograph entitled *Poles and Jews: A Failed Brotherhood* (Hanover, NH: University Press of New England, 1992).

9. The monopoly was banned in the Prussian partition in 1845, in the Austrian partition in 1889, and in the Russian partition in 1897.

10. One of the most visible strategies was the Polonization of the Jewish genocide.

11. In the postwar ethnographic research, the inn was not studied from the point of view of ethnic or national identity but was described from a class perspective, mainly as part and parcel of the social class of peasants within a coherent rural space. In contrast to this model,

the present volume's focus on an analysis of the inn as a much wider phenomenon relates to questions of cultural identity/hybridity; as such, the representation originates in the publication of William I. Thomas and Florian Znaniecki's *The Polish Peasant in Europe and America*, 5 vols. (Boston: Richard G. Badger, 1918–20).

12. Erica T. Lehrer, *Jewish Poland Revisited: Heritage Tourism in Unquiet Places* (Bloomington: Indiana University Press, 2013), 132–33.

13. Lehrer, *Jewish Poland Revisited*, see esp. chap. "Shabbos Goyim: Polish Stewards of Jewish Spaces," 123–58. The festival is a case that parallels the paradigm formulated by Diane Pinto in her article "A New Jewish Identity for Post-1989 Europe," in which she analyzes new and developing identities within the Jewish spaces in Europe, *Institute for Jewish Policy Research*, no. 1 (June 1996).

ACKNOWLEDGMENTS

THE PRESENT VOLUME ORIGINATED FROM the workshop organized by Bożena Shallcross and Iwona Kurz and supported by the Global Outreach Workshop at the POLIN Museum of the History of Polish Jewry. The workshop was held at POLIN in June 2019. A very special thanks goes to Antony Polonsky for his contribution to the workshop's deliberations and to Barbara Kirshenblatt-Gimblett for giving the participants an illuminating tour of the POLIN Museum's exhibits.

Financial support for preparing the present volume for publication came from the Maria Kuncewiczowa Fund at University of Chicago's Department of Slavic Languages and Literatures, and from the Jacobs School of Music and the Robert A. and Sandra S. Borns Jewish Studies Program at Indiana University, Bloomington.

We owe gratitude to Anna Francis, assistant acquisitions editor at Indiana University Press, for expertly guiding us through the entire publication process. We appreciate the exceptionally careful and insightful reading of the drafts by Gerard Siarny and the editorial assistance we received from Masha Fokina and Peyson Weekly. The thoughtful comments offered by the anonymous readers of the manuscript helped us shape and improve the final product. We are thankful for the contributions of Jillian Bray, who copyedited the manuscript, and Nancy Lightfoot and Carol McGillivray, who oversaw the production of the book, and for Enid L. Zafran's work on indexing the volume, and to Leyla Salamova for the design of the book's cover.

NOTE ON PLACE NAMES, PERSONAL NAMES, AND TRANSLITERATIONS

The chapters in this book explore practices and cultural artifacts that span some four hundred years and traverse the lands of today's Poland, Lithuania, Belarus, and Ukraine, referencing their many languages. Given this volume's focus on Polish culture, we favor the use of Polish geographic names, the exception being the capital city, which is referenced with the English Warsaw rather than the Polish Warszawa. Primary sources using alternative geographic spellings are rendered according to the source; bibliographic references to publication places have been revised throughout for consistency (e.g., "Warszawa" to "Warsaw").

Throughout this book, we give preference to Polish spellings of individuals' names, except where the spellings of some, such as Sholem Aleichem, are standardized in English. We retain the original spellings of authors' bylines in the text and the primary sources' original languages.

Transliterations of Yiddish follow YIVO guidelines, of Hebrew those of the *Encyclopedia Judaica*, with the modification that the ḥet is rendered as ḥ. An apostrophe separates two vowels with distinct vocalization, as in kolno'a (movie theater). No hyphens separate prefixes, such as hey or vav. For Russian, Belarusian, and Ukrainian, we use the simplified Library of Congress system, omitting the ligatures used in some instances when Cyrillic characters are rendered by more than a single Latin character.

The Jewish Inn in Polish Culture

PART I

Theatrical and Literary Phantasms

1

The Jewish Innkeeper in Polish National Ballet

Halina Goldberg

Tempers flared and a heated brawl ensued during an October 12, 1921, performance at the Grand Theater in Warsaw.[1] The disturbance interrupted what promised to be an enjoyable Wednesday evening featuring a triple bill of Pietro Mascagni's famous one-act opera *Cavalleria rusticana*, followed by a choreographed performance of Nikolai Rimsky-Korsakov's *Scheherazade* and concluding with a one-act Polish ballet titled *Karczma* (The inn) (for the playbill, see fig. 1.1). The theater was filled to the brim with a large audience who had flocked to see the first of two guest appearances by Maria Labia, the world-renowned Italian soprano who had stopped in Warsaw for just a few days and that evening took the part of Santuzza in Mascagni's opera. Labia's performance was splendid—the enthusiastic audience and critics alike were most favorably impressed by her warm, resonant voice and expressive acting—and the evening would have probably gone into the annals of Warsaw's principal theatrical stage as a successful one, were it not for the events that accompanied the concluding ballet. What happened then is described in both the Polish- and Yiddish-language press: when the performance of the Jewish innkeeper's dance started, young Jews present in the theater began to noisily protest. This, in turn, elicited an angry response from other members of the audience, and while the dance continued onstage, two brawling factions of the audience engaged in a screaming match accompanied by defiant applause on the one side and a deafening blare of whistles on the other. The police entered the theater and arrested the Jewish protesters.[2]

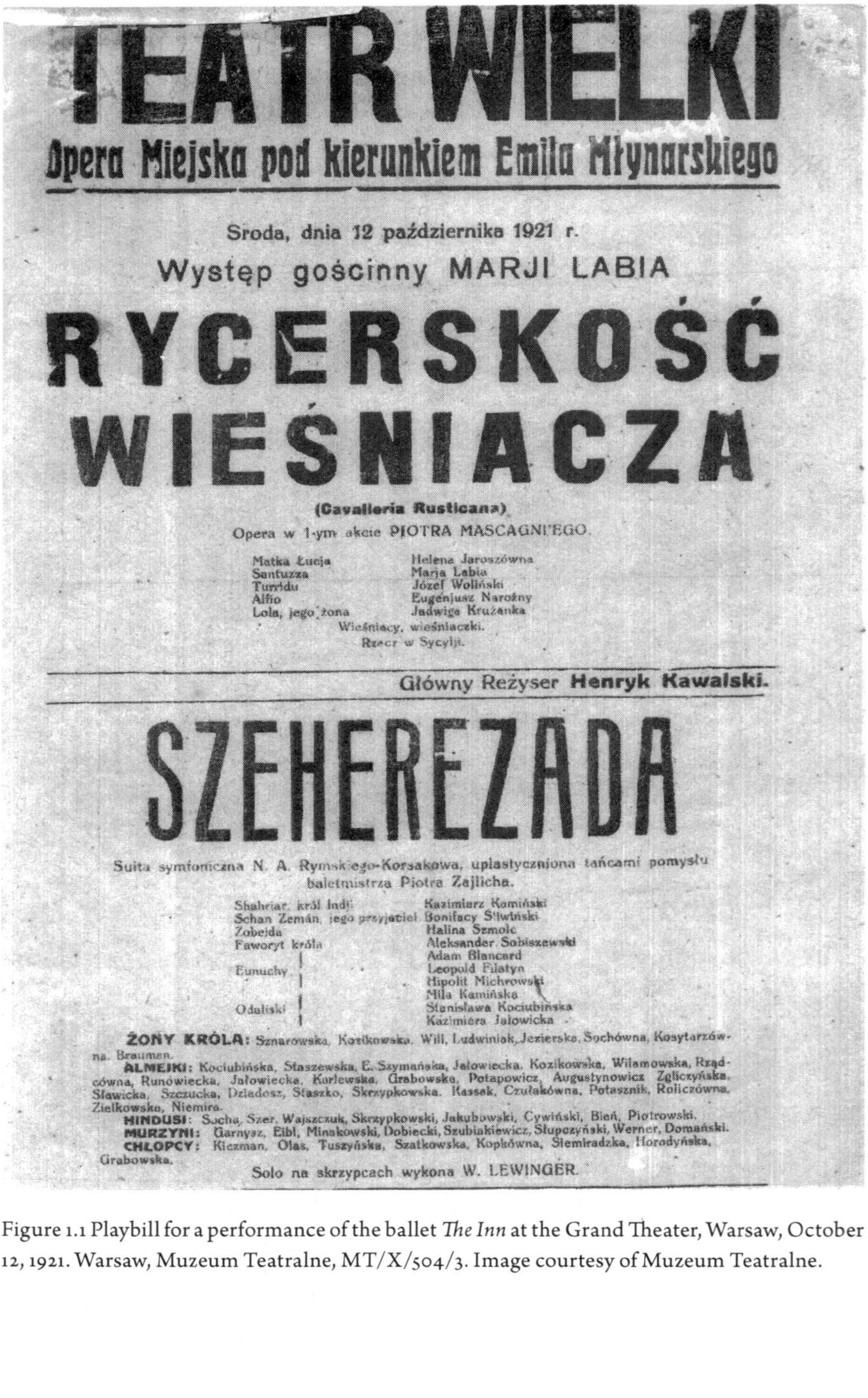

TEATR WIELKI

Opera Miejska pod kierunkiem Emila Młynarskiego

Sroda, dnia 12 października 1921 r.

Występ gościnny MARJI LABIA

RYCERSKOŚĆ WIEŚNIACZA

(Cavalleria Rusticana)

Opera w 1-ym akcie PIOTRA MASCAGNI'EGO.

Matka Łucja	Helena Jaroszówna
Santuzza	Marja Labia
Turridu	Józef Woliński
Alfio	Eugenjusz Narożny
Lola, jego żona	Jadwiga Krużanka

Wieśniacy, wieśniaczki.

Rzecz w Sycylji.

Główny Reżyser **Henryk Kawalski.**

SZEHEREZADA

Suita symfoniczna N. A. Rymskiego-Korsakowa, uplastyczniona tańcami pomysłu baletmistrza Piotra Zajlicha.

Shahriar, król Indji	Kazimierz Kamiński
Schan Zemán, jego przyjaciel	Bonifacy Śliwiński
Zobeida	Halina Szmolc
Faworyt króla	Aleksander Sobiszewski
Eunuchy	Adam Blancard
	Leopold Filatyn
	Hipolit Michrowski
Odaliski	Mila Kamińska
	Stanisława Kociubińska
	Kazimiera Jalowicka

ŻONY KRÓLA: Sznarowska, Kozikowska, Will, Ludwiniak, Jezierska, Sochówna, Kosytarzówna, Braumen.

ALMEJKI: Kociubińska, Staszewska, E. Szymańska, Jalowiecka, Kozikowska, Wilamowska, Rządcówna, Runowiecka, Jałowiecka, Korlewska, Grabowska, Potapowicz, Augustynowicz, Zgliczyńska, Sławicka, Szczucka, Dziadosz, Staszko, Skrzypkowska, Kassak, Czułakówna, Potasznik, Roliczówna, Zielkowska, Niemira.

HINDUSI: Socha, Szer, Wajszczuk, Skrzypkowski, Jakubowski, Cywiński, Bień, Piotrowski.

MURZYNI: Garnysz, Eibl, Minakowski, Dobiecki, Szubiakiewicz, Słupczyński, Werner, Domański.

CHŁOPCY: Kiczman, Olas, Tuszyńska, Szatkowska, Kopkówna, Siemiradzka, Horodyńska, Grabowska.

Solo na skrzypcach wykona W. LEWINGER.

Figure 1.1 Playbill for a performance of the ballet *The Inn* at the Grand Theater, Warsaw, October 12, 1921. Warsaw, Muzeum Teatralne, MT/X/504/3. Image courtesy of Muzeum Teatralne.

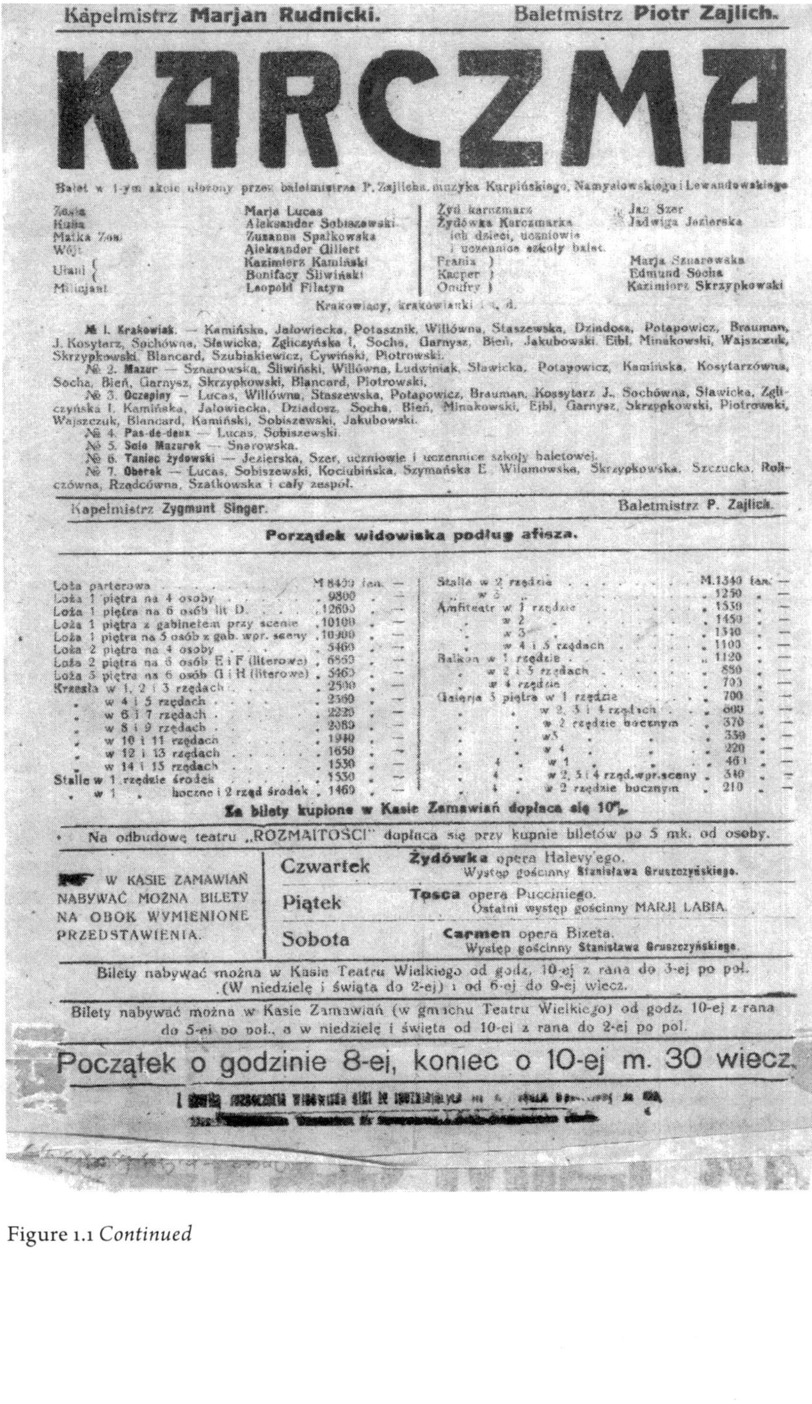
Kapelmistrz **Marjan Rudnicki.** Baletmistrz **Piotr Zajlich.**

KARCZMA

Balet w 1-ym akcie ułożony przez baletmistrza P. Zajlicha, muzyka Karpińskiego, Namysłowskiego i Lewandowskiego

Zosia	Marja Lucas	Żyd karczmarz	Jan Szer
Kuba	Aleksander Sobiszewski	Żydówka Karczmarka	Jadwiga Jezierska
Matka Zosi	Zuzanna Spałkowska	ich dzieci, uczniowie i uczennice szkoły balet.	
Wójt	Aleksander Gillert		
Ułani {	Kazimierz Kamiński	Frania }	Marja Sznarowska
	Bonifacy Śliwiński	Kacper }	Edmund Socha
Milicjant	Leopold Filatyn	Onufry }	Kazimierz Skrzypkowski

Krakowiacy, krakowianki i t. d.

№ 1. **Krakowiak.** — Kamińska, Jałowiecka, Potasznik, Willówna, Staszewska, Dziadosz, Potapowicz, Brauman, J. Kosytarz, Sochówna, Sławicka, Zgliczyńska I, Socha, Garnysz, Bień, Jakubowski, Eibl, Minakowski, Wajszczuk, Skrzypkowski, Blancard, Szubiakiewicz, Cywiński, Piotrowski.
№ 2. **Mazur** — Sznarowska, Śliwiński, Willówna, Ludwiniak, Sławicka, Potapowicz, Kamińska, Kosytarzówna, Socha, Bień, Garnysz, Skrzypkowski, Blancard, Piotrowski,
№ 3. **Oczepiny** — Lucas, Willówna, Staszewska, Potapowicz, Brauman, Kossytarz J., Sochówna, Sławicka, Zgliczyńska I, Kamińska, Jałowiecka, Dziadosz, Socha, Bień, Minakowski, Ejbl, Garnysz, Skrzypkowski, Piotrowski, Wajszczuk, Blancard, Kamiński, Sobiszewski, Jakubowski.
№ 4. **Pas-de-deux** — Lucas, Sobiszewski.
№ 5. **Solo Mazurek** — Snarowska.
№ 6. **Taniec żydowski** — Jezierska, Szer, uczniowie i uczennice szkoły baletowej.
№ 7. **Oberek** — Lucas, Sobiszewski, Kociubińska, Szymańska E. Wilamowska, Skrzypkowska, Szczucka, Rolliczówna, Rządcówna, Szatkowska i cały zespół.

Kapelmistrz **Zygmunt Singer.** Baletmistrz **P. Zajlick.**

Porządek widowiska podług afisza.

Loża parterowa	M 8400 fen. —	Stalle w 2 rzędzie	M.1340 fen. —
Loża 1 piętra na 4 osoby	9800 „ —	„ w 3 „	1250 „ —
Loża 1 piętra na 6 osób lit. D.	12600 „ —	Amfiteatr w 1 rzędzie	1530 „ —
Loża 1 piętra z gabinetem przy scenie	10100 „ —	„ w 2 „	1450 „ —
Loża 1 piętra na 5 osób z gab. wpr. sceny	10300 „ —	„ w 3 „	1340 „ —
Loża 2 piętra na 4 osoby	5460 „ —	„ w 4 i 5 rzędach	1100 „ —
Loża 2 piętra na 6 osób E i F (literowe)	6860 „ —	Balkon w 1 rzędzie	1120 „ —
Loża 3 piętra na 6 osób G i H (literowe)	5460 „ —	„ w 2 i 3 rzędach	880 „ —
Krzesła w 1, 2 i 3 rzędach	2500 „ —	„ w 4 rzędzie	700 „ —
„ w 4 i 5 rzędach	2360 „ —	Galerja 3 piętra w 1 rzędzie	700 „ —
„ w 6 i 7 rzędach	2220 „ —	„ „ w 2, 3 i 4 rzędach	600 „ —
„ w 8 i 9 rzędach	2080 „ —	„ „ w 2 rzędzie bocznym	370 „ —
„ w 10 i 11 rzędach	1940 „ —	„ „ w 3	330 „ —
„ w 12 i 13 rzędach	1650 „ —	„ „ w 4	220 „ —
„ w 14 i 15 rzędach	1530 „ —	„ 4 „ w 1	460 „ —
Stalle w 1 rzędzie środek	1530 „ —	„ 4 „ w 2, 3 i 4 rzęd. wpr. sceny	340 „ —
„ w 1 „ boczne i 2 rząd środek	1460 „ —	„ 4 „ w 2 rzędzie bocznym	210 „ —

Za bilety kupione w Kasie Zamawiań dopłaca się 10%.

Na odbudowę teatru „ROZMAITOŚCI" dopłaca się przy kupnie biletów po 5 mk. od osoby.

W KASIE ZAMAWIAŃ NABYWAĆ MOŻNA BILETY NA OBOK WYMIENIONE PRZEDSTAWIENIA.

Czwartek	**Żydówka** opera Halevy'ego. Występ gościnny **Stanisława Gruszczyńskiego.**
Piątek	**Tosca** opera Pucciniego. Ostatni występ gościnny MARJI LABIA.
Sobota	**Carmen** opera Bizeta. Występ gościnny **Stanisława Gruszczyńskiego.**

Bilety nabywać można w Kasie Teatru Wielkiego od godz. 10-ej z rana do 3-ej po poł. (W niedzielę i święta do 2-ej) i od 6-ej do 9-ej wiecz.

Bilety nabywać można w Kasie Zamawiań (w gmachu Teatru Wielkiego) od godz. 10-ej z rana do 5-ej po poł., a w niedzielę i święta od 10-ej z rana do 2-ej po poł.

Początek o godzinie 8-ej, koniec o 10-ej m. 30 wiecz.

Figure 1.1 *Continued*

The captivating story of this 1921 performance has been flagged in earlier scholarship, notably by the venerable historian of Yiddish literature and Ashkenazic Jewry Chone Shmeruk and the musicologist Bret Werb. Shmeruk's mention of the ballet *Karczma* appears in the context of a broader study: drawing on literary sources, he examines the *majufes* (a stereotypical Jewish song-dance) as a sociological phenomenon and a window into Polish-Jewish relations. Shmeruk bases his description of the ballet *Karczma* on two articles from the daily press—one in Yiddish and one in Polish.[3] Here is the entire excerpt in which Shmeruk contrasts the Jewish and gentile accounts of the event:

> [The ballet] included a scene called Mayufes, in which the dancers "turned the performance into a disgusting caricature that should not be allowed in even the cheapest cabaret, let alone a national theatre." With the Jews in the audience protesting loudly, the rest of the crowd shouted "Go on, Jews" and "On with the performance." The police came in and arrested ten young Jews. The same incident is described in a Polish daily; there the name of the scene is omitted, and the reporter writes only that, following a Polish folkdance, "the Jewish family who owned the tavern began a typical dance. Even though there was nothing offensive about the dance, deafening whistles were heard coming from the upper balconies. This is how the Jews protested this innocent dance." The Polish newspaper article stated that the Jews came to the performance carrying whistles, anticipating a demonstration; the Polish audience, however, applauded the dancers, and the performance continued.[4]

In his study, Shmeruk calls attention to the majufes as a gentile cultural phenomenon captured in Polish-language literature, and to the trauma this cultural phenomenon has inflicted on Jews, which can be gleaned in Yiddish-language writings. Indeed, the description of the Grand Theater performance as an "innocent dance" in the *Kurjer Warszawski* article is contrasted with *Der Moment*'s characterization of the scene as a "disgusting caricature that should not be allowed in even the cheapest cabaret, let alone a national theatre." Shmeruk is all but certain that the choreography deliberately caricatured Jews to amuse the Grand Theater's audience and highlights the insensitivity in the responses of gentile audiences and critics to the offense the Jews have taken to the majufes.

The goal of Werb's article is "to supplement Shmeruk's literary survey with examples of notated or recorded music."[5] In the section devoted to the ballet *Karczma*, Werb makes a couple of important observations gathered from Polish lexicographic sources. He reports that *Karczma* as choreographed by Piotr Zajlich premiered in December 1919. Werb also connects this ballet to the 1823 *A Cracovian Wedding in Ojców* (*Wesele krakowskie w Ojcowie*), for which music was provided in "collaborative effort" by major Polish composers Karol Kurpiński, Józef Damse, Józef Elsner, and Jan Stefani. Werb surmises that "this '*majufes*' scene had been created for Zajlich's 20th-century production, revealingly retitled *Karczma* (for by then the tavern had become the standard backdrop, in myth and cliche, for the meeting of Pole and Jew)."[6]

The ballet *Karczma* that so offended the Jewish audiences in 1921 was indeed a reworking of *A Cracovian Wedding in Ojców*, although setting a balletic wedding scene in a country inn and including Jewish characters was hardly a new idea. My examination of untapped archival sources endeavors to historicize the presence of the Jewish inn and its Jewish innkeepers in Polish ballet and to nuance and contextualize our understanding of the clashing reactions of Jewish and gentile audiences to the phenomenon.[7]

Celebrated as Poland's first national ballet, *A Cracovian Wedding in Ojców* (often shortened as *A Wedding in Ojców*) premiered in 1823. *A Wedding in Ojców* was arguably the most popular Polish ballet during the nineteenth century, and it continues to maintain its historic place in Poland's ballet repertory. The ballet's creators capitalized on the phenomenal popularity of two earlier national operas: the 1794 *Supposed Miracle, or Cracovians and Highlanders* (*Cud mniemany czyli Krakowiacy i górale*) and its 1816 sequel, *New Cracovians; Superstition or Cracovians and Highlanders* (*Nowe krakowiaki; Zabobon czyli Krakowiacy i górale*). The original *Cracovians and Highlanders*, considered Poland's first national opera, featured music by Jan Stefani to a libretto by Wojciech Bogusławski. Often called the father of Polish national theater, Bogusławski was a member of a conspiracy of politicians, military leaders, and members of the intelligentsia who organized against Poland's occupiers, resulting in an armed revolt against Russia and Prussia known as the Kościuszko Insurrection of 1794. In the days after its premiere, the patriotic and folkloristic music of *Cracovians and Highlanders* incited audiences to take up arms in the Kościuszko Insurrection, and the political allusions hidden under the surface of pastoral comedy remained current for decades to come.[8] The love story of the two main protagonists (Stach and Basia) unfolds during the wedding of another couple (Paweł and Zośka) in the first act, accompanied by the expected songs, rituals, and dances. Folkloristic dances and songs (mostly mazurkas and krakowiaks) accompany other salient moments in this opera in a manner characteristic of the genre of a singspiel (*śpiewogra*).

In the ensuing decades, the popularity of *A Wedding in Ojców* showed no sign of abating, and the opera has acquired a nearly mythical status. To capitalize on its appeal and update the story and music, in 1816 Jan Nepomucen Kamiński drafted a version that extended the narrative by one day, chock-full of events and featuring the same protagonists and overall sentiment as the original. The new singspiel, entitled *New Cracovians; Superstition or Cracovians and Highlanders*, included both favorite music by Stefani and new music by Karol Kurpiński. Here dances also accompany various moments of the story, but even though Stach and Basia's marriage is at the heart of the opera's happy ending, there is no wedding onstage. It was only logical that the audiences, enamored with the songs and dances from the two operas, would have wanted to experience in performance full-blown wedding festivities. This is what the 1823 ballet *A Wedding in Ojców* offered to them.[9]

A Wedding in Ojców was put on by Louis Thierry, the French-born director of the dance troupe associated with the National Theater. The musical score consisted of favorites from Stefani's and Kurpiński's versions, supplemented by new music by Józef Damse and possibly some favorites by Józef Elsner. The dances were choreographed mostly by Julia Mierzyńska, the prima ballerina of the troupe and also its director during the 1825–26 season.[10] In the premiere, Mierzyńska danced the part of the bridesmaid, and the solo number choreographed and performed by her remained in the repertory as "Mierzyńska's mazurka" ("Mazurek Mierzyńskiej") decades after she retired from the stage. Thierry took the part of the bridegroom, and Damse, who was well known for his singing and acting parts in singspiels, took the pantomimed character role of the bridegroom's father, who was also the organist. The new ballet found favor with audiences: by 1839, it had reached its hundredth performance at the National Theater (now renamed the Grand Theater), and by 1870, a total of 712 presentations were reported. Other cities, both in Poland and abroad, also saw performances of this popular work.[11]

A quick glance at the history of *A Wedding in Ojców*, however, puts into question the very idea of this ballet as "a work." While the overall contour of the story—featuring a bride and a bridegroom, their parents, other character types, and wedding attendants—and the musical and choreographic focus on beloved folkloristic dances can be found in all stagings of the ballet, even a cursory glance reveals that in each iteration there are differences: the names of the protagonists and the particular cast of character types changes with each choreography, and the specific musical choices also seem to vary. We have little record of the original version: there is no manuscript or printed score from the ballet's premiere aside from a couple of slim volumes that, in a typical manner, offered theatergoers take-home versions of their favorites, in this case piano transcriptions of two mazurkas by Damse.[12] The earliest extensive publications of music from the ballet are solo piano versions from nearly two decades later, each containing a somewhat different collection of musical numbers.[13] By then, Józef Stefani, the son of the composer of the 1794 opera, had his hand in shaping the music for Maurice Pion's new production.[14] A still different version is found in the print cited by Werb—a piano arrangement by Romuald Zientarski from 1856. This tendency to vary and recombine the musical numbers persisted throughout the ensuing decades, and by the time Zajlich staged the ballet in 1919, he incorporated trendy folkloristic compositions by Karol Namysłowski, the Jewish-born Leopold Lewandowski, and likely also music of other composers.[15]

These historical documents provide unmistakable evidence that the ballet *A Wedding in Ojców* did not have a fixed text, musical or otherwise. Each staging offered a unique version of the story with a new choreography and accompanied by a distinctive musical text.[16] (A quick and not exhaustive historical overview of stage works in this tradition can be found in the appendix, tab. 1.) Less than a true collaborative effort, the musical score was characterized by a layered authorship, in which some of the favorite numbers remained while each successive version introduced new and newly composed material to meet the public's insatiable thirst for fashionable tunes. There were also numerous spinoffs. For example, in 1839, Maurice Pion staged an offshoot titled *Stach i Zośka*, deemed more pleasing than *A Wedding in Ojców* by some.[17] Zajlich's scandalous *Karczma* of 1921 and *A Village Wedding* (*Wesele na wsi*), another ballet choregraphed by him, were also such spinoffs, as evidenced by the surviving inventories of all his stagings.[18]

The idea for *Karczma* did not materialize out of thin air; rather, it emerged out of decades of tradition. One enduring traditional element was the inn's continuing and central presence in the staging of both the operas and the ballets listed in table 1. Furthermore, a model for reimagining *A Wedding in Ojców* as *Karczma* was provided by an earlier version of *A Wedding in Ojców* that included Jews among its cast of character types. And finally, the deeply problematic representations of dancing Jews were found already in traditional nativity plays and throughout the second half of the nineteenth century in lowbrow theater. Likewise, the anger of Jewish audiences about the prevalence of Jewish caricatures onstage simmered quietly for half a century, erupting occasionally during theatrical performances, before it exploded at the Grand Theater in response to *Karczma*.

Given the significance of the tavern in the economic, civic, and social activities of a village (discussed in chaps. 3 and 4), it only makes sense that it was used as the setting for these national operas and ballets. The inn was specified by Bogusławski as the backdrop for acts 1 and 3 of his 1794 opera *Cracovians and Highlanders*, a staging that was preserved in Kamiński's 1816 remake. The first print of Kamiński's libretto included a lithograph of the stage as imagined by the doyen of contemporary Polish historical painters Michał Stachowicz: a vibrant dancing scene in front of an inn.[19] Both operas were supposed to take place in the historically significant hamlet of Mogiła.[20] As the actual village of Mogiła was owned by the neighboring Cistercian Abbey, it was not likely to have included Jewish innkeepers, musicians, or villagers. In fact, Kamiński's libretto references specific musicians by name, and there is no doubt they were not Jewish. The location of the 1823 ballet, only twenty miles northwest from Mogiła, was a village at the foot of another historical landmark, the ruins of the Ojców Castle, a fourteenth-century stronghold built by the legendary king Casimir the Great. The custom of staging the story in front of an inn was kept for the ballet, as evidenced by an 1851 lithograph representing wedding guests dancing a krakowiak in a scene from the ballet (see fig. 1.2). This image, like the earlier lithograph by Stachowicz, does not seem to include any Jewish characters.

The Jewish innkeeper and his family became a part of the story narrated in *A Wedding in Ojców* sometime late in the nineteenth century. This version is quite well documented in the archival materials related to an 1894 performance of the ballet in Kraków. The playbill (found in fig. 1.3) lists Szmul, the Innkeeper, and Ruchla, His Wife, among the cast of the play. It also has "A Jewish Dance" ("Taniec żydowski") itemized as the third number in the performance.[21]

The central role played by the Jewish couple in this version of the ballet is particularly noteworthy and is apparent in the libretto.[22] The first character to emerge from the inn in the opening scene of the ballet is the Innkeeper, rather predictably named Jankiel in the libretto (after the revered protagonist of *Pan Tadeusz*) instead of Szmul, followed by Ruchla. Their parts—like those of the parents of the bride and the Organist (who is the guardian of the Bridegroom)—are pantomime roles. Dance scenes are left

Figure 1.2 "Performance of *A Wedding in Ojców*." Lithograph by Claude Régnier and Eugene Cicéri lith. based on a drawing by Antoni Zaleski and J. Ważniewski. Printed by Lemercier, Paris (Paris: Wilczyński, 1851). Warsaw, Muzeum Narodowe, Gr.Pol.15396/49 MNW. Digital Collections of the National Museum in Warsaw. https://cyfrowe.mnw.art.pl/pl/katalog/929565. Public domain.

to the newly married couple, bridesmaids and groomsmen, and the pair of matchmakers.

Jankiel is present in every scene of the ballet. He ushers in the arriving guests, makes sure everybody has plenty of drink, observes the wedding rituals (especially the unveiling of the Bride—*oczepiny*), and mitigates conflict between the tipsy guests. When the Matchmaker gets angry at the Organist after the latter gives some vodka to the Matchmaker's child, Jankiel offers a performance by his children "who dance very beautifully," to distract his irritated guests from quarreling. The number, called "A Jewish Dance," is thus performed by children, a girl and a boy.[23]

There is nothing in the 1894 libretto that demonizes or demeans the Jewish characters. None of the stage directions ask the actors to caricature their movements or gestures. None of the actions portray them as buffoons

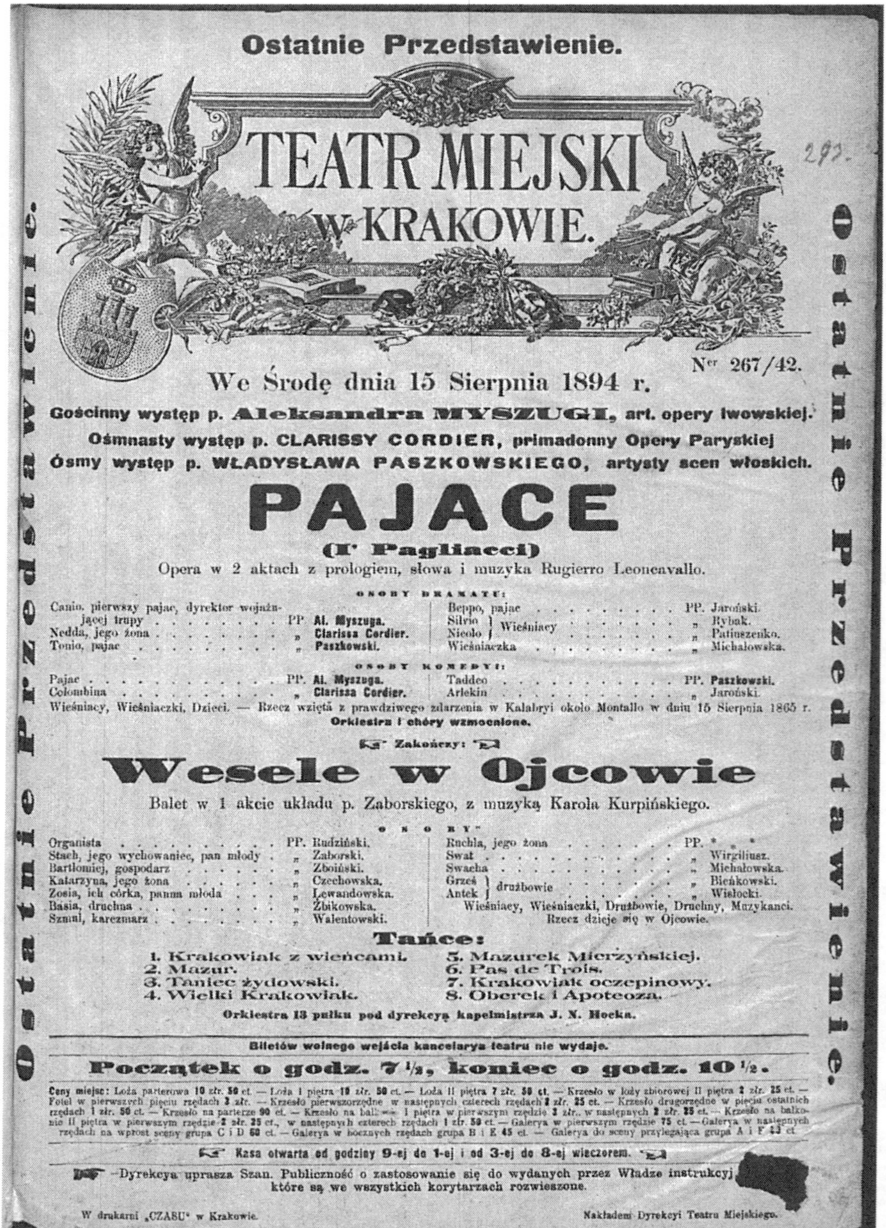

Figure 1.3 Playbill for a performance of the ballet *A Wedding in Ojców* in Kraków, 1894. Kraków, Archiwum Artystyczne i Biblioteka Teatru im. Juliusza Słowackiego, playbills, opr_25-289. Image courtesy of Teatr im. J. Słowackiego in Kraków.

(in fact, if anybody is portrayed as acting foolishly, it is the Organist). But the libretto only tells part of the story. Given that the choreographer of the 1894 version, Stanisław Zaborski, worked in garden and lowbrow theaters throughout Polish lands, it is easy to imagine that he might have been influenced by the unflattering depictions of dancing Jews that were common at the time in such venues.[24] Still, without documentation, we have no way of telling what was presented onstage and whether the acting or dancing underscored comic qualities of the Jewish characters. Likewise, we know nothing about the music of the "Jewish Dance."

The Kraków performance that featured a Jewish family onstage was not an isolated event. The difference in the names of the Jewish innkeeper appearing in the libretto and the playbill might preserve a trace of two distinct performances. Such performing variants would be disseminated by traveling artists. This role could have been easily fulfilled by Zaborski, whose itinerant professional life took him nearly every season to a Polish-language theater at a different location, from Kraków to Tarnów in Galicia, and from Warsaw to Łódź, Kalisz, and Lublin in the Russian partition.[25] A surviving playbill from an 1896 Lublin performance of *A Wedding in Ojców* also features a Jewish innkeeper, this time named Chaim, and No. 3 is a "Jewish Dance." The dancers—the innkeeper's progeny Lejbuś and Siora[26]—were played by children, who were identified in the playbill only by their first names, Kazio and Józia.[27]

By the time the innkeeper's family was included in the cast of *A Wedding in Ojców*, Jewish characters appeared in another popular ballet, *Pan Twardowski*, with the score by the Jewish-born and immensely successful composer of middlebrow music Adolf Gustaw Sonnenfeld and the libretto by Virgilio Calori, an Italian choreographer then active in Warsaw. In Calori's 1874 retelling of this beloved legend about the Faust-like, defiant, Polish nobleman-magician who makes a pact with the Devil and then cunningly escapes being taken to hell, there are two tavern scenes. The tavern named Rome (Pol. Rzym) is pivotal to the story, since only in Rome can the Devil take Twardowski's soul, and in entering this inn, the nobleman is tricked into submitting to the terms of the contract. In this, the penultimate scene in Calori's version of the ballet, there are no Jews, and the just-christened infant of the presumably gentile Innkeeper is essential to Twardowski's salvation.[28] Jews appear, however, in two other scenes of the ballet. In scene 4, portraying drunken merrymaking, ostensibly taking place in front of a tavern, a Jewish Violinist who just refused to play for Twardowski, through the latter's magic, ends up on the weathercock pole and "plays as if possessed" (see chap. 4 for convergences of the supernatural and violin virtuosity).[29] In later versions, a dancing Jewish Innkeeper is included in this scene.[30] One more passage, scene 5, includes three Jews, who come to collect rent from Twardowski but instead get a thrashing from his Famulus; in addition, two are magically compelled to spin and fly, while the third is made to stretch and shrink through Twardowski's spells.[31]

While Sonnefeld's ballet remained popular into the first decades of the twentieth century, in 1921 it was replaced by a version set to music by Ludomir Różycki, with a libretto by his wife, Stefania Różycka. In this version, the libretto specifies that a Jewish orchestra was playing in the scene in the Rome Inn, and other sources confirm that a Jew and two Jewesses performed a "Jewish Dance."[32] Różycki's score illustrates this dance with mistuned, comic music that shows close affinity to the bouncy polka-like tunes that accompanied Jewish caricatures in folkloristic and popular theater performances throughout the previous century.

By the late nineteenth century, there was an established convention of including a dancing Jew in traditional nativity plays and in the hugely popular one-act singspiel theater shows. In these middlebrow genres, the depictions of Jews were decidedly unflattering, mocking their appearances and movements and accentuating their intellectual and moral decrepitude. The story of these representations is rich and complex, and I explore it in another larger research project regarding the intersections between these representations and the majufes as a musical and cultural concept. In the following, I offer some of my key findings with pertinent examples.[33]

The Polish tradition of performing *szopka*—nativity puppet plays—goes back centuries. Next to the standard nativity cast, szopka scenes integrated another set of characters, among them the Devil, the Witch, and the Jew and the Jewess. Oskar Kolberg's magisterial nineteenth-century collection of Polish folklore contains many examples of szopka texts that include scenes with Jews. In the country version of the szopka, the Jew and the Jewess are called on to dance before being seized by the Devil and taken to hell.[34] Other versions of the scene make it clear that because of his rejection of Christ, the Jew is morally defective and hence subject not just to onstage thrashing but also eternal damnation in the hands of Satan.[35] Szopka was an influential genre, one that during the period under consideration migrated from its folk roots to principal Polish theaters, serving as a vehicle not just for entertainment but also for patriotic discourse and political

Figure 1.4 Jewish Innkeeper from a szopka, Christmas postcard "Merry Christmas," Włodzimierz Tetmajer, illustration to Lucjan Rydel's *Polish Bethlehem* (Kraków: J. Czarnecki, c. 1913). Warsaw, Biblioteka Narodowa, DŻS XII 8b/p.53/11a. The National Digital Library Polona. https://polona.pl/preview/b57cf75c-14c9-45ed-91f2-eac26cc2a7c0. Public domain.

satire. Like the rest of szopka's cast, the figure of the ridiculed dancing Jew was absorbed into this newer satirical genre. At least in some of these urban theatrical renditions of the szopka, the Jew was cast as an Innkeeper, most notably in Lucjan Rydel's celebrated and deeply patriotic *Polish Bethlehem* (*Betleem polskie*) from 1905 (see Włodzimierz Tetmajer's illustration representing the Jew from this play for a 1913 postcard in fig. 1.4). Wyspiański's play *The Wedding* (1901), discussed in chapter 7, elevates the szopka tradition, but the character of the Jew in this play again invokes stereotypical attributes of the Jewish innkeeper.

The nineteenth century witnessed a proliferation of Jewish characters on Polish theatrical stages. There were noble, tragic Jewish protagonists—Eléazar and Rachel in Halévy's opera *La Juive* (*The Jewess*), which was performed frequently and with great success in Warsaw and other Polish cities, and the complex eponymous heroes of Zapolska's plays *Małka Szwarcenkopf* and *Jojne Firulkes*. These intricate characters could not make up for the preponderance of the stereotypical comical types that populated the ubiquitous middlebrow musical plays. These greedy, immoral, dim-witted Jews appeared onstage by the 1840s, amusing and inciting intolerance in countless generations of viewers.[36] They also sang and danced onstage. The oldest of these plays and by far the most popular was Aleksander Ładnowski's *A Jew in a Barrel or Sealed Icek* (*Żyd w beczce czyli Icek zapieczętowany*), which first appeared onstage during the 1842–43 season.[37] *A Jew in a Barrel* was one of the most performed plays on Polish stages for nearly a century, as demonstrated by surviving copies, reprints, playbills, and mentions in the daily press.[38] Ładnowski capitalized on the success of this subject with ever-popular spinoffs titled *Sealed Berek* and *Unsealed Berek*. Similar plays by other "masters" followed.

A Jew in a Barrel serves as a good example of the context in which the dancing Jew appeared in these plays. The plot of the singspiel is simple: the greedy and lusty Jewish moneylender is hounding a poor Christian cooper who owes him money, and his loving wife, whom he wants to seduce.[39] The virtuous woman tricks the rich moneylender into hiding in a barrel, and he is then coerced with a thrashing and threats of drowning into paying his way to safety. Intermittently, as the avaricious Jew is hoaxed and outsmarted, the various protagonists sing onstage. In the most ridiculous and demeaning singing number, the moneylender's Jewish sidekick is called on to do the stereotypical ludicrous dance, which sources suggest was a sort of bouncy, clumsy polka.[40] As the century progressed, this caricatured dance and others like it, including the Jewish dance in the szopka, are increasingly identified by the term *majufes*, both in the performing sources and in the responses of the Jewish spectators.

Jewish audiences reacted to these representations of Jews onstage in a variety of ways. The frequent programming of these one-act comedies in garden theaters did not diminish the attendance of Jewish guests, a point emphasized by a critic who in 1871 complained about Alkazar theater's presentation of *A Jew in a Barrel*.[41] The review—printed in *Izraelita*, the Polish-language weekly of Warsaw's Jewish reformers—was the first of many published during the 1870s that protested the problematic representations of Jews in this and related plays.[42] In at least one case, Jews exercised their power as consumers of culture in order to force a change. In 1877, Anastazy Trapszo's troupe was invited to perform at a Purim ball in Łódź. *A Jew in a Barrel*, hastily selected as a last-minute substitution for the performance, emptied the room in a matter of minutes and became the reason for a boycott of the troupe. Since middle-class Jews were their main audience for the Polish-language theater in Łódź and because the boycott spread to other cities, it nearly caused the troupe to go bankrupt.[43] During the following year, the troupe presented at the Warsaw garden theater Arkadia a play that featured realistic and tragic Jewish characters. A review in *Izraelita* praised the troupe for choosing this work over *A Jew in a Barrel* and underscored how meaningful such a plot was to both Christian and Jewish members of the audience.[44] By the turn of the nineteenth century, demonstrations were occasionally staged during performances that featured Jewish stereotypes. In 1897, there were protests by socialist activists (from Jewish and Christian backgrounds) during a Kraków performance of *The Tempters of the People* (*Kusiciele ludu*).[45] In 1903, Jewish students in Warsaw and other Polish cities disrupted performances of the antisemitic play *The Golden Calf* (*Złoty cielec*).[46]

By the time the Grand Theater staged the ballet *Karczma*, the presence of a stereotyped Jew on a Polish stage and the implementation of this caricature through music and choreography had a nearly century-long tradition. For some fifty years, there was also a documented Jewish opposition to this practice. The sources I have examined show a whole range of depictions of the dancing Jew, from the mostly benign (at least on paper) characterization in the 1894 version of *A Wedding in Ojców* to the blatantly antisemitic *A Jew in the Barrel* (including its even more offensive offshoots) and szopka examples from Kolberg to Rydel. Portrayals of dancing Jews in Polish theater walked a thin line between comedy and racialized stereotyping and between entertainment and antisemitism.

Shmeruk was correct in pointing out that Jews and gentiles responded differently to these depictions. A closer look at the language used in the Polish- and Yiddish-language reviews, corroborated by the extant archival sources, reveals more about the diverging ways the reviewers interpreted such representations. Shmeruk remarks that when the "incident is described in a Polish daily; there the name of the scene [by which he means "Majufes"] is omitted." But the 1821 playbill makes it clear that the number was not titled "Majufes" but rather "A Jewish Dance." This is also the title for this dance in the documents from the 1890s performances. Moreover, Shmeruk's quote from the Polish-language newspaper translates the reference to the Jewish dance as "a typical dance," whereas the term used in Polish, *taniec charakterystyczny*, has a more specific meaning as "character dance." By the 1920s, character dance was a well-established category in classical ballet, made popular during the 1830s through Fanny Elssler's colorful folkloristic "national dances."[47] Thus, the author of the Polish-language review was offering an *aesthetic* justification for the dance: it was "innocent" because it was meant as a widely accepted genre of ballet. That the scene was conceived generically as a character dance is further confirmed by materials from Zajlich's archive. One inventory of his choreographed works contains handwritten comments regarding the genres of the individual works. Among annotations such as "classical" or "characteristic," the ballet *Karczma* is given the label "folkloristic characteristic" (*ludowy charakterystyczny*).[48] Furthermore, Jan Szer, listed on the playbill for *Karczma* as the Jewish Innkeeper (*Żyd Karczmarz*), was a soloist of Warsaw ballet especially admired for his character roles and parts that called for his mime skills.[49]

The contrasting Jewish response to *Karczma* was informed by decades of bitter experience with caricatures of dancing Jews on Polish stages and the ubiquity of majufes—a concept that by then became a shorthand for stereotypical sonic Jewishness—in everyday discourse. In emphasizing that such caricature "should not be allowed in even the cheapest cabaret, let alone a national theatre," the author of *Der Moment*'s article offers a particularly revealing commentary. Singspiels such as *A Jew in the Barrel* were considered lowbrow entertainment. Numerous surviving playbills confirm that such plays were typically performed together with a couple of other mediocre one-act comedies; that such programming was common as midnight entertainment during balls, especially during carnival; and that, starting in the later nineteenth century, these plays were often staged both in garden theaters that offered a lighter theatrical fare and in so-called people's theaters (*teatry ludowe*). The *Karczma* performance was different: it was presented in the Grand Theater in Warsaw, Poland's premier national stage, and the two other works on the program were internationally recognized masterpieces, *Scheherazade* and *Cavalleria rusticana*. Likewise, the 1894 Kraków performance of *A Wedding in Ojców* accompanied Ruggero Leoncavallo's *Pagliacci*. The organizers of these events must have seen this as perfectly acceptable because to them *A Wedding in Ojców* and its variant *Karczma* were genres of characteristic, folkloristic ballet. For the Jewish spectators, however, this was adding insult to injury—to allow caricatures of dancing Jews on the national stage in company of much-cherished artworks was to sanction and normalize them.

These stereotypes of Jewishness had broader implications that were increasingly recognized by the politically more alert among Jewish and gentile critics. Not only did such comical representations ridicule and humiliate Jews; more dangerously, they fed into specific stereotypes that were transformed within Polish social and political discourse into serious accusations against the Jewish minority. In the case of *Karczma* and the dancing innkeeper, these tapped into the highly volatile discourse regarding the role of Jewish innkeepers in spreading drunkenness among peasants.[50] Thus, antisemitic caricatures presented on theater stages fed into charges that were routinely used to justify denying Jews full political rights and to incite and rationalize violence against Jews.

In a larger geographic and chronological context, these stereotypes resonate with racialized representations of groups other than Jews. The inability of artists, audiences, and critics to recognize the problems with such depictions of Jews on the Polish stage parallels the persistent tone deafness to the problematics of blackface, yellowface, and Jewface representations we encounter in American culture. While studying the historical manifestations of these phenomena reveals much about the racial and ethnic circumstances of the past, such inquiry also illuminates our own shortcomings in failing to discuss and continuing to employ such representations. In recent years, academics and artists in the United States have been leading the efforts to use historical awareness and thoughtful staging as a starting point for revising our social attitudes toward these troubling representations.[51]

Similarly, the stereotypical representations of dancing Jews have not only been pervasive in Polish theatrical productions of the past, they also continue to surface in contemporary stagings (other instances of stereotypical modern representations of Jews and Jewishness are also mentioned in chaps. 10 and 11). In 2015, Cracovia Danza Ballet, a well-known Polish ensemble focused on historical dance, prepared a revival of *A Wedding in Ojców*, promising musical and choreographic authenticity steeped in painstaking archival research.[52] The "dancing Jew" has a cameo in this version: amid the performance brimming with the delightful and familiar tunes and lively choreographies of this national ballet, a traditionally dressed Jew emerges from a large coffer, and surrounded by bewildered wedding guests, he performs a clumsy dance to the accompaniment of alien-sounding music. After completing his dance, he spends several minutes extorting money for various gifts of dubious value from the ensnared Bride and Bridegroom, gets kicked out of the room, and finally reveals himself to be one of the peasants in Jewface.[53]

Cracovia Danza's production offers a useful case study: in searching for artistic "authenticity," the ensemble must have encountered information about Jewish characters having been included in the historical stagings of *A Wedding in Ojców*. But introducing a Jewish character into a twenty-first-century production also requires a careful examination of the social and political context of the original and a consideration of the potential impact on today's audiences to assure that the choreography, music, costume, and so on do not perpetuate harmful stereotypes.

This chapter seeks to provide the context that eluded Cracovia Danza's efforts at authenticity: to grasp the full impact of historical representations of Jews and the Jewish tavern in Polish ballet on their Jewish and gentile spectators. It does so both by placing such performances within the larger tradition of stereotyped portrayals of a dancing Jew to a largely gentile audience and by contextualizing this cultural phenomenon within the prevailing social, historical, and political discourses. It is also my hope that an awareness of these contexts for historical performances will help today's artists and audiences in seeking ethical and meaningful ways of engaging with the historical presence of Jewish characters in Polish national ballet.

Appendix

Table 1.1. Timeline Stage Works in the Tradition of *A Wedding in Ojców*

Date	Title	Composer(s)	Librettist	Choreographer
1794	*Cud mniemany czyli Krakowiacy i górale*	Jan Stefani	Wojciech Bogusławski	
1816	*Nowe krakowiaki; Zabobon czyli Krakowiacy i górale*	Karol Kurpiński [and Jan Stefani]	Jan Nepomucen Kamiński	
1823	*Wesele krakowskie w Ojcowie*	Jan Stefani, Karol Kurpiński, Józef Damse	Bonawentura Kudlicz Thierry (?)	Louis Thierry, Julia Mierzyńska, Maurice Pion
1839	*Wesele krakowskie w Ojcowie* (offshoot: *Stach i Zośka*)	Józef Stefani [and Jan Stefani, Karol Kurpiński, Józef Damse, Józef Elsner]	Bonawentura Kudlicz (Pion?)	Maurice Pion
1894	*Wesele w Ojcowie*	Karol Kurpiński [and Jan Stefani, Józef Damse, Józef Stefani, Józef Elsner]	Bonawentura Kudlicz (Zaborski?)	Stanisław Zaborski
1905 1911 1914	*Wesele w Ojcowie*	Karol Kurpiński, Karol Namysłowski, Leopold Lewandowski [and Jan Stefani, Józef Damse, Józef Stefani, Józef Elsner]	Bonawentura Kudlicz (Kulesza?)	Michał Kulesza

HALINA GOLDBERG is Professor of Musicology and Director of Robert F. Byrnes Russian and East European Institute in the Hamilton Lugar School of Global and International Studies at Indiana University Bloomington. She is author of *Music in Chopin's Warsaw*, editor of a special issue of the *Musical Quarterly* titled "Jewish Spirituality, Modernity, and Historicism in the Long Nineteenth Century: New Musical Perspectives," editor with Nancy Sinkoff of *Centering the Periphery: Polish Jewish Culture beyond the Capital* and the accompanying website (https://polishjewishmusic.iu.edu), and director of the digital project Jewish Life in Interwar Łódź (https://jewish-lodz.iu.edu).

Notes

This research was supported by the Fulbright-Hays Faculty Research Abroad Award. I am grateful for the generous help of librarians and archivists in Poland, especially the staff of Muzeum Teatralne in Warsaw, Dr. Diana Poskuta-Włodek from Archiwum Artystyczne i Biblioteka Teatru im, Juliusza Słowackiego in Kraków, and Mariola Nałęcz from Zakład Zbiorów Muzycznych Biblioteki Narodowej in Warsaw. All translations are mine, unless otherwise indicated, H.G.

1. In early nineteenth-century Warsaw, theater and opera shared the same stage, the "National Theater." After the failure of the November Uprising, the Russian authorities forbade the use of the name "National Theater," replacing it with "Grand Theater" ("Teatr Wielki"). In 1924, the name "National Theater" was returned to the dramatic stage built at the site of the former "Variety Theater," whereas the main opera house continued to be called the "Grand Theater."

2. The story can be pieced together from press announcements and reviews and the surviving playbill for the October 12, 1921, performance. *Kurjer Warszawski: wydanie poranne* 101 (1921), no. 283; *Kurjer Warszawski: wydanie wieczorne* 101 (1921), no. 283; *Kurier poranny* 44 (1921), no. 278; "A skandal in groysn teater" [A Scandal in the Great Theater], *Der Moment* 234 (October 13, 1921); playbill for a performance at the National Theater, Warsaw, October 12, 1921, Warsaw, Muzeum Teatralne, MT/X/504/3. On Maria Labia's career, see Harold Rosenthal, "Labia, Maria," *Grove Music Online*, ed. Deane Root, accessed December 30, 2019, https://doi.org/10.1093/gmo/9781561592630.article.15755.

3. Chone Shmeruk, "*Mayufes*: A Window on Polish-Jewish Relations," in *Polin: Studies in Polish Jewry Volume 10: Jews in Early Modern Poland*, ed. Gershon David Hundert (Liverpool: Liverpool University Press, Littman Library of Jewish Civilization, 1997), 273–86. Shmeruk's article was first published in Polish in *The Jews in Poland*, ed. Andrzej K. Paluch (Kraków: Jagiellonian University Research Center on Jewish History and Culture in Poland, 1992), and in Hebrew in *Tarbiz* 63, no. 1 (1993–94).

4. Shmeruk, "*Mayufes*," 280.

5. Bret Werb, "Majufes: A Vestige of Jewish Traditional Song in Polish Popular Entertainments," *Polish Music Journal* 6, no. 1, accessed December 30, 2019, https://polishmusic.usc.edu/research/publications/polish-music-journal/vol6no1/majufes/. The subject is also addressed in Werb, "Musical Afterthoughts on Shmeruk's 'Mayufes,'" in *Polin: Studies in Polish Jewry Volume 32: Jews and Music-Making in the Polish Lands*, ed. François Guesnet, Benjamin Matis, and Antony Polonsky (Liverpool: Liverpool University Press, Littman Library of Jewish Civilization, 2020), 63–82.

6. Werb, "Majufes."

7. Werb points to the absence of archival sources that is a result of the total destruction of Warsaw's National Theater during the Second World War. However, a closer exploration of the current archives at the National Theater and other document collections in Poland revealed some gems that have proven invaluable in writing this article.

8. A good English-language overview of *Cracovians and Highlanders* and its libretto's political allusions is found in Anna Parkitna, "Opera in Warsaw, 1765–1830: Operatic Migration, Adaptation, and Reception in the Enlightenment" (PhD diss., Stony Brook, 2020), 256–265.

9. The association between ballet and the "wedding" topic goes back to the Renaissance beginnings of this artform when narrative dance spectacles accompanied the lavish celebrations of aristocratic and royal nuptials.

10. Janina Pudelek and Jadwiga Kosicka, "The Warsaw Ballet under the Directorships of Maurice Pion and Filippo Taglioni, 1832–1853," *Dance Chronicle* 11, no. 2 (1988): 219–73; and "Wesele w Ojcowie," *Encyklopedia Teatru Polskiego*, accessed December 30, 2019, http://www.encyklopediateatru.pl/sztuki/8099/wesele-w-ojcowie. It is unclear how much Thierry and his anointed successor Maurice Pion contributed to this original version.

11. Pudelek and Kosicka, "Warsaw Ballet," 243–44.

12. Both preserved in the binders' volume from the 1820s in Biblioteka i Fototeka Instytutu Muzykologii UJ, 5197.

13. *Wesele w Ojcowie: balet układu P. Maurice Pion* (Wilno: n.p., [ca. 1840]), Biblioteka Narodowa Mus.III.104.521 Cim.; and *Zbiór krakowiaków z baletów* Wesele w Ojcowie *i* Stach i Zośka (Warsaw: Klukowski, [1842]), Biblioteka Narodowa Mus.II.17.826 Cim. These and other prints are referenced in Adam Tomasz Kukla, "Kwestia autorstwa muzyki do baletu na przykładzie *Wesela w Ojcowie*," *Muzyka* 64, no. 4 (2019): 37–64, where he also addresses the textual instability of this "work."

14. Several scores of new mazurkas composed by Józef Stefani for various performances of *A Wedding in Ojców* can be found in the collections of the National Library in Warsaw.

15. Ludomir Michał Rogowski, a conductor of the National Theater, is mentioned in relation to the 1923 *Wesele na wsi* by Irena Turska, *Przewodnik Baletowy* (Kraków: PWM, 1997), 370. In my research, I encountered no references to Moniuszko's arrangement of the ballet, which Werb mentions.

16. I might add that this is not surprising. Both genres, opera and even more so ballet, have historically been characterized by a great degree of textual fluidity. On this topic, see several chapters in *The Oxford Handbook of Opera*, ed. Helen M. Greenwald (New York: Oxford University Press, 2014), for example, Louise K. Stein, "How Opera Travelled," and Philip Gossett, "Writing the History of Opera." In comparison to other canonic work, the textual instability of *A Wedding in Ojców* is extreme.

17. *Czas: dodatek miesięczny* (October–December 1857), 280.

18. In Zajlich's documents, there are three such inventories, each listing all three ballets in succession. Warsaw, Muzeum Teatralne, D. 140 III k. 48. A playbill for *A Village Wedding* also survives in Warsaw, Muzeum Teatralne, P. 2413.

19. Jan Nepomucen Kamiński, *Zabobon, czyli Krakowiacy i Górale: Zabawka dramatyczna ze śpiewkami w 3 aktach* (Lwów: K. B. Pfaff, 1821).

20. There was a deep patriotic meaning to choosing this specific location. Mogiła (The Mound), today part of Kraków, is the site of the Wanda Mound, purportedly the grave of the legendary eighth-century Princess Wanda who committed suicide rather than marry a foreign prince.

21. Kraków, Archiwum Artystyczne i Biblioteka Teatru im. Juliusza Słowackiego, playbills, opr_25-289.

22. Kraków, Archiwum Artystyczne i Biblioteka Teatru im. Juliusza Slowackiego, file 84.

23. On dancing in taverns, involving children, mixed-gender, and interdenominational dancing, see Sonia Beth Gollance, *It Could Lead to Dancing: Mixed-Sex Dancing and Jewish Modernity* (Stanford, CA: Stanford University Press, 2021), esp. chap. 3, "The Tavern: Jewish Participation in Rural Leisure Culture."

24. "Stanisław Zaborski," *Encyklopedia Teatru Polskiego*, accessed December 30, 2019, http://encyklopediateatru.pl/osoby/82114/stanislaw-zaborski.

25. "Stanisław Zaborski," in *Encyklopedia*.

26. Most likely it was not a coincidence that the names Lejbuś and Siora were titular characters in Julian Ursyn Niemcewicz's novel in letters entitled *Lejbe i Siora, czyli listy dwóch kochanków* (1821), which discussed the question of Jewish assimilation to Polish society. Niemcewicz (1758–1841) was an eminent Polish writer, political figure, and supporter of the May 3 Constitution.

27. Kraków, Biblioteka Jagiellońska, 224660 IV 20/45. Zaborski was not part of the performance. The character of the Innkeeper's Wife is absent in this staging.

28. Wergiliusz Calori, *Pan Twardowski* (Warsaw: Druk i Nakład Drukarni Teatrów Warszawskich "Jan Cotty," 1874), 13–14.

29. Calori, *Pan Twardowski*, 7.

30. Program from a performance of Sonnenfeld's *Pan Twardowski* at the Grand Theater in Warsaw on January 6, 1916. Warsaw, Biblioteka Narodowa, DŻS XIXA 7.

31. Calori, *Pan Twardowski*, 10.

32. Opera program, *Pan Twardowski. Balet fantastyczny. Muzyka Ludomira Różyckiego. Choreografia baletmistrza Piotra Zajlicha. Dekoracje profesora Wincentego Drabika* [Warsaw: Drukarnia Teatralna F. Syrewicza, 1926], Warsaw, Biblioteka Narodowa, DŻS XIXA 6b; and J. R., "Teatr Wielki," *Robotnik*, May 12, 1921, 2. More recent performances continue to include the "Jewish Dance," as seen in the photograph of the "Jewish Dance" from the 1973 production of Różycki's *Pan Twardowski* (Act III) at the Warsaw Grand Theater, with Benon Dymecki as the Innkeeper and Krystyna Zgórska as the Innkeeper's Wife. Warsaw, Muzeum Teatralne, 4/222, https://archiwum.teatrwielki.pl/media//pan-twardowski-ludomir-rozycki-1973-06-24-17, accessed March 19, 2024.

33. According to my preliminary findings, which cannot be discussed in depth here, the term *majufes*, possibly derived from the Hebrew incipit of the Sabbath hymn (*zemirah*) "Mah Yafit," first appeared in Polish-language sources in the early nineteenth century, invariably used to mock the musical and cultural foreignness of Jews, especially those aspiring to achieve acculturation. The offensive and derogatory Yiddish term *mah yofis* or *mayufes* appears in Yiddish-language sources later and denotes Jewish humiliation and the subservience of assimilated Jews; in fact, the Yiddish term *mayofes-yid* or *mahyofesnik* carries a meaning akin to the American Uncle Tom. Since this chapter focuses on the representations of Jews in dance in Polish-language stage works, I use the Polish version of the term throughout.

34. Oskar Kolberg, *Lud*, ser. 5, *Krakowskie*, pt. 1 (Kraków: Drukarnia Uniwersytetu Jagiellońskiego, 1871), 204.

35. Kolberg, *Lud*, 212–15 and 224–25.

36. There were also some earlier Polish performances of plays in this vein, going back to the 1820s. These were translated from German and French and thus suggest a migration of the stereotyped image of a Jew on the theater stage. For a discussion of 1730 operatic performances in Hamburg that incited hostility toward Jews, see Jeanne Swack, "Anti-Semitism at the Opera: The Portrayal of Jews in the Singspiels of Reinhard Keiser," *Musical Quarterly* 84 (2000): 389–416.

37. Jerzy Got, *Repertuar teatru w Krakowie 1781–1843* (Warsaw: Instytut Sztuki Polskiej, 1969), 100.

38. For instance, a listing of the repertory for the 1862 season of Warsaw's Wielki and Rozmaitości Theaters mentions seven performances of *A Jew in a Barrel* (by comparison Moniuszko's *Halka*—already acclaimed as the Polish national opera—received eight, *Lucia di Lammermoor* seven, *Ernani* eight, *Troubadour* three, and *Rigoletto* only one). *Ruch muzyczny* (1862): 52, 828. There are also Chicago publications of this and related plays, which suggests that this theatrical tradition followed Polish audiences into diaspora. The presence of these Jewish characters on Polish stages and the astonishing popularity of *A Jew in a Barrel* are also referenced by Michael Steinlauf, "Polish-Jewish Theater: The Case of Mark Arnshteyn, a Study of the Interplay among Yiddish, Polish and Polish-Language Jewish Culture in the Modern Period" (PhD diss., Brandeis University, 1988), 53, 87n132, and 88n139.

39. Jews that appeared on German stages as far back as the early eighteenth century are depicted as having similar moral flaws. See Swack, "Anti-Semitism at the Opera," 395–400.

40. The various folk dances in this tradition, named variously *żyd*, *żydek*, *żydowski*, *żydowka*, *żydowska polka*, *gibany*, *kiwoń*, *kłaniany*, and *sydek*, are described in Grażyna W. Dąbrowska, *Taniec w polskiej tradycji. Leksykon* (Warsaw: Muza S. A., 2006), 295–97.

41. *Izraelita* 6 no. 30 (August 6 [August 18], 1871): 248.

42. *Izraelita* 10 no. 28 (July 4 [July 16],1875): 224–26; 11 no. 30 (July 23 [August 4], 1876): 237; 12 no. 8 (February 11 [February 23], 1877): 60–61; 12 no. 19 (May 5 [May 17], 1877): 155; 12 no. 25 (June 17 [June 29], 1877): 200.

43. Ludwik Solski, *Wspomnienia 1855–1893* (Kraków: Wydawnictwo Literackie, 1955), 125–28. The story is also reported in *Izraelita* 12 no. 8 (February 11 (February 23), 1877): 60–61.

44. *Izraelita* 12 no. 29 (July 15 (July 27), 1877): 230–31. The author of the review mistakenly names Mosenthal as the author, but the work was probably Johann-Heinrich Mirani's *Eine Judenfamilie*.

45. *Czas*, June 17, 1897, 3; June 22, 1897, 3; June 24, 1897, 3. Also see Ignacy Daszyński, *Pamiętniki* (Warsaw: Partia Razem, 2016), 45.

46. Maria Prussak, "Demonstracje żydowskich studentów (1903)," in *Teatr żydowski w Polsce*, ed. Anna Kuligowska-Korzeniewska and Małgorzata Leyko (Łódź: Wydawnictwo Uniwersytetu Łódzkiego, 1998), 98–105.

47. Lisa C. Arkin and Marian Smith, "National Dance in the Romantic Ballet" in *Rethinking the Sylph: New Perspectives on the Romantic Ballet*, ed. Lynn Garafola (Hanover and London: Wesleyan University Press, 1997), 11–68.

48. Warsaw, Muzeum Teatralne, D. 140 III k. 48.

49. "Jan Szer," *Encyklopedia Teatru Polskiego*, accessed December 30, 2019, http://encyklopediateatru.pl/osoby/70238/jan-szer. Werb draws attention to a possible connection between Szer's performance as a Jew in *Karczma* and a similar part he danced in the "Rome Inn" scene in Różycki's *Pan Twardowski*. See Werb, "Musical Afterthoughts," 72.

50. This topic is taken up, among others, in Glenn Dynner, *Yankel's Tavern: Jews, Liquor, & Life in the Kingdom of Poland* (New York and London: Oxford University Press, 2014).

51. Among the many examples of such musicological studies are W. Anthony Sheppard, *Extreme Exoticism: Japan in the American Musical Imagination* (New York: Oxford University Press, 2019); and Ayana O. Smith, *Inclusive Music Histories: Leading Change through Research and Pedagogy* (New York: Routledge, 2023). There are also studies exploring the history and implications of American Jewface: see Ted Merwin, "Jew-Face: Non-Jews Playing Jews on the American Stage," *Cultural and Social History* 4, no. 2 (2007): 215–33; and Rebecca Rossen, "Dancing Jews and Jewesses: Jewishness, Ethnicity, and Exoticism in American Dance," in *The Oxford Handbook of Dance and Ethnicity*, ed. Anthony Shay and Barbara Sellers-Young (New York and London: Oxford University Press, 2016), 66–90.

52. Some of these claims can be found on Cracovia Danza's website, http://cracoviadanza.pl/en/spektakl/58, accessed May 29, 2023. They are also repeated in press releases and interviews that accompanied the premiere.

53. An outdoor performance of *A Wedding in Ojców* by Cracovia Danza in Ojców Park, August 28, 2016, https://www.youtube.com/watch?v=14WWjvsZPUg&list=PLZeg2xwALuD_142kcq42a5zqVbxirBiFy, accessed May 29, 2023. In 2018, Cracovia Danza performed *A Wedding in Ojców* at the Grand Theater in Warsaw; the Jewish element was included in this staging in some form, as the précis promises a performance "complete with Jewish tunes," https://teatrwielki.pl/en/repertoire/calendar/2018-2019/the-wedding-at-ojcow-harnasie/termin/2018-11-23_19-00/, accessed May 29, 2023.

2

The Romantic Invention of the Jewish Inn

Bożena Shallcross

"FIVE INNS APPEARED BY THE roadway, and all of them dirty and shabby," observed the poet Władysław Syrokomla in his prose about excursions in the vicinity of the city of Wilno, in which he also confirmed the repetitious sameness of the inns' look as well as their surroundings: "A dilapidated tavern, a poor village, a pear tree in a field—are all the same as elsewhere."[1] Numerous other writers, travelers, and painters confirmed the ubiquity of real inns. Spreading like proverbial mushrooms, obviously they could not prosper amid such a fierce competition. Behind this visual and physical plethora of uniformity lurked numerous complications. To begin, this common element of the Polish-Lithuanian countryside was subjected to all kinds of legal rules, restrictions, and customs. Inns were built and owned by Polish gentry who, as holders of the *propinacja*—that is, alcohol monopoly—profited considerably from the privilege. But the majority of those who were directly involved in the business, either through leasing, managing, or serving there, were Polish Jews, who with their families were frequently the only Jews in a village or a town. One cannot overemphasize the strong connection that developed between the identity of a Jewish innkeeper and his inn.

The process of identification between the figure of a Jew and the inn (that paradoxically was not even his property but a landowner's) is reflected in all types of nineteenth-century writing. I approach this relationship through a hermeneutic perspective on the relation between Soplicowo's inn and its keeper Jankiel in Adam Mickiewicz's incomparable epic poem *Pan Tadeusz* (1834).[2] Mickiewicz, the poetic genius of Polish Romanticism, created there an everlasting portrayal of both the innkeeper and his inn. Yet, it was a minor Polish writer Franciszek Kowalski who invoked arguably the strongest identification between an inn and its Jewish innkeeper: "A roadside inn without a Jew is like a body without a soul; where there is an inn, there is a Jew."[3] This succinct definition not only captures a more general Romantic perspective on the deep, spiritual bond between a building and its inhabitant but also indicates an instance of an ethnic stereotyping through essentialization: the inn was fundamentally a Jewish phenomenon. Kowalski collapsed all possible distinctions between the inn and the Jew. For him, they constituted one entity. An inn without a Jewish innkeeper would have far-reaching negative consequences: such an inn would be a soulless shell devoid of the Jewish expression—the *locus* deprived of its *genius*. These characterless inns, devoid of a dominant and identifying Jewish presence, became a reality during the twentieth century when an economic and social development that originated in the earlier nineteenth-century revocation of the nobility's monopoly on alcohol gradually led to a degradation and disappearance of the Jewish inn. World War II and the genocide of Jews dealt the final blow to the cultural phenomenon.

Besides continuing the Romantic equivalence between the Jewish soul/self and his inn, Polish realist literature has developed a strong lineage of various evocations of the Jewish inn as a cultural site of the everyday or a shelter for those who were in transition—that is, outside the quotidian; the lineage was often permeated by an antisemitic bias and prone to satirical exaggeration.[4] Mickiewicz, who forged the most influential poetic image of the inn as a multifunctional site of encounters of all strata of the society that would not cross paths otherwise, conceived it as a common place for peaceful social gatherings, entertainment, and business dealings. (The poet's description of the inn can be found at the end of this essay in appendixes 1–2). Alexander Lindskog succinctly ascertains the Mickiewiczian representation in chapter 8 of the present volume: "The most famous such image is no doubt Jankiel's tavern in the Polish 1834 national epos *Pan Tadeusz*, where it serves as a center and frame, an anchoring-point and image of harmony and coexistence of the different social groups of the lost state, in which the Jew naturally has a place."[5] Ironically, this center was located off-center, on the outskirts, by the road, and it was in competition with the second Soplicowo inn.

The question why Mickiewicz decided to include in *Pan Tadeusz* such a common type of vernacular wooden building as central to the social life of the village contains a kernel of an answer: the inn had to be placed in the poem for it was a type of building indispensable in the countryside as it was known then. The poet saturated his entire epic work with images of an ordinary (*pospolite*)—neither beautiful nor sublime—life, a quality that was frequently viewed as negative by his contemporary readers and critics.[6] In celebrating the simple pleasures of the common and the everyday, the poet foregrounded the fact that an inn was an abode of the sympathetic Other, sympathetic because of the poet's all-too-uncommon positive general attitude toward Jews, Jewishness, and Judaism. Facing this aesthetic challenge, however, Mickiewicz turned the ordinary Jewish inn of Soplicowo into an extraordinarily whimsical and illusive building. In his intricate understanding of the Jewish inn, its auratic subtleties and visual extravaganza as well as other aesthetic qualities, Mickiewicz was ahead of his time—among other reasons, because he invoked its shabbiness and ugliness as autonomous aesthetic values, not just a mere negation of beauty.[7] However, some of his critics did not notice this careful planning of the inn's appearance and considered its unsightliness as an artistic failure because it had a biblical derivation. One critic took such a condescending point of view and wrote that in *Pan Tadeusz* "two Jewish inns stand opposite each other with the full unsightliness of Jerusalem's buildings."[8] For others, especially for the ethnographer Zygmunt Gloger, Mickiewicz's belief in the Judaic provenance of the inn was completely false.

Before Mickiewicz introduced the Jewish Other that dwelled in the inn, he presented the building itself as the Other, as a radically different, laugh-provoking yet dramatic and strangely alive space. Literary historians who wrote about architecture in *Pan Tadeusz* did not fully appreciate the possibilities hidden in the comparative Polish-Jewish elaboration of Jankiel's inn and approached its representation as a mere humorous depiction. For example, Henryk Biegeleisen argued in what was one of the earliest thoughtful readings of the inn's appearance that "similes in the entire description of the inn do not transcend the Jewish sphere, like its subject, adding to the greatly comical air of the inn."[9] Biegeleisen's observation that the poetic references point consistently (although not exclusively) to humor fused with Jewishness is a well-entrenched tradition in Mickiewicz studies, and few critics veer from it. In her recent reading of the Mickiewiczian inn, Grażyna B. Tomaszewska counterbalances the observation that Jankiel's inn is a light comic creation. According to her, the poet's superimposition of the image of an old praying Jewish man on the inn's exterior is not a case of odd personification but a disclosure of existential Jewish homelessness. Tomaszewska circumvents the satirical distortion of the inn and eloquently argues that Mickiewicz envisions the inn as a Jewish home whose fate is "eternally uncertain, exposed to loss, whose being one has to avow in prayer."[10] Clearly, her argument reflects the somewhat proto-existential stereotype of the Wandering Jew. These two readings—Biegeleisen's and Tomaszewska's—can be (almost too easily) pitched against each other: the first narrows the description's meaning to its comic aspects; the second probes its depth in terms, purportedly, of solemn meditation on Jewish fate. Nonetheless, Tomaszewska's interpretation of the old inn as a symbolic representation of the Jewish home whose existence is always threatened overlooks the poet's effort at emphasizing the continuity of the Jewish art of building as having its archetypal roots in both Noah's Ark and the Temple of Solomon.

But first, some basics. Jankiel leases from Judge Soplica two inns: one new and one old; in doing so, he keeps potential competition at bay. The inns are located across from each other at the Soplicowo road, a practical choice for such a fixture of convenience. Out of the two, it is the old building that preoccupies the narrator of the epos, who in the previous parts of the text revealed a Romantic predilection for historical, or simply old, architecture. The description of this inn's exterior precedes Jankiel's appearance. This order of introduction—first the inn, second its inhabitant—follows the poet's earlier order of representing the characters in *Pan Tadeusz*; for example, young Zosia's bedroom reveals, despite her absence, ample information about her. This approach is facilitated by the quintessentially Romantic medium—the language of traces that, projected on the interiority of Zosia's private space in the Soplicowo manor, turned her room into her intimate portrayal. This aesthetic formula, predicated on an indirect representation of a dweller through her or his dwelling's decor, choice of furniture, portraits, and knickknacks, and so on was mastered by Honoré de Balzac, who in his prose frequently relied on the premise according to which what was in the exterior was also in the interior, and vice versa. Jankiel the innkeeper, likewise, makes his appearance in *Pan Tadeusz* after a vivid and elaborate presentation of his inn, but the actual mimetic link between his inn and him is far more precarious.

Mickiewicz saturated the description of the inn with comparisons; indeed, this embedded descriptive passage contains more similes than other descriptions in *Pan Tadeusz*, creating through the strategic accumulation an additional rhetorical figure of amplification to the point of the description appearing as one huge simile.[11] What is the point behind this amplification? For Tadeusz Dworak, who studied comparisons in *Pan Tadeusz*, the description of the inn through frequent similes enhanced its *couleur local* and added humor and charm to the inanimate objects;[12] like Biegeleisen, he narrowed the similes' topical dimension to mosaicism, Jewishness, and a stylized figure of a Jew. Such objectives do not transcend the standard effect attributed to similes by rhetoric, and, indeed, there is more in Mickiewicz's description than this reading.

At first glance, the old and decrepit inn does not invoke the Romantic sublimity of a ruin. Hardly a noble ruin, it rather is an example of shabby poverty in its vernacular variation. Old vernacular buildings, not the least because of their locally sourced material, tend to blend in with their environment and become an organic whole with the nearby surroundings, their ecology, and what is culturally familiar. Indeed, one reason for this organic blending was landlords' commission of local builders and craftsmen, whose skills determined their product's overall vernacular character; such builders tended to employ a homegrown stylistic tradition, craft, and materials.[13]

However, Jankiel's inn and its figurative space are impacted by several architectural traditions, as shown in the amply detailed exterior appearance. Its style proves to be much harder to pinpoint despite its overall vernacular frame and the use of wood as material. On the one hand, the building is anchored in local village life; on the other, it stands out because of its patina and ancient genealogy. No wonder critics' response to this building varied. For example, the art historian Zdzisław Kępiński considered the inn to be analogous to Masonic architecture built in Polish lands in the beginning of the nineteenth century,[14] while the literary historian Marta Piwińska interpreted Jankiel's inn as a sample of the purest embodiment of Sarmatian baroque.[15] Her view concurs with the general observation made by historians of architecture that wooden Jewish buildings in small towns preserved the traditional *styl krajowy* (Polish national style) mostly through a use of arcades, pillars, balusters, decorative trims, "broken" roofs, and so on. Not surprisingly, Gloger, who rejects Mickiewicz's conviction that the inn had Judaic genealogy, views the inn as a purely Slavic construct. Gloger reads Mickiewicz quite literally as materially emphasizing local provenance of the raw building material.[16]

Contrary to these unidirectional stylistic attributions, I find it impossible to discern one style in the literary construction of the inn, let alone unify it conveniently under the umbrella term of the *styl krajowy*. Mickiewicz invented the inn, as I contend, in an entirely new manner, as a patinaed mixture of several different architectural styles and references to some well-known buildings that, according to the narrator, reflect on the overall character of the inn whose roots conceptually are in Judaic tradition.

Let us unpack the narrative of the old inn's genealogy concocted of overlapping architectural comparisons, all taken from places and periods other than the narrative present of Soplicowo. At multiple points, the similes indicate how valuable are the building's associations with Jewishness. In this sense, Mickiewicz's similes are aggrandizing and tend to circumvent the inn's basic vernacular character. Moreover, certain features of the building are hinted at and approximated—through comparison—but not described in detail. These strategies have one consequence: the inn's description is not mimetic. The narrator's plan to use some comparisons to upgrade the inn's architecture downgrades the mechanics of mimesis. Since the inn's description does not embrace imitation understood as a mirror reflection of the world, I would say that this gesture foregrounds instead "the art of the lamp," of the inner light of the poet directed toward the outside world, to use the literary critic M. H. Abrams's well-known distinction.[17] One might say that the light of the poet extends to the later dulcimer concert as a divinely inspired improvisation by Jankiel, the master of masters.

Besides this marginalized vernacularism, the inn is compared with at least two ancient architectural models. They return in the poem like echoes from a distant, biblical past and space; their reflexive, ontologically weak status stems from the fact that these prototypes do not exist as physical constructions. In turn, this status further underscores the inn's visionary rather than mimetic mode. Mickiewicz chose Noah's Ark as one of the prototypes, a decision that did not resonate in any architectural refinement in the inn's appearance; after all, as far as we know, Noah merely built a simple container that served as a vessel for paired representatives of the animal world. The comparison with Noah's Ark cleverly justifies the inn's dual functionality as an accommodation for travelers and a shelter for animals such as travelers' horses.

The second major comparative model that the poet fancies—the First Temple of Solomon in Jerusalem—belongs to the higher register.[18] This simile brings the inn closer to the religious sphere yet creates a certain comical tension between the archetypal sacred Temple and a more prosaic boxlike Ark. The Temple's actual design remains unknown, except for the information given in the Hebrew Bible's Book of Kings. Since the current archaeological research—due to the political situation—cannot support the biblical description of Solomon's Temple, the simile addresses, for the contemporary reader, a genealogical void, an immaterial trace, or an echo of a structure that in all probability was built but is known mainly through its biblical description. The reader is not left with an empty referral but with a phantasm of a semisacred building that is both Jewish and deeply entrenched in the more universal cultural imaginary.

These genealogical strategies, usually perceived as merely humorous, reveal the presence of a somewhat awkward cultural ambition in constructing this edifice. They strive to establish a higher social prestige for a simple Jewish country inn by inserting some of the oldest architectural references that frame and ennoble the general status and origin of the inn-type building. This framing, avoiding a purely historical speculation, embraces a Judaic lineage that contradicts the usual appearance of common inns, which is attested by nineteenth-century travel writers and ethnographers. Performed through comparison, the framing both expands and transcends the sphere of solely Judaic references when the narrator finds in the Soplicowo inn's curved shape a reflection of the famous Leaning Tower of Pisa. As an imagined and barely approximated construct, Jankiel's inn must transcend even the most basic law of gravitation, otherwise its half-rotten and crooked columns would not inspire confidence in those seeking shelter inside. Such a building, viewed by a practical eye, is not habitable. Looked at from the purely poetic perspective, however, the inn's inhabitability is a moot matter, for Mickiewicz did not consider this practical question worthy of an inclusion in the representation. For the poet, the inn—like the nearby manor—was imaginable but unbuildable and, like the nearby manor, hardly a home. The narrator embraced yet another perspective: the dispensation of the building's realness for the sake of material temporality manifested in the inn's decaying wood. Contemplating the distinction between buildable and unbuildable structures, an architectural historian Robert Harbison introduced yet another option: buildings such as the infinite constructs in Franz Kafka's prose.[19] This third option is closer to and somewhat overlapping with Mickiewicz's vision; the poet as the builder of the precarious textual inn belongs to the Kafkaesque literary club. Jankiel's inn is not a substantial structure that conflates two media, textual and architectural—or to shorten it, architextural—because it is not buildable. Rather, it is a fancifully symbolic entity endowed with a long genealogy and protean qualities. The distinction between the mirror and the lamp forcefully reappears in this part of the poetic mechanism of phantasmatic representation.

While rejecting the notion that the inn's rotten pillars have a Greek classical lineage, the narrator allows its descriptive potential to absorb another architectural trace echoing, this time, the much later Gothic style. Once again, this particular reference carries a certain risk of destabilizing the narrator's reliability, for he introduces the round arches adorning the inn's arcade as Gothic—"They're topped with arches (also made of wood) / Half-rounded, copying the Gothic mode."[20] Obviously, Gothic arches are sharp, never round. Whether the mention of half-rounded "Gothic" arches results from a deliberate confusion on the narrator's part (meant to enhance the comic effect through intentionally ignorant narrative voice) or a simple lapse in his knowledge, the invocation's mention of Gothic style contributes to the overall sense of the inn's cultural hybridity.

Thus, the inn—shifted toward the poetic discourse on architectural styles, building practices, and their circulation—is construed as a porous structure subjected to diverse claims. Laths, timber, straw, wooden ornaments made with an axe—they all generate the vernacular dimension of the building, its first descriptive layer. The second, cosmopolitan, so to speak, dimension is engendered by the entangled similes that conjoin Phoenician style with Gothic, and compare the inn to Noah's Ark, to a barn, and to a *szkoła* (Pol. school; in Yiddish, the word *shul*/school refers to a synagogue as a place of study).[21] Despite this genealogical complexity, the narrator makes another, even loftier, aspirational statement, according to which Jews disseminated the inn's peculiar style only within Polish architecture: "A style unknown / To architects in any place. / The Jews it was who brought it here to us." (119).[22] If taken seriously, this exclusive transfer from the Holy Land to Polish land should strengthen the inn's artistic identity as unique and essentially Jewish. This is not quite the case, as the building is too eclectic. The gesture of transfer creates, nonetheless, the textual layer that dialectically cements the entire structure. So strengthened, the inn incarnates a shareable Christian-Jewish space, shelter, and tradition.

The inn, being a complex attempt at multicultural appropriation that produced an architectural hybrid, is simultaneously transformed into a comic-fantastic architecture with two basic functions: a bizarre, architecturally eclectic enclave and a shelter for travelers. The slightly exaggerated ornamental excess of the building's exterior, accentuated through the numerous cultural similes, makes the inn's appearance a case of dissimilarity that complicates its common architectural type. Its overall incompatible aspects create disruptive energies, especially in the architectural, temporal, and religious spheres that feature in the inn's representation. Additionally marked with its accumulated patina of time, the building appears to be heterochronic. Michel Foucault asserts that the nineteenth century cherished spaces of heterotopias and heterochronies, which were considered "different," unusual, destabilizing.[23] And such was Jankiel's inn: a site radically othered to become a dwelling of the Other.

Amid the emphasized, accumulated deterioration that almost threatens its existence, Jankiel's inn is identified and seemingly unified through an optical illusion or pareidolia: in the irregular structure of the inn the eye perceives the figure of an old praying Jew. This type of optical perception organizes the architectural complexities of the inn into a more coherent visual pattern. The individually decrepit parts of the inn's elements that are falling apart—the old roof, its thatched cover, leaning pillars, and the blackened walls—gain one cohesive meaning through this deliberately anthropomorphizing image. As the last visual imprint of the inn, this inscription is most uncanny: the building's somewhat shaky structure, resembling an old Jew rocking in prayer, acquires features of a dynamic, (nearly) mobile object. I ask again: What sort of shelter could such a building offer? It would be hard to find an answer in the inn's architextuality, which is schematically represented as lacking a vertical structure. The philosopher Gaston Bachelard understands verticality in a house's symbolic structure as indispensable for its perception as a safe shelter.[24] The inn is a single-story building; following Bachelard, it does not suggest safety and security. Yet it has a surplus of other religious and spiritual values. Therefore, the insertion of the old praying Jew's image signals who is the *spiritus movens* of the place. In creating this personification, the narrative suggests a spiritual connection between prayer and its embodiment, for the practice of simultaneous praying and rocking engages both the soul and the body. The decorative elements of the inn's facade interweave with the image of the praying Jew: "At the end are knobs, a little like a box / That Jews strap to their foreheads when they pray, / Called 'tzitzt' in their tongue."[25] Art historians call this sculptural, vertical ornament, here translated as "knobs," *campanula*, as its shape is reminiscent of hanging bellflowers. The ornament takes on a religious tint when associated with tefillin as a part of phylacteries: the leather box of tefillin contains passages from the Torah inscribed on parchment and is worn by pious Jews on their foreheads. In the poem, this religious artifact is misidentified as tzitzit (*cyces* in Polish) which is a name for another, separate religious artifact—that is, the fringes of the prayer shawl known as tallit or a *katan*. These fringes, however, appear not on praying men's foreheads but on their shoulders and below. As a result of this double merger of Judaic artifacts, the campanula, intended to be a tefillin, becomes a tzitzit. Although seemingly erroneous, this fusion indicates how freely the sacred coalesces with the profane in the poem. Through these strategies, the seemingly ordinary roadside building becomes extraordinary—close to spiritual phenomena—as if suffused by a religious spirit. The image of the praying Jew proves that the inn is created as not quite a real thing but rather as Mickiewicz's phantasmatic product of a distinct, exilic longing and loss.

The sense of the inn's mournful spirituality quickly dissipates when its interior is revealed as a place where quite different "spiritualia" are present and served. Inside, in succession, simple rooms and furniture reflect their primary functions. Contrary to the incongruous but decorative exterior, the interior is generic in its layout and basic in its furnishing. It is simple, orderly, clean, and altogether vernacular. The organization of the space reflects the layout commonly used in inns across pre- and postpartition Poland, although its orderliness demonstrates how Mickiewicz veers away from the stereotypical view of Jewish inns as shabby and dirty. The old inn's interior is halved (but not gendered like in synagogues): one half is for those in transit, the other for the locals. Such division bespeaks of practicality that accordingly accommodates everyone from the village and beyond. Unlike the nearby gentry manor, the inn's space is open, as it serves the public as a business, yet it is not quite egalitarian, because of the spatial distancing and hierarchy among peasants, petty gentry, and others. The interior illustrates a set of social relations where little attention is paid to its detailed decor or anything else. This is a stage prepped for the crucial debate about the future of free Poland, and this debate is taking place under the watchful eye of Jankiel. Reflecting the specific representation of social order, as well as a pars pro toto image of public political discussion in the partitioned Polish-Lithuanian lands, the arrangement demonstrates how the vernacular character of the inn's interior is incompatible with its complicated exterior. The class division is so clearly delineated in this embodiment that it leaves no room for considering the Balzacian principle, according to which exterior parallels interior.

Standing in the middle of the inn, the innkeeper wears a black gaberdine adorned with silver clasps and a silk sash that emphasize the dignity of his person. His traditional but expensive outfit (silver, silk) bespeaks his identity and prosperity in a few strokes of a brush. Jankiel does not echo the personification of the "outer" Jew inscribed in the facade and lost to the world; this innkeeper is not immersed in prayer. Contrary to the outer image, Jankiel the "inner" Jew conveys the sober presence of mind (in the sense that he is minding his own business); exuding stability and solemnity, he is polite and honest yet towers over his seated, drinking guests. This characterization echoes the seventeenth-century agronomist and writer Jakub Kazimierz Haur, who in his agrarian treatise entitled *A General Agricultural Economics*, describes an ideal innkeeper as attentive, sober, and polite.[26] Additionally, a model tavern-keeper should have at his disposal musicians and serve good food. Mickiewicz's innkeeper does not have to aspire to these high standards; he already met them all.

Within his own space of the inn, the man exudes dignity; while outside, especially among the quarrelsome local gentry group, he represents the voice of reason and peace. In a telling moment, he uses a clever tactic and calls himself "Żydzisko" ("Ja sobie Żydzisko"); mainly through the use of the suffix *-isko*, *-sko* added to "Żyd" (Pol. Jew), the word strategically implies that Jankiel is not somebody to be afraid of, but rather someone quite familiar and honest.[27] For the Polish ear, this is a strong self-definition uttered not to jeopardize a sense of the Polish noblemen's superiority but to affirm Jankiel's nonthreatening presence among them. For the sake of the situation, he hides his knowledge, his conspiratorial connections, and his talent at commanding people. The "Żydzisko" expression diplomatically tones down his status and agency as well as strategically deemphasizes the creative persona for which he is renowned. He employs this cautious strategy, in which he is aided by the narrator, until the wedding dulcimer concert, during which he undergoes a powerful transformation and through his display of musical talent, wins the entire audience's enthusiastic esteem. The interplay between his identity and the social context simultaneously nuances and undermines the idea of Romantic inclusiveness that Mickiewicz propagates in *Pan Tadeusz*.[28]

In general, Jankiel's social significance rests on carrying out the various, often quite demanding functions ascribed to him by the "host of the poem," as the literary historian Kazimierz Wyka called the narrator. Jankiel is an innkeeper, a musician of some repute, assistant to the rabbi (*podrabinek*; diminutive of *podrabin*), the head of his family, and Father Robak's reliable and efficient emissary.[29] He is also a skillful fixer whose ability to negotiate peace among quarreling gentry is a condition for the more stable functioning of gentry solidarity (*bracia szlachta*). As for his spiritual depth—a quality not mentioned in the practical instructions published by Jakub Kazimierz Haur—it is demonstrated much later and elsewhere in the poem: in his famous improvisation on dulcimer during Zosia's and Tadeusz's wedding. Besides accurately reflecting the virtues of an ideal innkeeper, Jankiel surpasses them all during his dulcimer concert, through which he demonstrates that he is a virtuoso Polish-Jewish performer, a divinely inspired *improvisatore* whose mastery additionally comes across through artful citations of popular Polish tunes that re-create the audience as an affective community.[30]

This perception of Jankiel did not escape Cyprian Kamil Norwid, a careful contemporary reader, who portrayed him in the moment of concentration, perhaps preceding the performance (see fig. 2.1).[31] The image appears to be deliberately unfinished, as Norwid did not include in its pictorial space the item of importance—the dulcimer—and, therefore, engaged the genre of the fragment, so central to Romantic aesthetics. In a stroke of genius, Norwid made his Jankiel's tefillin appear slightly loose on his left arm as if partly undone; as a result, Jankiel holds in his right hand the tefillin's end, the tzitzit's fringes, and the mallets. Conjoined, the items metonymically bespeak the bond between his body, his piousness, and his music as a performative unity.

Jankiel's "Concert of Concerts" is a masterful performance envisioned as an experience ennobling and aestheticizing Jankiel.[32] All the roles ascribed to Jankiel converge at several points, including Jewish spiritual superiority—a perennial trope in Judaism that Mickiewicz prefers to see in terms of Israel's seniority.[33] I would argue that the poem tries yet does not entirely succeed in making a case for the innkeeper's dual identity—that of a good Jew and a "good Pole," because of one qualifying word: *though* in the brief phrase "though a Jew" (*choć Żyd*).[34] This word creates a tension that reflects Jankiel's otherness and lower rank within the vertical social structure of Soplicowo. Only from the pivotal point of his liberating musical performance that spiritually dominates his audience does Jankiel exercise his spiritual and artistic agency as the master. This moment of spiritual power is fleeting, as brief as the dulcimer concert, after which he sheds his transformed persona and returns to the usual status of a respected Jewish innkeeper and a patriot who deferentially kisses General Dąbrowski's hand.

Mickiewicz's inn is not just a crumbling, bizarre construct; it is a performative inn, very much like Jankiel the innkeeper is also a virtuoso dulcimer performer. Performativity, heterochrony, openness, and ambiguity

Figure 2.1 "Jankiel," Cyprian Kamil Norwid, from ink drawing of "Jankiel and Shylock," 1848. Warsaw, Muzeum Narodowe, Rys. Pol. 159761 MNW. Digital Collections of the National Museum in Warsaw. https://cyfrowe.mnw.art.pl/pl/zbiory/898867. Public domain.

manifested in the inclusion of diverse references connect but do not conflate the dwelling with its dweller. The inn's exterior is anthropomorphized to look like an old praying Jew, while the inn's interior is overseen by a Jewish man, one not in a praying trance but one busy taking attentive care of his guests' immediate needs and political future.[35] In this way, Mickiewicz went against the general trend of representing Polish-Jewish inns and their keepers as a typical cultural phenomenon. Under his pen, both his creations turned to be uniquely influential in imagining the ever-illusory national unity.

Appendix 1

The new inn made an uninspired impression:
The old one had been built in ancient fashion
Dreamed up by the carpenters of Tyre, and then
Spread through the world by the Jews—a style unknown
To architects in any other place.
The Jews it was who brought it here to us.
It's shaped like a ship in front, a temple behind;
The ship part is a Noah's Ark on land,
Or, as the vulgar say, a barn—a house
For sundry creatures (horses, oxen, cows,
Billy goats); while flocks of poultry dwell upstairs
With crawling insects too, and snakes in pairs.
The oddly formed rear section brings to mind
The Temple of Solomon on the Mount, designed
By Hiram's carpenters—who for their part
Had been first to learn the builder's art.
Synagogues are still built this way; in turn,
Their shape is seen in that of inn and barn.
A roof of thatch and unplaned boards juts high,
Like a ragged Jewish hat, into the sky.
Above are long rows of wooden galleries
On moldering pillars that are mysteries
Of architecture—leaning to one side
Like Pisa's famous tower, still they abide,
Shunning, in fact, the models of ancient Greece
For the pillars lack both capital and base.
They're topped with arches (also made of wood)
Half-rounded, copying the Gothic mode,
Formed not by burin or with chisel, but by
The carpenter's ax, deployed most artfully.
They curve like the arms of sabbath candlesticks.
At the end are knobs, a little like a box
That Jews strap to their foreheads when they pray,
Called "tzitzit" in their tongue. In summary
The crooked inn resembles from afar
The figure of a Jew swaying in prayer:
The roof a hat, the thatch a straggling beard,

Smoke-blackened walls the gown; in front, secured
Like tzitzit there, an ornament is carved.[36]

Appendix 2

Inside, synagogue-like the inn was halved:
One part, with small cramped room, was set aside
For gentlemen and ladies on the road;
The other half was one enormous hall.
Long wooden tables stood along each wall;
By them, but lower, stood chair by little chair
Like children round their father.
Sitting there
Were peasants cheek by jowl with every sort
Of lesser gentry. The overseer sat apart.
Sunday it was; they'd been to Mass, then after,
They'd come to Jankiel's inn for drink and laughter.
Each had raw vodka in a frothing cup,
A barmaid ran about, topping them up.
In the middle stood Jankiel, keeper of the inn,
With silver clasps on his floor-length gaberdine,
Left hand tucked in his silken belt, the right
Stroking his long gray beard in solemn thought.
He kept a careful eye on everything,
Gave orders, welcomed new folks entering,
Conversed, calmed those too heatedly debating—
Not serving though, but merely circulating.
Everyone knew him for an upright man.
He'd managed the inn for many years; no one,
Peasant or gentry, ever complained
To the manor. Why would they? He'd every kind
Of top-rate drink: he kept book carefully
But honestly; he welcomed jollity,
Loathed drunkenness. He loved all gatherings
And hosted wedding parties, christenings,
He'd have a village band—with double bass
And bagpipes—play each Sunday at his place.
He was musical, and famous for his flair
On his nation's instrument, the dulcimer.

He used to tour the manors, amazing all
With music and song—he'd a fine voice as well.
Though Jewish, he spoke the Polish tongue quite clearly,
And Polish songs he loved especially dearly.[37]

Bożena Shallcross is Professor of Polish literature in the Department of Slavic Languages and Literatures and was formerly the Core Faculty of the Institute on the Formation of Knowledgeat the University of Chicago. She is a member of twelve editorial boards, including *Slavic Review* and *Teksty Drugie*. She has authored several monographs, translated or edited several other books, and published a number of articles. Her latest monograph, entitled *The Holocaust Object in Polish and Polish-Jewish Culture*, also appeared in Polish and Russian translations. Most recently she published "Anamnesis of Joy" in *Fabrica Litterarum*, "War and Violence: How to Rescue a Wartime Artifact" in *The Cambridge Handbook of Material Culture Studies*, and "Scandalous Glass House: On Modernist Transparency in Architecture and Life" in *Centering the Periphery: Polish Jewish Culture Beyond the Capital.*

Notes

1. Władysław Syrokomla, *Wycieczki po Litwie w promieniach od Wilna*, vol. 2 (Wilno: Nakładem A. Assa, 1860), 69. Władysław Syrokomla was a pseudonym of Ludwik Kondratowicz (1823–62), a second-generation Polish Romantic poet, writer, and translator. Syrokomla is also considered as one of the earliest poets writing in modern Belorussian.

2. Adam Mickiewicz (December 24, 1798–November 26, 1855) was the leading voice in Polish Romantic poetry and drama (*The Forefathers' Eve*); widely recognized for his artistry outside the realm of partitioned Poland, in Europe and Russia, he remains the most impactful poet in Polish literature. From 1829, after five years of exile in central Russia, he lived abroad, mostly in Paris, where he gradually replaced his writings by political and religious activities amid his struggle for economic survival. He died in Istanbul, where he went to organize a military unit called the Jewish Legion that consisted of Jewish conscripts escaped from the Russian army. For a detailed account of Mickiewicz, his life, and output, see Roman Koropeckyj, *Mickiewicz: The Life of a Romantic* (Ithaca, NY: Cornell University Press, 2008).

3. "Karczma na trakcie bez Żyda, jest to ciało bez duszy; gdzie karczma, tam Żyd." Franciszek Kowalski, *Wspomnienia* (1819–1823) (Kijów: Nakładem Idzikowskiego, 1850), 62. Franciszek Kowalski (1799–1862) was a Polish writer, pedagogue, and translator of Molière and Walter Scott.

4. In particular, the genre of travel writing abounds in highly critical reports about the "karczma" experiences, saturated with antisemitic bias. This negative perspective, developed over the years through generalized observations and exaggerated judgments, informed the stereotype of a Jewish innkeeper as a greedy host who cheated on his customers and was responsible for their alcoholism. According to the stereotype, the Jewish inn was a dirty, crowded, and noisy space where service and food left much to desire. This is the gist of Józef Ignacy Kraszewski's depiction of Jewish inns and their keepers; see *Wspomnienia Wołynia,*

Polesia i Litwy, vol. 1 (Wilno: Teofil Glucksberg, 1840), 152–53. See especially the chapter "Karczmy, żydzi, drogi."

5. See *infra*, chapter 8.

6. Cyprian Kamil Norwid issued the strongest criticism of the nobility's life as banal: "They eat, drink, and hunt mushrooms," praising Jankiel as "the only serious character." Cyprian Norwid, "Letter to Włodzimierz Cybulski," *Pisma wszystkie*, vol. 9, *Letters, 1862–1872*, ed. Wiktor J. Gomulicki (Warsaw: Państwowy Instytut Wydawniczy, 1971), 271. Henryk Markiewicz writes that Stanisław Ropelewski "in a sole—in the emigration—extensive evaluation of *Pan Tadeusz* posed many objections against the poem, but without reservations praised a masterful comparative description of the inn and the Jewish figure," which "will keep their memory for posterity." Henryk Markiewicz, "Perypetie Jankiela," in *W ogrodzie świata: profesorowi Aleksandrowi Fiutowi w siedemdziesiąte urodziny*, ed. Tischner Łukasz and Józef Wróbel (Kraków: Wydawnictwo Uniwersytetu Jagiellońskiego, 2015), 397.

7. Karl Rosenkranz's *Aesthetics of Ugliness* was published four years before Baudelaire's *Fleurs du Mal*, a poetic affirmation of melancholy shabbiness.

8. Michał Grabowski, *Pamiętniki domowe*, vol. 1 (Warsaw: Nakładem S. Orgelbranda, 1845), 75. Such claims resonate with the recurring accusations of Jews being aesthetically insensitive and incapable of creating beauty that have been explored in modern scholarly discourse—e.g., by John M. Efron, *German Jewry and the Allure of the Sephardic* (Princeton, NJ: Princeton University Press, 2016).

9. Henryk Biegeleisen, *"Pan Tadeusz" Adama Mickiewicza: Studyum estetyczno-literackie* (Warsaw: T. Paprocki, 1884), 138.

10. Grażyna B. Tomaszewska, "*Pan Tadeusz* a pochwała niedoskonałości," in *Pan Tadeusz: Poemat—Postacie—Recepcja*, ed. Andrzej Fabianowski and Ewa Hoffman-Piotrowska (Warsaw: Wydawnictwa Uniwersytetu Warszawskiego, 2017), 85.

11. Tadeusz Dworak, "Analiza porównań w *Panu Tadeuszu*," *Pamiętnik Literacki* 38 (1948): 273.

12. Dworak, "Analiza porównań w *Panu Tadeuszu*," 257.

13. The landlords' wealth permitting, they would hire architects who built manors in a neoclassical style with columned porticos in the front facade. This is not the case of the Soplicowo manor, which is a more modest building.

14. See Zdzisław Kępiński, *Mickiewicz hermetyczny* (Warsaw: Państwowy Instytut Wydawniczy, 1980), 342.

15. Marta Piwińska, "Staropolska 'nauka budownicza' w *Panu Tadeuszu*," *Rocznik Towarzystwa Literackiego imienia Adama Mickiewicza* 25 (1990): 109–22.

16. Zygmunt Gloger, *Budownictwo drzewne i wyroby z drzewa w dawnej Polsce*, vol. 1 (Warsaw: Druk W. Łazarskiego, 1907), 91.

17. M. H. Abrams, *The Mirror and the Lamp: Romantic Theory and the Critical Tradition* (New York: Oxford University Press, 1971).

18. We know the design of the Temple only from its biblical description, according to which Hiram I, the king of Tyrus, a close associate of King David, sent his builder, also named Hiram, to Jerusalem at King Solomon's request to assist his builders. Mickiewicz referred to the distant connection in the phrase "tyryjscy cieśle" (the carpenters of Tyre); Adam Mickiewicz, *Pan Tadeusz or the Last Foray in Lithuania*, trans. Bill Johnston (Brooklyn, NY: Archipelago, 2018), 119.

19. Robert Harbison, *The Built, the Unbuilt and the Unbuildable: In Pursuit of Architectural Meaning* (Cambridge, MA: MIT Press, 1992), 162.

20. The half-rounded arch is a typical Romanesque feature and does not define or characterize Gothic architecture, which uses the pointed arch.

21. This conflation of building types is asserted in the following way in the original: "Żydzi go naśladują dotąd we swych szkołach, / A szkoł rysunek widny w karczmach i stodołach." Adam Mickiewicz, *Pan Tadeusz czyli ostatni zajazd na Litwie*, ed. Leon Płoszewski (Warsaw: Spółdzielnia Wydawnicza Czytelnik, 1948), 107. Johnston uses the word *synagogue*: "Synagogues are still built this way; in turn, / Their shape is seen in that of inn and barn" (120).

22. Mickiewicz, *Pan Tadeusz*, 119.

23. Michel Foucault, "Of Other Spaces: Utopias and Heterotopias," trans. Jay Miskowiec, in *Facing Value: Radical Perspectives from the Arts* (Amsterdam, Stroom Den Haag: Valiz, 2017), 164–71.

24. Gaston Bachelard, *The Poetics of Space*, trans. Maria Jolas (Boston: Beacon, 1994).

25. Mickiewicz, *Pan Tadeusz*, 120–21.

26. Jakub Kazimierz Haur, *Oekonomika ziemiańska generalna* (Kraków: Drukarnia Dziedzice Krzysztofa Schedla, 1675), 282. See also Piotr Kowalski, *Theatrum świata wszystkiego i poćciwy gospodarz: o wizji świata pewnego siedemnastowiecznego pisarza ziemiańskiego* (Kraków: Wydawnictwo Uniwersytetu Jagiellońskiego, 2000).

27. The English translation of the phrase from Book VII lost the panache with which Jankiel imposed xenophobia on his identity: "I am just a Jew" (237) renders a more neutral meaning.

28. Jerzy Fiećko argues that the presence of very negative antisemitic references in *Pan Tadeusz* shows the extent to which Mickiewicz wanted to expose the circulation of such stereotypes among the Polish gentry. See Jerzy Fiećko, "Co robi Żyd w narodowej epopei?: Jankiel i konteksty" in *Pan Tadeusz: Poemat, Postacie, Recepcja*, ed. Andrzej Fabianowski and Ewa Hoffman Piotrowska (Warsaw: Wydawnictwa Uniwersytetu Warszawskiego, 2016), 288.

29. Alexander Hertz justly observes that the more Jankiel is engaged in Polish affairs, the more he steers away from his religious Jewish community. Aleksander Hertz, *The Jews in Polish Culture* (Evanston, IL: Northwestern University Press, 1988).

30. For more details about the mechanism of improvisation in Jankiel's concert, see Bożena Shallcross, "'The Wondrous Fire': Adam Mickiewicz's *Pan Tadeusz* and the Romantic Improvisation," *East European Politics and Societies* 9, no. 3 (1995): 523–33. Much has been written about the prototypes for the character of Jankiel; see chapter 4. In this chapter, however, I am pursuing his uniqueness as interwoven with his inn and his functions, rather than exploring the discourse about his provenance.

31. The splendid drawing is a double portrait, as to the right of Jankiel is that of another literary character, Shylock. For reasons unknown, most publications of this drawing reproduce only the half with the figure of Jankiel.

32. For the contemporary reader, the "Concert of Concerts" also gestures to Jankiel's emancipation as anticipating the pattern of liberation in biographies of numerous Polish Jewish artists during the long nineteenth century.

33. Abraham G. Duker, "The Mystery of the Jews in Mickiewicz's Towianist Lectures on Slavic Literatures," *Polish Review* 7, no. 3 (Spring 1962): 40–66.

34. The word *though* is omitted in Johnston's translation.

35. Dominique Bauer, "Interior Spaces as Traces in Balzac's *La Comédie Humaine*," *Palgrave Communications* 3, no. 17043 (2017), doi:10.1057/palcomms.2017.43.

36. Mickiewicz, *Pan Tadeusz*, 119–21.

37. Mickiewicz, *Pan Tadeusz*, 121–22.

PART II
Contractual Frameworks

3

Jewish Tavern Here and There

Regional Differences in Forms of Rural Lease-Holdings before and after the Partitions

Judith Kalik

The image of the Jewish tavern has been a favorite subject of Polish literature, as can be seen from the chapters in this volume that deal with works by Mickiewicz (chap. 2), Wyspiański (chap. 7), and Stryjkowski (chap. 8). Historical research on the Jewish tavern similarly dominates studies of the history of rural Jews in early modern Eastern Europe, and the picturesque figure of the Jewish tavernkeeper stands at the center. However, in literature and history alike, the Jewish tavern of the prepartition Polish-Lithuanian Commonwealth is usually described without attention to regional differences in forms of lease-holding. In the postpartitions period, on the contrary, different parts of the former Commonwealth (Kingdom of Poland, Austrian Galicia, Russian Ukraine, and Belarus) are studied separately, without substantial comparison among them. Some regional differences surely have been observed, such as the practical absence of the Jewish leaseholders in Greater Poland[1] and the great concentration of Jewish rural leaseholders in Podlasie and eastern Mazowsze.[2] Different forms of leaseholds, such as the general leasehold and sublease, also have been discussed, but again, not in regional context.[3]

Let us begin with the terminology. A scholarly investigation of the regional differences in leaseholding must acknowledge the three kinds of leaseholders distinguished in the sources: leaseholders proper (Pol. *arendarz*), innkeepers (*karczmarz*), and tavernkeepers (*szynkarz*). For example, according to a 1795 census of the shtetl of Pukhovichi in the district of

Igumen of Minsk Gubernia—already under Russian rule—there were four leaseholders, eleven tavernkeepers, and one "poor woman at the inn" (Rus. *pri karchme*), while in the villages that belonged to this community there were two leaseholders, ten tavernkeepers, and six innkeepers.[4] Historians of Polish Jewry Murray Rosman and Glenn Dynner use different English translations for these latter two occupations: "tavernkeeper" for *karczmarz* and "barman" for *szynkarz*.[5] This terminology is appropriate only for the urban context, but it is hardly suitable when applied to the rural countryside. There were obviously no "bars" in villages (though as we read in chap. 5, by the late nineteenth century, when Jews migrated to big cities, the various functions of the tavern were transferred to courtyards and cafés). The rural inn (Pol. *karczma*), however, consisted of a guesthouse with one or more rooms for hosting occasional carriage travelers, a tavern (Pol. *szynk*) where alcoholic drinks (mostly vodka) and food were served, and stables were also available.

There were two types of inns with stables in nineteenth-century Belarus: the drive-through inn and the T-shaped inn. In the drive-through inn, the stables were in the central section of the building, with the szynk on one side of this section and the living quarters of the guests and of the innkeeper's family, the kitchen, and the shop on the other. In the T-shaped inn, the stables with the living quarters of the innkeeper's family were attached to the main building, which itself consisted of two equal compounds: one side comprised the guest rooms; the other included the szynk and a kitchen.[6] (For a symbolic representation of the inn's architecture, see chap. 2.)

The word arendarz (leaseholder) was the general term for leaseholder of any kind; it was also informally applied to inn- and tavernkeepers. The urban leaseholders were probably innkeepers, since there was at least one inn at Pukhovichi, where the abovementioned "poor woman" lived, but no innkeepers are mentioned in the census. Rural leaseholders, however, are terminologically distinguished from either inn- or tavernkeepers in the same text. A similar situation also prevailed in a restricted region of the prepartition Crown Poland, which I have in previous work called the "leaseholders' belt,"[7] a strip of land stretching from Podlasie in the north to the Carpathian Mountains in the south. Numerous leaseholders appear as individual taxpayers in the poll-tax assessment lists in this region, which consisted of Węgrów and Tykocin, autonomous major communities in the north; Przemyśl regional council in the south; and Lublin, Chełm-Bełżec, and Ordynacja Zamoyska regional councils between them. These leaseholders are also terminologically distinguished from inn- and tavernkeepers: "leaseholder David with two tavern-keepers in Dobrzyń,"[8] "leaseholder and innkeeper in Żurawce near Przemyśl,"[9] and "village of Pysznica: the widow of a leaseholder with her son and an innkeeper in the royal estate" (see fig. 3.1).[10] These leaseholders were not the general leaseholders who leased propination rights for an entire estate or cluster of estates and then sublet them to individual inn- and tavernkeepers in individual villages, since they were always identified with specific villages and not with estates. Most probably, noble landowners leased their villages to numerous rural Jewish leaseholders in this region.

In a few cases, an explicit expression that indicated the practice of leasing villages to Jews is used: "David holding the villages Horodyszcze, Dubicz, and Hilibicz,"[11] "Icko holding the village Rudziniec and other small villages."[12] Leasing villages to the Jews was probably widespread practice farther east of Podlasie, in the former Grand Duchy of Lithuania. For example, the leasehold of Solomon Maimon's grandfather stated, "He selected for his residence one of these villages on the river Nieman, called Sukoviborg, where, besides a few peasants' plots, there was a water-mill, a small harbor, and a warehouse for use of the vessels that come from Königsberg, in Prussia. All this, along with a bridge behind the village, and on the other side a drawbridge on the river Nieman, belonged to the leasehold, which was worth a thousand gulden, and formed my grandfather's *Ḥazakah* (Heb. tenure)."[13]

However, this was not the case in Ukraine, east of the "leaseholders' belt," where only inn- and tavernkeepers are mentioned in the poll-tax assessment lists. Especially interesting is the regional council of Ruś, where leaseholders are listed only in villages that belonged to two Jewish communities: Lisko, an enclave of Ruś cut off from its central part by the Przemyśl regional council, and Drohobycz, which in the Polish administrative structure belonged to the Przemyśl district, but within the framework of Jewish autonomy was part of the regional council of Ruś. It seems that the rural inn- and tavernkeepers flourished farther east, while the urban leaseholders prevailed in Little Poland, and practically no Jewish leaseholders were found in Greater Poland.

The terms of leasing villages to the Jews are known, since a few such leasing contracts have survived. For example, Dominican nuns of Bielsk Podlaski leased two villages (Miców and Wysłów) in 1748 to Solomon Kotowisz for one year. These villages were held by the nuns as a pledge (Pol. *zastaw*) for a loan that a noble received from them. The lease included a mill, an inn, and a forest. Two servants, one from each village, were

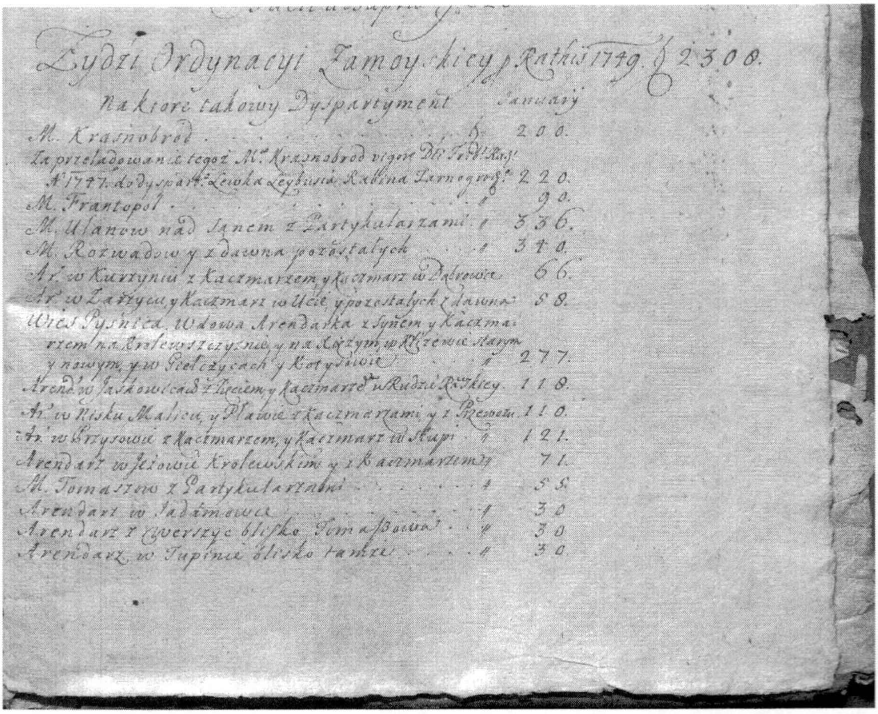
Zydzi Ordynacyi Zamoyskiey p. Rathis 1749. 2300.

Na ktore takowy Dyspartyment — Janua[ry]

M. Krasnobrod	200.
Za przeladowanie tegoz M. Krasnobrod vigore ... 1747 do dyspart. Lewka Leybusia Rabina Tarnogrodz.	220.
M. Frantopol	90.
M. Ulanow nad Sanem z Partykularzami	336.
M. Rozwadow y z dawna pozostalych	340.
Ar. w Kurtyniu z Kaczmarzem y Kaczmarz w Dabrowce	66.
Ar. w Zarzycu y Kaczmarz w Ucie y pozostalych z dawna	58.
Wies Pysnica Wdowa Arendarka z Synem y Kaczmarzem na Krolewszczyznie, y na Rzeczym w Krzewie starym y nowym, y w Pielczycach y Kotydnowie	277.
Arend. w Jaskowicach z Ruzem y Kaczmarz w Rudzie R...	118.
Ar. w Nisku Malicu, y Plawie z Kaczmarzami y z Przewozu	110.
Ar. w Brzysowie z Kaczmarzem, y Kaczmarz w Stupi	121.
Arendarz w Jeżowie Krolewskim y z Kaczmarzem	71.
M. Tomaszow z Partykularzami	55.
Arendarz w Jadamowce	30
Arendarz z Cycertzyc blisko Tomaszowa	30
Arendarz w Tupince blisko tamze	30

Figure 3.1 Jewish innkeepers and leaseholders listed in Ordynacja Zamoyska in 1749. Archiwum Skarbu Koronnego, Ordynacja zamoyska, 1749, syg. 40, p. 445. Warsaw, The Central Archives of Historical Records (Pol: Archiwum Główne Akt Dawnych; AGAD).

provided to the Jewish leaseholder to assist him in his work.[14] However, neither the real extent of the practice of leasing villages to the Jews nor its geographical and chronological limits have been recognized.

To find an overall explanation for the existence of this leaseholders' belt, we should identify the common socioeconomic characteristics of this region. Small estates of lower and middle nobles typified this area, especially Podlasie, eastern Mazowsze, and the Carpathian highlands, where the largest concentration of rural leaseholders is found. Often these nobles owned one or two villages, and sometimes a single village was divided between two or even three such owners, each with his own Jewish leaseholder. Unlike magnates, such poor nobles had no interest in fostering a retinue of noble leaseholders for the purpose of political lobbying in local dietines (Pol. *sejmiki*). Being either unable or unwilling to manage their villages by themselves, they found an easy solution in leasing these villages to Jews.

This phenomenon has largely escaped scholars' attention because of their preoccupation with relationships between magnates and Jews. This is hardly surprising, as the magnates' family archives are readily accessible, but poor nobles have left little or no documentation.

The patterns of leaseholds inside this "leaseholders' belt" were not uniform. In the territory of the Jewish autonomous major community (Heb. *kehilah rashit*) of Węgrów, in eastern Mazowsze and Podlasie, Jewish rural leaseholds were unstable, rarely lasting longer than two consecutive years, and usually the leaseholders and the villages they leased changed every year in a bewildering pattern. However, leaseholds in the regional council of Przemyśl in Red Ruthenia lasted much longer, sometimes for a decade or more. For example, Wulf Siehiński appeared in the Jewish poll-tax lists as a leaseholder of the royal estate of Medyka (Pol. *starostwo medyckie*) from 1741 to 1752.[15] There are good reasons to assume that further east the situation was the same, meaning that in the Grand Duchy of Lithuania (east of Podlasie) leaseholds were unstable, while in Ukraine (east of Przemyśl) they were much more durable. This does not necessarily mean that the Jewish community's policy of enforcement of the so-called tenure had failed in the north and had been successful in the south, since the rights of tenure could be sold if leaseholders themselves were not interested in long leaseholds.

The lists of rural Jews in Minsk Gubernia prepared for the purpose of their eviction in 1808 stand out in their peculiar sex and age composition. People of both sexes of working age (twenty to fifty years old) constituted an absolute majority of the population (61.4%), while children were in the minority (28.9%).[16] This stands in sharp contrast with the composition of the general Jewish population of the same *gubernia* observed in the first national census of the Russian Empire. According to this census, taken in 1897, the respective numbers were 34.4 percent of the working age and 53.6 percent children.[17] It is hardly conceivable that the difference can be explained by the change in the structure of the population during the nineteenth century, since the "reversed pyramid" structure was characteristic of both Jewish and non-Jewish populations in the preindustrial age.

To understand whether this peculiar age and sex composition was typical for the rural Jewish population throughout the Pale of Settlement or whether this pattern was restricted to Belarus, we should compare the data from Minsk Gubernia with the age and sex composition of the rural Jews in Ukraine (see tab. 3.1). Similar eviction lists were also composed in 1808 for the Kiev Gubernia. The difference between them and the eviction lists from

Table 3.1. Composition of the Rural Jewish Population of Minsk and Kiev Gubernias, 1808–1858, by Age and Sex (in %)

Age Groups	1808 Rural Jews in Minsk Gubernia[18]			1808 Rural Jews in Kiev Gubernia[19]			1858 Jewish Farmers in Minsk Gubernia[20]		
	M	F	Total	M	F	Total	M	F	Total
0–9	6.5	17.4	12.3	23.4	29.9	26.7	19.1	34.0	26.7
10–19	15.6	17.4	16.6	13.2	14.5	13.8	21.9	17.7	19.8
20–29	22.8	21.5	22.1	19.1	23.5	21.3	26.9	22.5	24.7
30–39	25.4	22.5	23.8	19.8	19.5	19.7	14.9	13.6	14.2
40–49	18.8	12.7	15.5	19.1	10.5	14.8	9.2	6.8	8.0
50–59	10.1	4.8	7.3	4.7	1.6	3.1	7.1	5.4	6.3
60+	4.4	3.2	3.7	0.4	0.2	0.3	0.7	0	0.3

Belarus is striking: children under ten constitute the most numerous group of the population. However, the eviction lists from Kiev do not display the "reversed pyramid" structure of the age composition of the Jewish population either, since teenagers are less numerous than people in their twenties. It should be considered that these lists do not count all rural Jews but rather only those who voluntarily agreed to be resettled in Jewish agricultural colonies in Kherson Gubernia. For this reason, the age and sex composition reflected in these lists is most like the distribution of people of both sexes by age in the Jewish agricultural colonies in Minsk Gubernia in 1858.

The Jewish agricultural colonies of Minsk Gubernia were relatively new settlements, which explains the disproportional representation of people in their twenties and the absence of the elderly among colonists. One can also notice the proportion of men aged forty to sixty made up a proportion of their gender twice as large as did similarly aged women, while in all other age groups their proportion was nearly equal. Presumably, rural women of this age together with their teenage children preferred to be resettled in towns and shtetls rather than to join the agricultural settlers. However, the difference between the age groups of children among rural Jews of Minsk Gubernia in 1808, on the one hand, and rural Jews of Kiev Gubernia in the same year and Jewish farmers in 1858, on the other hand, is striking. The majority of the traditional rural Jews of Minsk Gubernia were probably temporary residents of the countryside, while the rural Jews of Kiev Gubernia resided in villages permanently, just as the Jewish farmers did in 1858. In Poland, the situation was like that of Ukraine.[21] Thus, in the villages near

Piotrków Trybunalski in central Poland, the average Jewish family consisted of 4.7 people in 1826, and the number of children per family was 4.9 from 1808 to 1850. It seems that the family strategy of young Jewish couples in the shtetls and towns of Belarus was to invest their dowry money into a rural leasehold to accumulate capital for opening their own businesses in a shtetl. Such a pattern of behavior would explain the predominance of working-aged people among the rural population of Minsk Gubernia in 1808, as well as the small number of children.

This constant exchange of population between town and village distinguished rural Jews of the former Grand Duchy of Lithuania from their Ukrainian and most of their Polish counterparts, who were, probably, permanent rural dwellers. The combined evidence of the eighteenth-century Jewish poll-tax lists and of the eviction lists of 1808 shows that probably in eastern Mazowsze, Podlasie, and the Grand Duchy of Lithuania rural leaseholds were usually short-term contracts. It is difficult to tell what caused the difference in leaseholds' duration in these regions and Ukraine. Most likely the leaseholds in grain-producing Ukraine were simply much more profitable than in the marshlands of Podlasie, Belarus, and Lithuania, which were less suitable for the cultivation of cereals.

Our observation that the rural Jews of Minsk Gubernia were temporary residents in villages—based on the peculiar age structure of the Jewish rural population in 1808—may explain the puzzling contrast between the sweeping success of the Hasidic movement in Ukraine and Poland and its only marginal penetration into Belarus and Lithuania. Spending just a few years of their life in the countryside, the Jews of Belarus and Lithuania managed to keep abreast of traditional Jewish education. They were thus sympathetic to the Vilna Gaon's teachings and found the Hasidic courts a less attractive option, while the permanent rural population of Ukraine and Poland were cut off from urban centers of education, and so were rapidly enchanted by Hasidic alternative worship through personal devotion and ecstatic prayer. The disproportionate number of boys and girls of school age among the rural Jews is particularly instructive. According to the eviction lists, there were 13.8 percent of boys and 19 percent of girls between the ages of three and fourteen among the rural Jews, showing that most boys attended Jewish primary schools (*kheyder*) in shtetls.

The third difference in forms of leaseholds concerns the distinction between the Catholic and Orthodox parts of the Commonwealth. Since the second half of the seventeenth century, leasing of inns and taverns, where alcohol was sold to the locals, became a typical Jewish occupation.

In taking over this sector of the economy, Jews displaced other groups that were also interested in competing for leaseholds. Before the profitability of *propinacja* (propination) leases became clear in the sixteenth century, the majority of rural inn- and tavernkeepers had been hereditary peasant leaseholders in Poland and Lithuania, and Orthodox and Uniate married priests in Ukraine and Belarus.

Though the Jews ousted hereditary peasant leaseholders from the propination, peasant tavernkeepers continued to exist in the eighteenth century, especially in royal estates. Thus, the possessor of *starostwo krzeczowskie* (the royal estate of Krzeczów), Adam Schwarzenberg-Czerny, dismissed in 1756 two Jewish tavernkeepers in a village of Przyborów and transferred their propination rights to two peasants: Daniło, in whose house one of the taverns was located, and Cisak, who built the tavern at his own expense. However, the conflict was triggered not by the competition between Jews and peasants but by a competition among the Jews: one of the Jewish tavernkeepers bought vodka not from the local Jewish distiller but from a Jewish distiller from another village. He was fined one hundred *grzywny* for this offense but claimed in court that the fine was only fifty grzywny. The chieftain (Pol. *wójt*) of the village was called to testify against him, but he refused, and finally the tavernkeeper paid only half of the original fine.[22]

Of course, Catholic monasteries and parish churches often kept their own taverns, but the problem of lost tavern leases was much more acute for married Orthodox and Uniate priests who had to support their large families, and for whom leasing taverns and inns provided a secure source of income. Their displacement by the Jews caused serious problems. For example, in 1690 the Orthodox parish priest of Ostrów signed an agreement with the *starosta* of a royal estate, which was later confirmed by King Jan Sobieski. It specified that Jewish leaseholders were to pay annually thirty *złoty* to the parish priest to compensate him for the damage he incurred when his liquor concession was removed. For his part, the parish priest committed neither to produce nor to sell liquor in his parish, or vodka or beer in his church. Jewish leaseholders were obliged not to sell vodka on Sundays and major Christian holidays.[23] However, the Orthodox and Uniate married priests ousted by the Jews from their lease of the lord's propination often transgressed such prohibitions to sell liquor in order to support their large families. These constant violations of the lord's monopoly on propination leased to the Jews often created favorable conditions for soaring violence. Thus, the bishop of Belarus, Jerzy Konisski, complained in a letter to Radziwiłł in February 1762 that it was unjust to subject the parish priest in Pupowiec to a Jewish leaseholder in matters of propination and milling.[24] He then stated that a new Jewish leaseholder came to the priest's house and asked him whether he had any vodka in his possession. The honest priest had shown him a quart of vodka meant for his own consumption. In response, the Jewish leaseholder turned his house upside down, though he did not discover anything. He later returned to the priest accompanied by Cossacks (in fact, armed servants of Radziwiłł dressed as Cossacks), confiscated all his property, and even sealed the church. The bishop asked Radziwiłł for the sake of God to restrain his Jewish leaseholder.[25]

This document, as well as many similar ones, shows that the legend about the Jews leasing the Orthodox churches arose out of the widespread practice of sealing the churches as a sanction against the violation of the lord's propination rights by a priest. In other words, the continuing competition between the Jews and Orthodox priests for propination rights, not a theological approach to the Jews that differed from that of Catholics, was largely responsible for the atmosphere of mutual violence characteristic of relations between the Orthodox Church and the Jews in the Polish-Lithuanian Commonwealth.[26]

The fourth difference distinguishes Left-Bank Ukraine under Russian rule since 1654 from the rest of the territories that remained in the Polish-Lithuanian Commonwealth. After the victory of the Cossack uprising of 1648, the propination rights passed from the Polish magnates to the Cossack regiments, but, contrary to all expectations, Cossack commanders continued to lease these rights to the Jews. In 1719, the Cossack colonel Balcer even prohibited leasing taverns to Cossacks and peasants, allowing it only to the Jews following the policy of the previous colonel Yeropnik.[27] These Jewish leaseholders in Left-Bank Ukraine under the Russian rule usually did not produce alcohol themselves; rather, they bought it for sale in the taverns and inns from the Cossacks. Thus, for example, the Jewish tavernkeeper in a village of Sosnitsa, Joseph Markovich, bought in 1723 from the *sotnik* (centurion) Vasil Doroshenko one *kufa* (forty buckets) of simple vodka for twenty talers and one *barilo* (fifteen buckets) of good vodka for eleven *złoty*, one *kufa* of mead for four rubles, and two barrels of beer for three rubles and one *złoty* (see fig. 3.2).[28] In the Polish-Lithuanian Commonwealth, in contrast, the still continued to be an integral part of the Jewish inn. Thus, in 1726, two drunk customers of the Jewish inn in a village called Ptaszkowa in Little Poland, Grzegorz Jaskułka and Jakub Michalik, broke a still during a fight. The Jewish leaseholder demanded

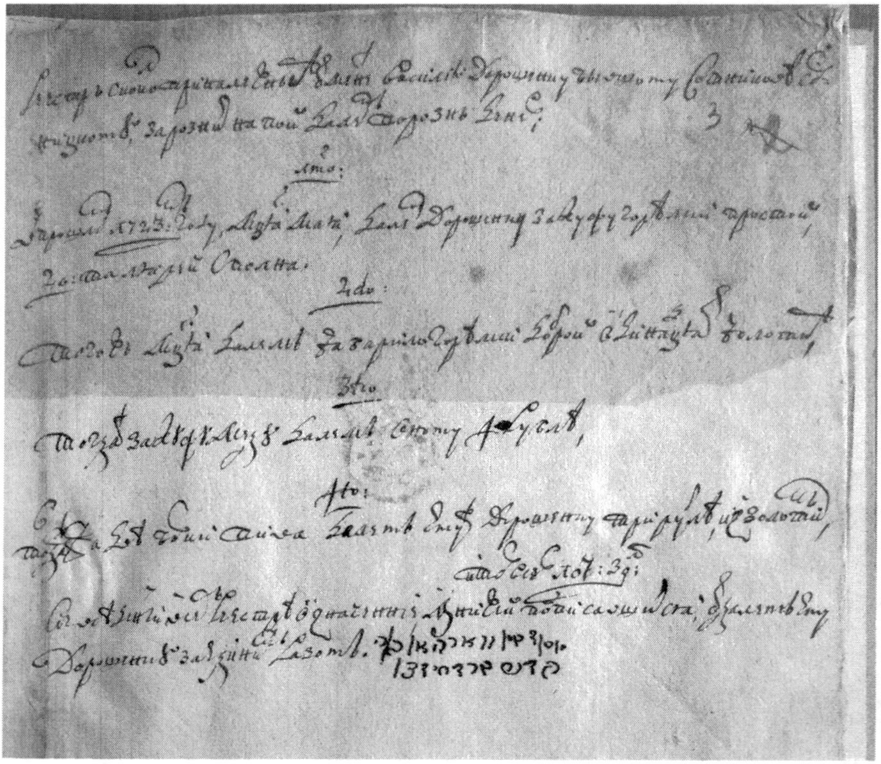

Figure 3.2 The purchase of vodka by Joseph Markovich, a Jewish tavernkeeper in a village of Sosnitsa, from Vasil Doroshenko, in 1723. F 51, op. 3, spr. 2007, Sosnitsa, 1726, p. 3. Kyiv, The Central State Historical Archive in Kyiv (Ukr. Центральний державний історичний архів України або ЦДІАУ; Tsentralnyi derzhavnyi istorychnyi arkhiv Ukrainy; TsDIAK).

compensation, but after a judicial inquiry, he admitted that he dealt a heavy blow to Jakub Michalik's mouth. The court sentenced Michalik to pay two grzywny to the Jew, but the latter had to pay three grzywny to the court and to apologize to Michalik.[29] Only in the mid-nineteenth century, with the introduction of the industrial alcohol distilleries, was the production of alcohol finally detached from the Jewish inn and tavern in the other parts of the former Polish-Lithuanian Commonwealth.[30]

The fifth difference isolates the Sub-Carpathian region in Western Ukraine (Eastern Galicia) from the rest of the Commonwealth. In other parts of the Polish-Lithuanian Commonwealth, especially in Ukraine, local landlords leased taverns and inns to the Jews using their monopoly on production and sale of alcohol for profit, because of a large surplus of grain. However, in the narrow valleys of Sub-Carpathian Galicia, there was no surplus of grain, but there was a large surplus of salt. Salt was produced there through its extraction from natural brine brought by underground streams from the Carpathian Mountains and collected in natural ponds called locally "windows" (Pol. *okna*). Brine was pumped from these ponds and boiled in open pans in numerous salt refineries, called locally "salt baths" (Pol. *bania solna*), where salt was extracted through evaporation of water. Local Jewish innkeepers were interested in selling salt to fertile lowlands, such as Podolia, in exchange for grain. To obtain salt, many of them became leaseholders of salt refineries. In some cases, several Jews were involved in such transactions. Thus, for example, in a village of Wujsk near Sambór, the Jewish leaseholder of the village leased the salt refinery to another Jew, who in turn subleased a part of it to a third Jew. There was also a fourth Jew in the village who served as an innkeeper.[31] Dov Ber of Bolechów describes in his memoirs even more complicated circulation of goods: his father bought timber from peasants in the Carpathian highlands, sold it to the leaseholder of salt refineries (Pol. *żupnik*) for salt, sold this salt to peasants from lowland Podolia for grain, produced vodka from this grain, and sold it to Hungary for wine.[32] Jewish leaseholders of salt refineries themselves regularly sold salt for grain to local peasants, and even asked the treasury to postpone their leasehold payments until St. Michael's Day after the harvest, when the peasants were ready to pay their debts.[33] Significantly, with the reintroduction of the state monopoly on the production and sale of alcohol in the Second Polish Republic in 1924, all alcohol distilleries in former Galicia were located north the river Dniester in lowland Galicia.[34]

In conclusion, we may remark that the literary image of the Jewish tavern widely discussed in many other chapters of this volume correlated with the reality in a complicated way. On the one hand, the Jewish tavern was indeed a focal point of the interaction between different strata of the Christian society.[35] The Jewish leaseholder stood in its center, and the rural microcosm provided a fertile ground for the deep acculturation of the rural Jews.[36] On the other hand, this image, as any other stereotype, ignored many important regional and chronological differences in the development of the Jewish tavern and inn. There were several different types of Jewish taverns in various parts of the Polish-Lithuanian Commonwealth before and after the partitions. These differences, among other things, help us to explain some issues that seem, at first glance, distanced from the Jewish tavern and inn, such as the successes and failures of the Hasidic movement in different parts of the former Polish-Lithuanian Commonwealth and the mutual hostility between the Orthodox clergy and the Jews.

JUDITH KALIK is a research associate at the Goldstein-Goren Diaspora Research Center of the Tel Aviv University and teaches at the Departments of History and of Russian & Slavonic Studies in the Hebrew University of Jerusalem. She is author of *The Polish Nobility and the Jews in the Dietine Legislation of the Polish-Lithuanian Commonwealth* (in Hebrew); *Scepter of Judah: Jewish Autonomy in the Eighteenth-Century Crown Poland*; *Movable Inn: The Rural Jewish Population of Minsk Guberniya in 1793–1914*; with Alexander Uchitel, *Slavic Gods and Heroes*; and with Alexander Kulik, *Jews in Medieval Poland: A Documentary History* (forthcoming).

NOTES

1. Jerzy Topolski, "Uwagi o strukturze gospodarsko-społecznej Wielkopolski, czyli dlaczego na jej terenie nie było żydowskich karczmarzy," *Żydzi w Wielkopolsce na przestrzeni dziejów*, ed. J. Topolski and K. Modelski (Poznań: Wydawnictwo Poznańskie, 1995), 71–82.
2. Józef Maroszek, "Żydzi wiejscy na Podlasiu w XVII i XVIII wieku w świetle przemian struktury rynku wewnętrzego," *Studia Podlaskie* 2 (1986): 56–71.
3. Adam Teller, "Ḥakhira kelalit veḥokher kelali be'aḥuzot beit Radziwiłł bame'a ha-18," *Yazamut yehudit be'et haḥadashah. Mizraḥ Eiropa ve'ereẓ Yisra'el*, ed. Ran Aaronsohn and Shaul Stampfer (Jerusalem: Magnes, 2000), 48–78.
4. Национальный Исторический Архив Беларуси [Natsional'nyĭ Istoricheskiĭ Arkhiv Belarusi] (NIAB), F 333, op. 9, d. 31, 101–14.
5. Murray Jay Rosman, *Lords' Jews: Magnate-Jewish Relations in the Polish-Lithuanian Commonwealth during the Eighteenth Century* (Cambridge, MA: Harvard University Press, 1990); Glenn Dynner, *Yankel's Tavern: Jews, Liquor, and Life in the Kingdom of Poland* (Oxford: Oxford University Press, 2014).
6. Сергей Сергачев [Sergeĭ Sergachev], "Архитектура корчмы в Белоруссии" [Arkhitektura korchmy v Belorussii], *Архитектурное наследство* [Arkhitekturnoye nasledstvo], 1985: 3, 3c. 148–56.
7. Judith Kalik, "Jewish Leaseholders (*Arendarze*) in 18th-Century Crown Poland," *Jahrbücher für Geschichte Osteuropas* 54 (2006): 229–40.
8. Archiwum Główne Akt Dawnych, Archiwum Skarbu Koronnego (AGAD, ASK), dz. 84, syg. 12, Węgrów, year 1722.
9. AGAD, ASK, dz. 84, syg. 30, Przemyśl, year 1740.
10. AGAD, ASK, dz. 84, syg. 40, Ordynacja Zamoyska, year 1749.
11. AGAD, ASK, dz. 84, syg. 21, Tykocin, year 1731.
12. AGAD, ASK, dz. 84, syg. 21, Tykocin, year 1731.
13. Solomon Maimon, *An Autobiography*, introduction by Michael Shapiro, trans. J. Clark Murray (Urbana: University of Illinois Press, 2001), 6.
14. Центральний Державний Історичний Архів України м. Львів [Tsentral'nyĭ Derzhavnyĭ Istorychnyĭ Arkhiv Ukraïny m. L'viv] (TsDIAUL), F. 140, s. 1. od. 36, 1–2.
15. AGAD, ASK, dz. 84, syg. 31, 33, 34, 38, 39, 40, 43.
16. Judith Kalik, *Movable Inn: The Rural Jewish Population of Minsk Guberniya from 1793 to 1914* (Warsaw/Berlin: De Gruyter, 2018), 180.

17. Яков Б. Шабад [Yakov B. Shabad], "Минская губерния" [Minskaya guberniya], *Еврейская энциклопедия* [Evreĭskaya ėntsiklediya], ред. Авраам Гаркави, Лев Каценельсон [red. Avraam Garkavi, Lev Katsenel'son] (С-Петербург [S-Peterburg]: Брокгауз-Ефрон [Brokgauė-Efron], 1908–13), vol. 11, 78–82.

18. NIAB, F 138 op. 1 d. 5.

19. DAKO F 2 op. 3, spr. 1960.

20. NIAB F 333 op. 9 d. 271, 478, 659, 662, 733.

21. Tomasz Jankowski, "Ludność żydowska Piotrkowa Trybunalskiego, 1808–1870" (PhD diss., University of Warsaw, 2014), 62.

22. Bolesław Ulanowski, ed., *Księgi sądowe wiejskie*, vol. 2, Starodawne prawa polskiego pomniki XII (Kraków: Nakładem Polskiej Akademii Umiejętności, 1921), no. 7515, 683.

23. AGAD, MK 232, kk. 683v.–684.

24. It is unclear whether it was addressed to Michał Kazimierz Radziwiłł, who died in May 1762, or to his son Karol Stanisław.

25. AGAD, AR, V. 7132, 5–7.

26. Илья Галант [Il'ya Galant], "Арендовали ли евреи православные церкви на Украине?" [Arendovali li evrei pravoslavnye na Ukraine?], *Еврейская старина* [Evreĭskaya starina], 1909: 1, 81–89; Judith Kalik, "The Orthodox Church and the Jews in the Polish-Lithuanian Commonwealth," *Jewish History* 17 (2003): 229–37.

27. Центральний Державний Історичний Архів України м. Київ [Tsentral'nyĭ Derzhavnyĭ Istorycnyĭ Arkhiv Ukraïny m. Kyïv] (TsDIAK), F 51, op. 3, spr. 334, 7–8. I wish to thank my former student Oleg Zhidkov for providing me with this and the following sources (see note 31).

28. TsDIAK F 51, op. 3, spr. 2007, 3.

29. Bolesław Ulanowski, ed., *Księgi sądowe wiejskie*, vol. 1, Starodawne prawa polskiego pomniki XI (Kraków: Nakładem Polskiej Akademii Umiejętności, 1921), no. 4156, 564.

30. Kalik, *Movable Inn*, 168.

31. AGAD, ASK 84, syg. 18, 22, 27, 28, 30, 31.

32. Mark Wischnitzer, ed., *Zikhronot Rabi Dov mi-Boliḥov (5483–5565)* (Berlin: Kelal, 1922), 27.

33. Wischnitzer, *Zikhronot Rabi Dov mi-Boliḥov*, 101.

34. TsDIAL F 758 op. 1, spr. 2, 29.

35. Judith Kalik, "The Inn as a Focal Point for Jewish Relations with the Catholic Church in the Polish-Lithuanian Commonwealth," in *Jews and Slavs*, vol. 21, ed. Wolf Moskovich and Irena Fijałkowska-Janiak (Jerusalem and Gdańsk: Hebrew University of Jerusalem, Center for Slavic Languages and Literatures and Gdańsk University, Institute of Slavic Phililogy, 2008), 381–90.

36. Judith Kalik, "An Interaction of the Rural Jews with Different Social Strata in the 16th–18th Centuries Polish-Lithuanian Village," *Jewish History Quarterly* 273 (2020): 49–68.

PART III
Communal Spaces in Transition

4

Jewish Musicians in the Polish Inn during the Nineteenth Century

Benjamin Vogel

Old Polish taverns, like taverns elsewhere in Europe, were traditionally the center of the "cultural life" of the village—a place for social meetings, dancing, and family celebrations on holidays and Sundays. They served as a sort of village drawing room. Glenn Dynner references the acclaimed Polish writer Józef Ignacy Kraszewski (1812–87) when commenting that the "tavern had been 'a heart of a village,' where locals sinned, married, grieved, fought, and loved."[1] The innkeeper was expected to provide music in the tavern, for which he paid and which he often performed himself, but the guests also paid the musicians, especially for playing specific pieces upon request.[2] However, music, understood as stimulating the urge to drink, was prohibited in taverns on all days except Sundays. Moreover, the number of taverns was to be restricted according to town size, and there could be only one per village.[3] After 1848, the inns in the Polish Kingdom had to be placed at least fifty-five feet from nearby churches because wedding guests or mourners went straight to the tavern to celebrate their happiness or drown their sorrows in beer and vodka.[4]

The subject of the following discussion is what instruments and in what configurations were heard in inns managed by Jewish and gentile innkeepers. The information on this topic is limited to mere surviving shreds of evidence in written documents (periodicals and literature) and in iconographic sources. Unfortunately, authors of those sources were often unreliable in their descriptions, betraying flawed knowledge of the instruments and of playing techniques. There is also a scholarly lacuna regarding the tavern performances of klezmers—the traditional Jewish musicians employed by Jewish communities for centuries in religious and familial celebrations.[5]

At the turn of the nineteenth century, restrictions introduced in the region of Galicia prohibited Jews from running village inns. Similar limitations were introduced in the territory of the Polish Kingdom in the mid-nineteenth century. Although those constraints were not strictly obeyed, they nonetheless substantially diminished Jewish participation in the innkeeper profession in comparison to the eighteenth century. Given these circumstances, one can surmise that claims relating to large numbers of Jewish innkeepers in Polish lands during these periods and their roles in inducing drunkenness among peasants are greatly exaggerated.[6] One can also assume that such restrictions had some influence on employing specific Christian or Jewish bands (Pol. *kapela*; Yid. *kapelye*) in taverns. Despite these restrictions, music nonetheless remained an essential part of the tavern experience and of the social life of country and, later, town taverns.

The Instrumentarium of Jewish and Christian Bands

Typically, Jewish bands playing in inns consisted of no more than three to four people, and most often these were duos—for example, a fiddler and a dulcimer player—or such musicians playing solo. Standard ensembles consisted of a violin (sometimes a second violin), a dulcimer, a bass instrument (double bass or cello), and a tambourine, and later also cymbals. In a rare description of musicmaking in a Jewish inn at the end of the eighteenth century, Hubert Vautrin—a French Jesuit who spent several years in Poland—describes peasants from neighboring villages gathering during Carnival in an inn to partake in some simple entertainment: alcohol, bread, and dancing to a "Jewish village musician with his dulcimer or violin, [who] makes them turn confusedly to the beat in a cramped space."[7] In the second half of the nineteenth century, wind instruments—most often a clarinet—appeared in such small bands.

We can compensate for the dearth of written documentation by using iconographic sources to get a sense of the typical casts. A merrymaking scene from a tavern, drawn in 1818 by Kazimierz Żwan, shows two Jewish musicians, playing a dulcimer and a bass (see fig. 4.1). In a 1778 drawing by Jean Pierre Norblin de la Gourdaine, one can see a fiddler and a dulcimer player performing for a group of listeners that includes small children (see

Figure 4.1 "The Inn" (*Karczma*), steel engraving by Kazimierz Żwan, 1818. Warsaw, Biblioteka Narodowa, G.50918/II. The National Digital Library Polona. https://polona.pl/item-view/4749a792-fab8-4240-99f0-e64bc21b37c1?page=0. Public domain.

fig. 4.2). An 1819 watercolor by the same artist depicts a similar scene, in a private residence (as indicated by the furniture, including a large bed covered by a down blanket, with a chamber pot underneath the bed), whose inhabitants—a couple with four children—listen to a band composed of a dulcimer player, two violinists, and possibly another musician, partly hidden by the figure of the hostess, with a bassetto or a drum (see fig. 4.3). Another watercolor, attributed to Norblin and titled *An Inn in Częstochowa in 1800*, represents a tavern filled to the brim, where a bass player and fiddler can be seen in front of the stove, on the right, in the back of the painting.[8] In the 1830 watercolor from the Israel Museum in Jerusalem, we see a four-person band composed of double bass, cymbals, dulcimer, and violin (see fig. 4.4). The same watercolor was clearly used as the basis for the decoration of a clay pitcher from Mikulov in Moravia, preserved in the collection of the Jewish Museum in Prague, this time with a date of 1836.[9] The part of the pitcher that is invisible in the photograph probably contains the picture of the fiddler and the dulcimer player.

Figure 4.2 "Jewish Concert. Poland" (*Concert juif. En Pologne*), Jean Pierre Norblin de la Gourdaine, watercolor, 1778. Kraków, Muzeum Narodowe, Zbiory Czartoryskich, MNK XV-Rr.-1163. Reproduced by permission of Muzeum Narodowe w Krakowie.

The xylophone virtuoso Mikhl Yekhiel Guzikov (known also as Joseph Gusikov) (1809–37), a member of the klezmer family from Szkłów (today Шклоў in Belarus), who became popular among Jewish musicians and internationally famous, was performing all around Europe with a band consisting of his three brothers playing two violins and a cello (shown in fig. 4.5).[10] The band leading the Jewish wedding in the drawing from about 1840 and the later oil painting (*Jewish Wedding*, after 1858, National Gallery in Warsaw) by Wincenty Smokowski also comprises a violinist, a dulcimer player, and a bass player.[11] Finally, in Adam Lerue's lithograph, entitled *Market Square in Kazimierz* (1857, after an earlier sketch from nature in 1852), one can see two musicians standing in the town square (see fig. 4.6). According to Wojciech Włodarczyk, one of the musicians is playing the violin and the other a trumpet.[12] Despite the relatively big (oversized) bell

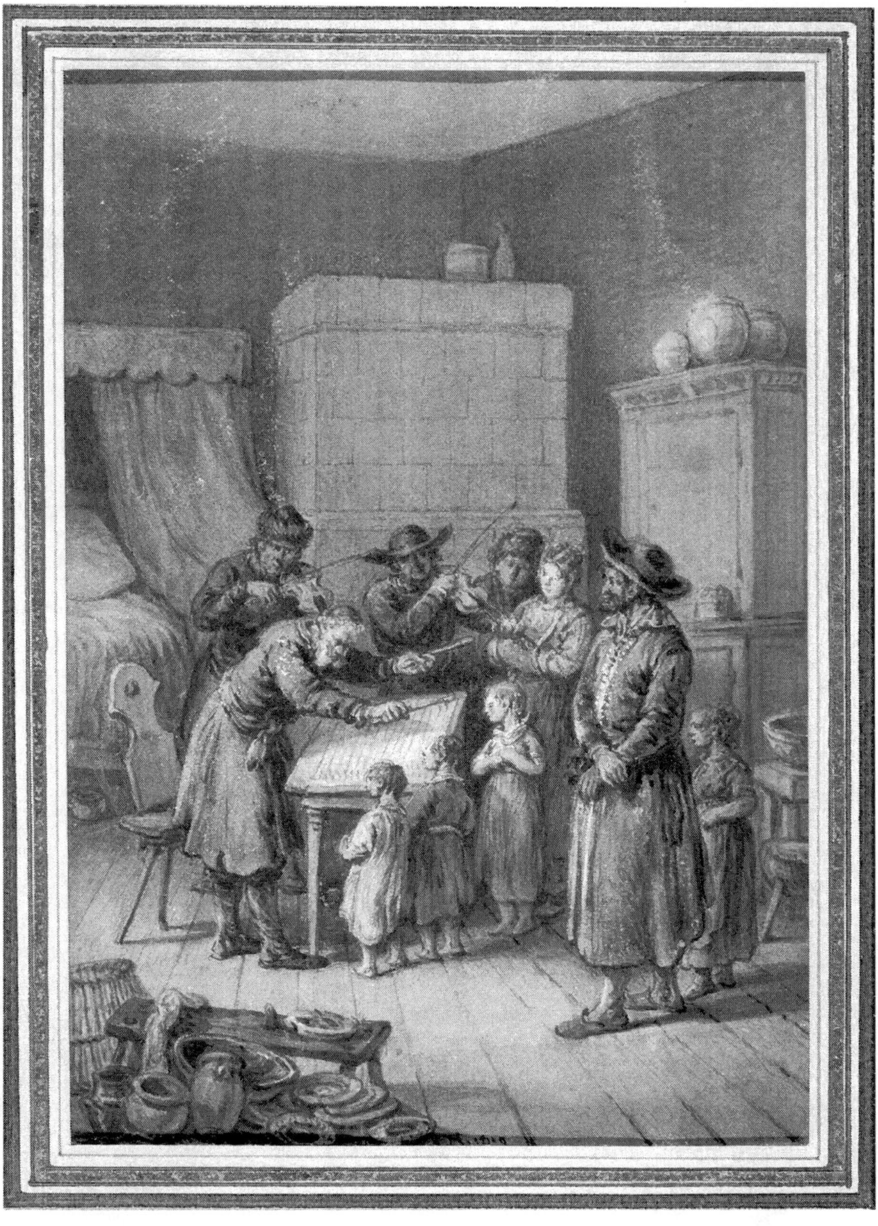

Figure 4.3 "Jewish Orchestra," Jean Pierre Norblin de la Gourdaine, watercolor, 1819. Warsaw, Muzeum Narodowe, Rys.Pol.1991 MNW. Digital Collections of the National Museum in Warsaw. https://cyfrowe.mnw.art.pl/pl/katalog/893856. Public domain.

Figure 4.4 "Jewish Kapelye," watercolor, artist's name illegible, 1830. Jerusalem, The Israel Museum, P66.11.22820.s. Image courtesy of The Israel Museum.

of the latter instrument, the position of the player's hands clearly indicates that the instrument is a clarinet, and the outfit (which seems to be a skirt and a caftan) makes it likely that the musician is a woman.

Bigger bands, using numerous bowed string instruments (including violas, cellos, and double basses) as well as various wooden and brass wind instruments, were hired sporadically for family ceremonies and weddings of wealthier inhabitants in villages and towns.[13] According to Soviet folklorist Moshe Beregovski (1892–1961), "In the last quarter of the nineteenth century a *kapelie* consisted of the following instruments: one or two first violins, one or two second violins, cello or bass (both, in larger bands), flute, clarinet, horn (often bass horns as well), Turkish drum with plates, and small drum."[14] Numerous bowed and wind instruments increased the cast of the bigger bands to as many as twelve or even fifteen musicians.[15] Dulcimer, the instrument of Mickiewicz's Jankiel, the paradigmatic Jewish musician discussed in chapter 2, became less common, forced out by the lively and fashionable wind instruments. One of the few exceptions was the band of Jankiew (Jankev, Jacob) Cymbalista from Przemyśl, consisting of

Figure 4.5 "Guzikov, Polish Jew" (*Guzikow żyd polski*), pen drawing, c. 1835. Kraków, Archiwum Narodowe, Zbiór Ambrożego Grabowskiego, sygn. 29/679/47, ryc. 206. Image courtesy of Archiwum Narodowe w Krakowie.

Figure 4.6 Detail of *Market Square in Kazimierz Dolny*, Adam Lerue, *Album Lubelskie* (Warsaw: Adolf Pecq & Co., 1857), tab. 33. Warsaw: Biblioteka Narodowa, A.2714/G. XIX/III-29 cz. 1. The National Digital Library Polona. https://polona.pl/preview/ae943718-28da-416b-8d32-47e1aadd68be. Public domain.

four violinists, a bass player (on cello?), and a dulcimer player. The makeup of this band is revealed in an undated photograph from the end of the nineteenth century, preserved in the YIVO archives.[16]

Other important examples of Jewish music ensembles are preserved in photographs from the collection of the YIVO Institute for Jewish Research—founded in 1925 in Berlin and Wilno (with the participation of Albert Einstein and Sigmund Freud, among others), with its archives first located in Wilno, and in 1940 relocated to New York. The institute has a photograph from about 1900–1905 showing Alter Goizman's eleven-person band from Cudnów in the Wołyń region (now Чуднів, Ukraine).[17] The band consists of four violins, double bass, transverse flute, clarinet, two trumpets, trombone, and a drum. Another photograph from YIVO, dated to 1912, shows the eight-person Faust family band from Rohatyń (Ukr. Рогатин) in Galicia, playing two violins, viola, double bass, transverse flute, trumpet, clarinet, and another unidentified instrument.[18] In a 1905 photograph of the Szpilman family band from Ostrówek, then in Radom governorate, fourteen musicians are seen, playing four violins, cello, double bass, drum, two transverse flutes, two clarinets, two trumpets, and trombone.[19] In the YIVO archives, there is also a picture of an unknown klezmer band from Russia, probably dating from before World War I, and thus possibly from eastern territories of the former Poland. The band consists of nine musicians playing a drum, three violins, clarinet, trumpet, cornet, baritone saxhorn, and a tuba.[20] An interwar-period photograph of the Hasidic band from Nowy Dwór near Warsaw, under the direction of a certain Spielfidel, shows ten musicians, of which five hold violins, and others are shown with cello, trumpet (cornet?), and trombone. Two musicians are without instruments.[21] Sixteen klezmer instruments were shown in the picture taken before 1928 of the no-longer-extant wooden Aron kodesh (Heb. Torah ark) from the Włodawa synagogue (restored after a fire around 1920, burned again in 1934). The decorations consist of tuba, transverse flute, signal horn in trumpet form with one coil, mandolin (cittern?), snare drum with drumsticks, cymbals, valves helicon, viola, trumpet with rotary valves, triangle, tambourine, two flutes, cello, and a harp. Some of those instruments were sculptured, and some, mostly brass, were actual instruments.[22] The instruments shown in the Włodawa synagogue were probably only a part of the klezmer instrumentarium because the full set would not fit the Torah ark. The instruments were intended to illustrate Psalm 117 *Praise the Lord (Hallelu Et Adonai).*

Such complex and varied instrumental ensembles were created for the needs of the numerous Jewish theaters that emerged in the last decades of the nineteenth century and thrived in the urban landscapes described in chapter 5. In their repertoire, vaudeville productions prevailed, which demanded musical accompaniment, overtures, and all kinds of interludes. During the twentieth century, such ensembles were employed in recording music for the movies, including films on specifically Jewish subjects that were also produced in Poland. Smaller bands continued to play in inns and taverns, and wealthier families were routinely able to hire such bands for special family events and weddings.

The illustration that decorates the dust jacket of Glenn Dynner's book *Yankel's Tavern* leads us to another iconographical source on klezmer musicians in taverns run by Jews.[23] This idyllic picture by Gustaw Pilatti (1874–1931) shows the tavern's interior, with two pairs of Christian peasants in local folk costumes, one pair sitting with a baby on their knees, the other dancing to music played by a Jewish fiddler. In the center, the Jewish innkeeper is pouring vodka into a glass. Dynner rightly points out that the representation is deliberately idealized and stylized and that it offers an unrealistic depiction of the two religious groups' coexistence. Various online art auctions offer colorful copies of this painting as the *Wilanów Frieze* (*Fryz Wilanowski*) that portrays Wilanów peasants' merrymaking in a Jewish tavern. Although the name might suggest that the *Wilanów Frieze* is found in the Wilanów Palace in Warsaw (a frieze being a type of longitudinal painting adorning important buildings), this image has nothing to do with the palace, instead depicting the residents of the nearby village Wilanów (now a district of Warsaw). Pillati painted thirty such friezes portraying peoples and their customs in various parts of Poland. They were issued as lithographs in 1928 by Andrzej Chlebowski, the owner of Warsaw's publishing house "Świt," who had them lithographed at the printing shop of Wierzbicki i S-ka.[24] Most of Pillati's friezes were also used to illustrate Polish regional costumes in Jadwiga Makosińska's 1931 publication devoted to Polish ethnography.[25]

Other friezes included in Makosińska's publication offer a glance at Christian folk bands from various regions of Poland during the period after the First World War. The *Kraków Friezes* are found on pages 10 and 12. The first presents a cart embellished with flowers, with young couples and a band composed of a violinist and a double bass player. The second frieze shows guests dancing at the wedding, accompanied by the same band plus a boy with a tambourine. Page 31 shows the *Łowicki Frieze*, where wedding dances are accompanied by a band composed of a violin, a double bass, and a drum. The piper and highlanders dancing *zbójnicki* (the highlander bandit's dance) are depicted in the *Zakopane Frieze* on page 53. And finally, in the *Cieszyński Frieze* on page 74, Pillati presents a speeding horse-drawn peasant wagon with wedding guests and a band (or a part of it) consisting of a trumpeter and a (tenor?) saxhornist. Such a cast was characteristic for Silesia, where brass bands became popular in industrial plants, following the fashion for military bands.

There were some marked differences between Christian and Jewish bands playing in taverns. Christian bands used bagpipes, which did not appear in klezmer bands. Bagpipes were also accompanied by smaller folk fiddles with higher tuning (compatible with bagpipe's pitch), so-called *mazanki* in the Greater Poland region, and *złóbcoki* in the Podhale region. Furthermore, in the last period of klezmer bands in the Polish lands, they did not use the newly popular accordions, in contrast to the Christian bands. Once-ubiquitous dulcimers were found in both types of bands. Jewish bands usually used stringed bowed instruments made by luthiers or luthier factories (with the individual parts of the resonance box glued together). Christian bands typically used instruments of lesser quality, made from inferior materials as imitations of master violins (glued together or gouged out—the bottom with walls and sometimes with a neck made from one piece of wood with a glued belly), produced by the village carpenters or the musicians themselves. Christian bands playing in taverns usually had an ensemble of three to five people (violin, second violin, bagpipe or dulcimer, bass, drum), even during major family and wedding festivities. Most often, however, the ensembles were duets—for example, bagpipe and violin or dulcimer and violin. It was also common to enlarge the ensemble by allowing a willing and relatively musical guest to accompany the violinist or piper on a bass or a drum.

The instrumentarium of village bands underwent considerable changes in the second half of the nineteenth century. During the American Civil War (1861–65), shipments of bowed string instruments mass-produced in Germany could not reach North America. These were made in the numerous German centers of cottage manufacture, in villages where labor was distributed among families that made individual violin parts, other families that glued them together, and still others that covered them with varnish. Unable to be sold in North America, such instruments hit the European market at discounted prices, also finding their way into the hands of village musicians in the Polish lands. It had positive and negative influences on traditional folk music. For example, the small fiddles *mazanki* and *złóbcoki* that traditionally performed alongside bagpipes were forced out by ordinary violins with strings shortened with binding like with capo tasto to match the bagpipes' higher pitch.[26] Double basses or cellos replaced folk basses manufactured by village carpenters. Likewise, the village-made drums, usually tambourines, were replaced with factory-made big drums, often with attached cymbals (such percussion appeared also in Jewish bands). And finally, the adoption of the popular accordion, with tempered major-minor tuning, killed tonal diversity of the old village bands. Wooden and brass wind instruments became common in both Jewish and Christian bands starting in the mid-nineteenth century or a little earlier, probably under the influence of military bands in which both Jews and gentiles played during military service. They often returned home with such vintage, used instruments.

Musicians and Repertories

The surnames (and nicknames) of Jewish musicians often reflected their profession (musical or other), specialty in the band, or their physical features. Very common was the above-mentioned name Szpilman, which means "a musician." One can translate Spielfidel, also mentioned above, as "a fiddler player," and the surname of Jankiew Cymbalista denotes "a dulcimer player." Among the members of the klezmer brotherhood in Lwów in 1629 one finds Jakub Szmuklerz (haberdashery maker), Zelman Czapnik (hatter, cap maker), Jeruchim Pasamannik (Pasamonik? haberdashery maker), Eizyk Bass (bass player), Abuś Cymbalista (dulcimer player), and Chasz Ślepy (the blind one).[27] Mendel Bass and Wolf Zimbler (dulcimer player) played in the previously mentioned Faust band. The presence of surnames or nicknames related to professions other than music attests to the fact that many musicians had a second profession, when making music was not a sufficient source of income. They often supplemented their income as hairdressers, tailors, or glaziers.

The repertoire of these bands included almost all types of music, from typical klezmer pieces for family occasions and Jewish religious holidays to music that was used by their Christian neighbors for similar occasions. It included fashionable urban repertory of dances and operatic arias. Klezmers, called in the old times "usuals," could ad-lib anything, which meant playing any piece on demand, from memory and without a score. Klezmers only became musically literate by the end of the nineteenth century when Jews were finally allowed to attend music schools. In his recent book describing musical life in the province of the Polish Kingdom, Wojciech Tomaszewski gives an example of a dance party that took place on January 4, 1855, at the estate of a Mrs. and Mr. "W. P. G." in Kiełczew near Koło. For this occasion, the hosts hired two bands from Łęczyca, one led by E. Kordelas and another, directed by Nusbaum: "Mr. *Kordelas* who distinguished himself with both his playing and the selection of his companions continued to accompany dance with excellent polkas, mazurkas, and gallops, to the general satisfaction of the dancers and listeners. In another room, Mr. *Nusbaum* played happy *szumkas* along with the zestful singing of 'Jim is drinking to Jacob' [Pol. 'Pije Kuba do Jakuba']."[28] The *szumka* was described in 1831 as a "happy dance similar to the mazurka"[29] and in 1993 as a "happy, lively Ukrainian song; a former fast folk dance in Ruś, in 2/4 bar, similar to *kołomyjka* [Ukr. *kolomyika*]."[30]

Imagining the Jewish Musician in the Arts

Some instruments used in klezmer music and the virtuoso musicians that played them became the stuff of legends and subjects of literary fiction. The dulcimer, an inconspicuous stringed instrument, hit by handheld little hammers, is one such storied object. Dulcimer strings, a few for each tone, are stretched over the usually trapezoidal, or sometimes rectangular, resonance box, and make a loud, sometimes buzzing sound reminiscent of the bellowing, sustained voice of bells. Such types of instruments were known in the ancient Middle East, from where they then came to Europe during the Middle Ages and gained considerable popularity. They were likely brought to Polish lands by Jews, who transferred them to local rural musicians. They became common during the nineteenth century, especially in the eastern territories of the former Polish-Lithuanian Commonwealth (where they were also often used by Roma musicians). They must have been known as early as the beginning of the seventeenth century, since records mention Chaim, a dulcimer player from Poland, who had served in Wallenstein's German army during the Thirty Years' War (1618–1648) and died in 1636.[31] The oldest preserved record of the use of dulcimer by traveling Jewish musicians comes from 1694.[32]

Jankiel, a dulcimer player brought to life by Adam Mickiewicz in his 1834 national epic poem, *Pan Tadeusz: The Last Foray in Lithuania*, discussed in chapter 2, has become a mythical figure in his own right. Deeply respected and known for his honesty, Jankiel is not only the leaseholder of two taverns but also a deputy rabbi of Nowogród and a secret emissary to the Polish Legion in the Napoleonic army. To generations of Mickiewicz readers, he was known, above all, as a dulcimer master. In the famous excerpt of Book XII of the *Pan Tadeusz*, Jankiel gives a concert illustrating the fate of Poland during the partitions. Mickiewicz probably modeled his figure on the Będzin rabbi Jakub Nathan, known as a Polish patriot during the period of partitions.[33] Another person who might have been referenced here was Jankiel Liberman, a traveling musician who was known as a dulcimer player and who, like literary Jankiel, became an innkeeper. Mickiewicz met and heard Liberman perform in Saint Petersburg in 1830.[34] In Jankiel's "Concert of Concerts," some even imagine Fryderyk Chopin's improvisations.[35] Among the numerous iconographic attempts to present the figure of Jankiel, the least known but probably the most suggestive one is Norwid's drawing from 1846 (the drawing is also discussed in chap. 2 and reproduced in fig. 2.1).[36] Here, Jankiel is deeply pensive, without the dulcimer but with striking sticks in his right hand and a thread twisted around his left hand, and the thread's other end drawn to the right hand as if spinning a story "on knitting needles," which he wants to transform into the sounds of his dulcimer. For Norwid, Mickiewicz's Jankiel stands above all other personae of *Pan Tadeusz*. He makes this sentiment clear in a letter written in 1866 where he concludes, "Poland's favorite and famous national poem, in which the only respectable and serious character is who? . . . a Jew (Jankiel). The rest: daredevils, jesters, storytellers, gluttons who eat, drink, pick mushrooms and wait for the French to come and make them a homeland."[37]

The Warsaw musician Mordechaj (Mordko) Fajerman was later seen as the embodiment of the literary Jankiel and was extremely popular in Poland's capital (Fajerman is shown in fig. 5.3). Born in Kałuszyn in 1781, Fajerman moved to Warsaw after a town fire and lived there until his death around 1880. He performed in the streets and courtyards (which took on many of the functions of the country inn as people migrated to urban centers—a process discussed in chap. 5), delighting Warsaw residents with great performances of Polish dances, mazurkas, polonaises, and popular melodies. He also enjoyed recognition and popularity among professional musicians. Although Fajerman was called the "last dulcimer player of Warsaw," his instrument was not the dulcimer; rather, like Guzikov's, it was a xylophone. This instrument consists of wooden (or glass) tiles that emit sounds of different pitches, arranged in two rows. Like the dulcimer, it is played using small hammers.

Another storied figure of klezmer music is the "Jewish violinist" or more appropriately "fiddler" (since the string instruments they played did not always rise to the rank of "a Stradivarius"). During the eighteenth and nineteenth centuries, when outstanding violinists were worshipped by their audiences, legends often attributed the masterful virtuosity of Niccolò Paganini, Karol Lipiński, Henryk Wieniawski, and others to a pact with the devil. There were many Jews among such virtuosos of the concert stage, but even more among musicians in taverns. The figure of an extraordinary virtuoso violinist playing for ordinary, simple people reflected the leading role of the violinist in a klezmer band. In one of his most famous short stories, entitled *Janko the Musician* (1879), the Nobel-winning Polish writer Henryk Sienkiewicz describes a young country boy, possessed by music, who makes a violin from wooden shingles and horsehair, but the instrument unfortunately "did not want to play as beautifully as those in the tavern."[38]

In Yiddish literature, the virtuoso klezmer playing the violin was also a hero of many stories, novellas, and theater plays. He was even the subject of countless paintings—for example, by Marc Chagall (*The Green Violinist*, *The Blue Violinist*, *Fiddler on the Roof*, and many others). The father of Yiddish literature, Sholem Aleichem (1859–1916), wrote the most famous stories on this subject. In his short, playful novel *On the Fiddle* from 1902, a music teacher gives a "shortened" history of music, as follows:

> The fiddle, you understand me, is an instrument that is older than all instruments. The first fiddler in the world was Tubal Cain, or Methuselah, I no longer recall accurately. . . . The next fiddler was King David. After him, there was a third, Paganini he was called, also a Jew; all of the best fiddlers in the world have been Jews. For example, Stempeny [*sic*] . . . Paganini, they say, sold his soul to Ashmodeus for a fiddle. Paganini hated playing for great men, royalty and popes, no matter how they used to pay him. He preferred to play for poor people in all the taverns, in all the villages, or even in the woods for the beasts and the birds. What a fiddler Paganini was![39]

Sholem Aleichem created a picture of a Jewish Paganini, a virtuoso fiddler playing for the simple people, in his novel *Stempenyu, a Jewish Romance*, published in the Yiddish language in Kyiv in 1888:

> Stempenyu was a nickname of sorts he'd inherited from his father. His old man, God rest him, was a klezmer known as Berl Bass or Berl Stempener, after the village of Stempeni not far from Mazepevke. He played the double bass and was also a decent *badkhn*, with a gift for rhymes. He was an inveterate swindler, who disguised himself as a beggar at every wedding. . . . Klezmer music had been in Stempenyu's family going back several generations. Berl Bass or Berl Stempener, as we already know, played the bass; his father, Reb Shmulik Trumpet, played the trumpet; his grandfather, Reb Fayvush Cymbaler, played the cymbalon, and his great-grandfather,

> Reb Ephraim Violin, well . . . In short, Stempenyu was the result of ten generations of klezmer—and he was not in the least ashamed of it, as the simple laborer is sometimes ashamed of his lot.[40]

Stempenyu's playing embodied the essence of klezmer music, music that appealed to the soul of listeners. This was because Sholem Aleichem identified the sound of Stempenyu's violin with the Jewish language:

> He would snatch up the fiddle, and drawing the bow across it in the most careless fashion, he would succeed in making it speak at once. It needed but a single movement of his elbow, and the little fiddle was speaking to us all. And how it spoke! In the most unmistakable accents! Really, with words that we all understood, in the plainest fashion, as if it had a tongue, and as if it were real living, human being! It would moan, and wail, and weep over its sad fortune as if it were a Jew. And, its cry was shrill and heartrending. It was as if every note found its way upward from out of the deepest depths of the soul.[41]

The character of Stempenyu appeared many times in stage adaptations of the novel by Sholem Aleichem, in other works by him already presented on American stages (when the writer migrated to the USA), and in local bookstores. In this manner, he became a sort of klezmer icon in Jewish musical culture. In 1932, Joseph Achron composed a three-part suite for violin and piano, called *Stempenyu*, in which he endeavored to present the spirit and mastery of klezmer music. This piece was performed by Joseph Szigeti, Jascha Heifetz, and many other great violinists in the 1930s on world concert stages.[42] Stempenyu was also the prototype for the eponymous *Fiddler on the Roof* in the world-famous 1964 musical, loosely based on another of Sholem Aleichem's stories, the 1894 *Tevye the Milkman*, as well as for the violinist in the movie version of the musical from 1971 (Isaac Stern played the violin solo). Similarly, Stempenyu's inspiration can be traced to the 1998 movie titled *Train de vie* (*Train of Life*), as well as to the persona adopted by Isaac Perlman, who toured with klezmers and recorded the 1995 album *Klezmer: In the Fiddler's House*. The archetype of a brilliant Jewish violinist was also the backdrop for multitudes of Wunderkind violinists of humble origins, who sought fame in the nineteenth and early twentieth centuries in Ukraine and Belarus, giving rise to their Jewish contemporaries mocking this phenomenon as "bathe and send to Paris!"

In the twentieth century, the role of Stempenyu's violin was taken on by the more agile and expressive clarinet. Early on, the klezmer spirit was attributed to the celebrated virtuoso performer and band leader Benny Goodman, although his musical pedigree was purely in jazz. However, during the revival of klezmer music in the United States, such mythical musicians were clarinetists from Europe and several generations of klezmer tradition, such as Dave Taras (1897–1989) called "the Benny Goodman of klezmers," Naftule Brandwein (1884–1963) called "the Charlie Parker of klezmers" or even "the king of klezmers," and Giora Feidman (born in 1936).

***

Klezmer musicians in Polish taverns had a function that could be compared to electric audio equipment. Their music drew clients from around, neighbors and strangers, who came to rest in the inn, to dance, or just to listen. On the other hand, the musicians offered specific musical entertainment, bringing the sounds of neighboring towns or of the broader world into the village and transporting the sounds of the village into the city (for more on this, see chap. 5). Especially in the case of weddings or other larger family and religious ceremonies that employed larger klezmer bands, klezmers were able to get the event's participants and bystanders into the music (and dance), and even encourage a state of excitement. When the village musicians migrated to urban centers, their function, musical style, and instruments changed as they took on new roles not only in the town taverns and coffeehouses but also in theater, on the dance floor, and in the movies. While these changes were taking place, the nostalgic and idealized image of a Jewish village musician continued to nourish the musical, literary, and visual imagination in Jewish and gentile cultures of the twentieth century in the old and the new worlds.

BENJAMIN VOGEL is Professor Emeritus of Musicology at the Universities of Warsaw, Szczecin (Poland), and Lund (Sweden). He is author of, among others, *Musical Instruments in the Culture of the Kingdom of Poland* (in Polish), *Piano Industry in Polish Lands from the Mid-18th Century to World War II* (in Polish), *Chopin's Piano* (2018), and "'There on the Willows We Hang Our' . . . Violins: On Old Macewas, Synagogues and Klezmorim" in *Muzykalia 7 / Judaica 2 – De Musica* (2009).

NOTES

1. Glenn Dynner, *Yankel's Tavern: Jews, Liquor, & Life in the Kingdom of Poland* (Oxford: Oxford University Press, 2013), 22.

2. Wojciech Kalwat, "Staropolskie karczmy. Brud, paskudne jedzenie, niewygodne posłania . . . i jedne z najważniejszych miejsc w dawnej Rzeczypospolitej," Ciekawostki Historyczne.pl, last modified February 2, 2023, https://ciekawostkihistoryczne.pl/2023/02/25/staropolskie-karczmy/.

3. Dynner, *Yankel's Tavern*, 73.

4. Dynner, 22, 92; Jan Słomka, *Pamiętnik włościanina: od pańszczyzny do dni dzisiejszych* (Kraków: Krakowska Drukarnia Nakładowa, 1912), 110.

5. The term *klezmer* was applied mainly to musicians from Central and Eastern Europe. Until the mid-nineteenth century, klezmers were musically illiterate, but they were known for their ability to play vast repertories from memory and for their skill in improvising and embellishing when playing an unfamiliar tune. From the mid-nineteenth century on, klezmer bands were also frequently hired by gentiles, performing dance and concert music. In today's jargon of Polish pop musicians, a klezmer is a musician who can play everything ad-lib. For more, see Walter Zev Feldman, *Klezmer: Music, History, and Memory* (New York: Oxford University Press, 2016); and the periodical *Polin: Studies in Polish Jewry* 32: *Jews and Music-Making in the Polish Lands* (2020).

6. Joanna Rodziewicz, "Rola karczmy w życiu dawnej wsi polskiej," *Rolniczy Magazyn Elektroniczny* no. 54 (2019), https://rme.cbr.net.pl/index.php/archiwum-rme/377-marzec-kwiecie-nr-54/kultura-i-tradycje-ludowe40-7681/339-rola-karczmy-w-yciu-dawnej-wsi-polskiej, accessed January 12, 2025; Dynner, *Yankel's Tavern*, 52–65.

7. Hubert Vautrin, *L'observateur en Pologne* (Paris: Giguet et Michaud, 1807), 292.

8. Zygmunt Batowski, *Wystawa dzieł Jana Piotra Norblina (1745–1830)* (Warsaw: Towarzystwo Zachęty Sztuk Pięknych w Król. Pol., 1910), 24. Norblin's authorship is uncertain, and the work has also been attributed to Aleksander Orłowski. An engraving based on this watercolor was reproduced in the journal *Kłosy* 21, no. 540 (1875): 293. The National Gallery in Warsaw holds an identical watercolor titled *Zabawa w karczmie* (*Karczma w Częstochowie*) from 1800, attributed to Aleksander Orłowski: https://cyfrowe.mnw.art.pl/pl/katalog/756604.

9. Dana Veselská, "Svatební obřady aškenázských Židů—historie a současnost," *Folia Ethnographica* 40, *Supplementum ad Acta Musei Moraviae* (2006): 112.

10. Guzikov was admired by luminaries such as Karol Lipiński, Fryderyk Chopin, Franz Liszt, and Felix Mendelssohn, while French ladies introduced a fashionable hairstyle with side curls called *coiffure à la Gusikov*.

11. Banach, *Tematy muzyczne*, fig. 96.

12. Wojciech Włodarczyk, "Powiślańscy Żydzi w dawnych wiekach," *Powiśle Lubelskie* 56, no. 6 (2013): 2–6, https://rtpwilkow.files.wordpress.com/2013/11/pow-lub-6-2013.pdf.

13. Beniamin Vogel, "Klezmerzy Księstwa Warszawskiego," *Studia Musicologica Stetinensis* 2 (2010): 183–88; Vogel, "'Na wierzbach zawiesiliśmy nasze . . . skrzypce.' Rzecz o dawnych instrumentach, macewach, synagogach i klezmerach," *Muzyka* 52, no. 2 (2007): 75–113; "'There on the Willows We Hung Our' . . . Violins: On Old Macewas, Synagogues and Klezmorim," *Muzykalia* VII/*Judaica* 2 (2009), http://demusica.edu.pl/wp-content/uploads/2019/07/vogel_muzykalia_7_judaica22.pdf.

14. Moshe Beregovski, *Old Jewish Folk Music: The Collections and Writings of Moshe Beregovski*, ed. and trans. Mark Slobin (Syracuse, NY: Syracuse University Press, 2000), 301.

15. Henry Sapoznik, "Overview," in *Klezmer Music 1910–1942*. Folkways Records. FW34021, FSS 3402. 1981, 5, compact disc.

16. Henry Sapoznik, *The Compleat Klezmer* (New York: Tara, 1988).

17. Sapoznik, *Compleat Klezmer*, 63; Sapoznik, *Klezmer Music*, 5. He was also known as Yehiel Goyzman (Hausman) or Alter Chudnover (1846–1913).

18. Sapoznik, *Klezmer Music*, 1.

19. Sapoznik, *Compleat Klezmer*, 51; Henry Sapoznik, *Klezmer! Jewish Music from Old World to Our World*. 2000, Yazoo CD 7017, compact disc, overview.

20. *Oytsres-Treasures, Klezmer Music 1908–1996*. 1999. Wergo LC 06356, compact disc, overview, 25; *Klezmer Pioneers: European & American Recordings, 1905–1952*. 1993. Rounder Records 1089, compact disc, overview.

21. Isachar Fater, *Muzyka żydowska w okresie międzywojennym* (Warsaw: Rytm, 1997), 204.

22. Vogel, *Na wierzbach*, 89, 108; Vogel, "There on the Willows."

23. It is reproduced also as a black-white image on p. 29 of the book.

24. The caption of Dynner's reproduction of the *Wilanów Frieze* informs us that this is Pilatti's lithograph "published by A. Chlebowski, in the journal 'Świt,' and printed by B. Wierzbicki and Sons, Warsaw, n.d. (Moldovan Family Collection)." See Dynner, 29. Since the monthly magazine *Świt* was issued by Polish Catholic abstinence organizations in the years 1904–39 to support the temperance movement, one could surmise that it was an insert in the form of a poster intended to accuse Jews of intoxicating and exploiting peasantry. In this instance, however, the reference is not to the name of a journal but the name of the Andrzej Chlebowski's Publishing House in Warsaw, at 71 Krakowskie Przedmieście (A. Chlebowski, Towarzystwo Wydawnicze "Świt"), the publisher of Pillati's lithographs.

25. Jadwiga Makosińska, *Etnografja Polski w nauczaniu geografji objaśniona na fryzach ludowych Pillatiego* (Lwów-Warsaw: Książnica-Atlas, 1931), 29–30. Even though the frieze represents an idealized picture of Jewish-gentile coexistence, Makosińska spares no accusations of real and imaginary culpability on the part of the Jews, including responsibility for alcoholism among the peasants.

26. Beniamin Vogel, *Der Einfluss des professionellen auf den nicht professionellen Instrumentenbau in Polen, Studia instrumentorum musicae popularis* VI (Stockholm: Musikhistoriska museet, 1979), 175–77.

27. Zbigniew Chaniecki, *Organizacje zawodowe muzyków na ziemiach polskich do końca XVIII w.* (Kraków: Polskie Wydawnictwo Muzyczne, 1980), 133, 154.

28. "*P. Kordelas* odznaczający się i grą i doborem współtowarzyszów, grał wciąż do tańca doskonałe *polki*, *mazury* i *galopy*, z powszechnem zadowoleniem tak tańczących, jak i słuchających. P. *Nusbaum* grał wesołe szumki w innym pokoju, przy ochoczem: *Pije Kuba do Jakuba*." Wojciech Tomaszewski, *Kronika życia muzycznego na prowincji Królestwa Polskiego w latach 1815–1862* (Warsaw: Biblioteka Narodowa, 2007), 249.

29. Łukasz Gołębiowski, *Gry i zabawy różnych stanów w kraju całym . . .* (Warsaw: Nakładem autora, 1831), 324.

30. Władysław Kopaliński, *Słownik mitów i tradycji kultury*, 4th ed. (Kraków: Państwowy Instytut Wydawniczy, 1993), 1146.

31. Abraham Zevi Idelsohn, *Jewish Music in Its Historical Development*, 3rd ed. (New York: Schocken, 1975), 455.

32. Idelsohn, 457–58.

33. Stanisław Jędrzejek, "O rabinie Jakubie i Świętej Pani z Zagórza," in *Wspomnienie o Stanisławie Jędrzejku* (Katowice: Infograf, 2005).

34. Chaim Löw, "Rodowód Jankiela. W stulecie *Pana Tadeusza*," *Muzykalia* XI, *Judaica* 3, http://demusica.edu.pl/wp-content/uploads/2019/07/low_muzykalia_11_judaica31.pdf.

35. Idelsohn, *Jewish Music*, 457–58.

36. "Jankiel," Cyprian Kamil Norwid, from ink drawing of "Jankiel and Shylock," 1848. Warsaw, Muzeum Narodowe, Rys. Pol. 159761 MNW. Digital Collections of the National Museum in Warsaw. https://cyfrowe.mnw.art.pl/pl/zbiory/898867.

37. See Henryk Piątkowski, "Norwid o *Panu Tadeuszu*. Trzy listy poety z r. 1866," *Wiadomości Literackie* (1925): 29, 81; Cyprian Norwid, "Letter to Włodzimierz Cybulski," in *Pisma wszystkie*, ed. Wiktor J. Gomulicki, vol. 9, *Listy 1862–1872* (Warsaw: Państwowy Instytut Wydawniczy, 1971), 271.

38. Norwid, "Letter to Włodzimierz Cybulski," 271.

39. Joshua S. Walden, "The 'Yidishe Paganini': Sholem Aleichem's Stempenyu, the Music of Yiddish Theatre and the Character of the Shtetl Fiddler," *Journal of the Royal Musical Association* 139, no. 1 (2014): 89.

40. Sholem Aleichem, *My First Jewish Novel, Stempenyu*, trans. Daniel Kennedy, 2016, introduction, http://www.yiddishbookcenter.org/language-literature-culture/yiddish-translation/my-first-jewish-novel-stempenyu.

41. Aleichem, *Stempenyu*, 6.

42. Published among others by the Viennese Universal Edition in 1932 and dedicated to Joseph Szigeti.

5

From Taverns to Courtyards and Cafés

How the Shtetl Migrated into Fin de Siècle Warsaw

Beth Holmgren

The primarily Jewish-operated taverns in the provincial Kingdom of Poland were remarkably multifaceted establishments, as described by Glenn Dynner and Judith Kalik—contributors to the present volume—and other historians such as Yohanan Petrovsky-Shtern.[1] As Kalik notes in chapter 3, the tavern comprised a public guest-house and stables, and offered food and lodging to Jewish and gentile travelers—provided, of course, that said travelers could pay. For its local patrons—the Jews in the shtetl, Christian nobles in the manor house, and Christian peasants in the village—the tavern functioned, in Dynner's formulation, as "the epicenter of village and small town life." By serving food and drink and offering musical entertainment, the tavern provided the one public secular site for indulging one's appetites, celebrating special events, and crossing borders between religious communities and social classes.[2] Kalik likewise identifies the tavern/inn "as a focal point of social life, providing often the only place different social strata could interact."[3] As an establishment permitted to sell alcohol, the tavern also vented "the repressed libido of the shtetl," according to Petrovsky-Shtern, with liquor flowing in and secrets consequently spilling out.[4] Such secrets occasionally touched on political conspiracy and more regularly involved criminal activities (prostitution, gatherings of thieves).[5] In general, the tavern facilitated the exchange of local gossip and regional or continent-wide news, given its mix of regular patrons and passing travelers. Much as it offered the lone option for travelers in search of accommodation, so the tavern became the shtetl's one-stop shop for refreshment, entertainment, some goods and services, lubricated socializing, and worldly information, though what was on offer tended to be limited or random. In chapter 3, Kalik notes that long before massive Jewish immigration to the cities, the tavern's functions encompassed a guesthouse, stables for guests' horses, and a dining / common room.

By the last two decades of the nineteenth century, however, the provincial inn's local clientele was rapidly dwindling. Between 1881 and 1914, hundreds of thousands of Jews from the Kingdom of Poland and the Pale of Settlement had migrated to Warsaw, the third-largest city in the tsarist empire, because they were desperate for employment, better trade opportunities, and, in some cases, the pursuit of radical ideals. Taverns existed in the big city, but they were by no means the only, or even the main, communal spaces in which Jewish newcomers learned to adapt to a fast-modernizing metropolis that intimidated them with its size, noise, fast pace, densely crowded streets, towering tenement buildings, and tremendously diverse population.

Building on Jürgen Habermas's reading of the café as part of "the public sphere of bourgeois culture" in Europe, historians Scott Ury and Shachar M. Pinsker trace the emergence of a "Jewish public sphere" (Ury) or "thirdspace" (Pinsker) in the Yiddish-language coffeehouses established in early twentieth-century Warsaw. In Ury's analysis, the coffeehouse, triangulated with the Yiddish theater and Yiddish newspapers, was "rooted on an ethno-lingual plane" and at once educated and variously politicized a Yiddish-speaking and reading clientele.[6] This essay presents a prelude and a complement to these scholars' important work, focusing on the "Warsaw education" of thousands of in-migrating Jews accustomed to the provincial inn's necessarily limited display of diversity. Specifically, I analyze the impact of the tenement courtyard connecting working- and lower middle-class residents to the street, a space that familiarized the newly settled with the overwhelming variety of Warsaw residents, including imposing types of established Varsovian Jews, and the city's growing network of cafés that ranged from well-appointed locales in the city's gentile-majority Downtown (Śródmieście) to emerging coffeehouses in the Jewish-majority Nalewki district.

The All-Warsaw Courtyard: The City Invades and Initiates

For so many poor newcomers, their tenement apartment buildings and especially their courtyards afforded them their first relatively stable vantage point on city life. The courtyard was utilitarian at best. It usually contained the building's communal well and communal toilet. But the daily visits of an array of vendors, artisans, performers, and beggars to the courtyard introduced the city to those recently arrived (by migration or age) and served, entertained, and reoriented them. The nonfiction stories of Isaac Bashevis Singer (1902–91) are particularly revealing on this point since he, the son of a provincial Hasidic rabbi, vividly captures the shock and thrill of moving from his sleepy shtetl of Radzymin to Nalewki. In "The Trip from Radzymin to Warsaw," the boy narrator is gobsmacked by the noise and unruly crowds of the city street, which he can only compare to a hometown disaster: "The gutter was filled with people. The throngs, the yelling, the pushing reminded me of the fire I had witnessed in Radzymin some weeks before and I was certain a fire had broken out here in Warsaw, too."[7]

The yelling, pushing throngs also moved through his family's shared domestic space—the large collective-use courtyard that almost all of Warsaw's tenements buildings were built to enclose.[8] The young Singer can observe this courtyard from the perch of his apartment's balcony, a place where he "was both inside and outside at the same time."[9] In his story, "The Suicide," Singer takes note of his gentle father's religious resistance to the courtyard:

> Here in the house, amidst the holy books, the peace of the Sabbath reigned again, but the street outside was full of shouting, turmoil, theft, robbery, war, and injustice. A year or two before we had come to live in Warsaw, there had been a revolution. People still spoke about "bloody Wednesday" and the bomb Baruch Schulman had thrown at a policeman. Jewish boys were still in jails or working in prison camps deep inside Russia. Father himself never stepped out on the balcony, except on very hot summer evenings, when the heat indoors was unbearable. The balcony was already a part of the street, of the crowd, of the Gentile world and its savagery. He even frowned at my going out on the balcony.[10]

In Singer's imagination, the courtyard, referred to as "the street" here, connected him with not only a violent gentile world but also the Jewish heroes who had bombed the police and marched in protest during the 1905 demonstrations—heroes who now suffered grievous punishment in Siberian exile and local jails such as Warsaw's infamous Citadel Fortress. As soon as Singer's father dozed off for the afternoon, the boy raced down to the courtyard, eager to experience its drama and to learn more about the Jews' valiant, rebellious past.

While Singer was drawn to the courtyard as a place of compelling and enlightening danger, other boys of Warsaw—assimilated and unassimilated

Jews and poor gentiles—relished the courtyard for its routine parade of tradespeople, artisans, and entertainers, who transformed the space every day into a multicultural market and stage. Józef Galewski (1882–1966), the famed set designer for interwar Warsaw's theaters and cabarets, recalls this sequence from his working-class boyhood: a black-clad Jewish peddler buying and selling junk, a sooty vendor delivering coal, Slovak artisans advertising their skill in mending pots, and a Roma woman offering to tell fortunes.[11] Writer Benedykt Hertz (1872–1952), the son of a Jewish insurgent in the 1863 uprising against the Russians, remembers early morning Jewish peddlers and artisans—rag buyers and repairers of broken glass and china—and recalls musicians who busked for coins from the children on the ground and the housewives and female servants standing in the windows and on the balconies above them. These performers included motley orchestras of Czech musicians wearing Austrian uniforms and playing Austrian music, and Italian organ grinders decked out more elegantly in soft fedoras and velvet jackets.[12] (Fig. 5.1 shows such a performance in early twentieth-century Warsaw.) Most eagerly anticipated were the shabby family troupes of acrobats, who would roll out a dirty rug, strip down to their leotards, and start juggling, tumbling, doing contortions, and walking about on their hands. When the acrobats left, the local boys often tagged along after them, vicariously experiencing what it was like to make one's living on an ever-changing courtyard stage.[13]

For children, housewives, and servants (servants were often first-generation Varsovians from peasant villages), the courtyards in Nalewki and gentile-majority districts functioned as an extension of the big city, filtered insofar as the tenement guards (as instructed and bribed by the Russian police) vetted those who entered the courtyard gate. The city courtyard afforded a relatively safe daytime space for greater and more diverse entertainment and refreshment than any provincial tavern could provide. Dynner lists the "buns, doughnuts, cottage-cheese cakes, [and] pickled herring" for purchase in the taverns, but the clever vendors in Warsaw also packed candy and pastry in their baskets to tempt children who had a few *grosze* to spend.[14]

Experiencing the daily parade in the courtyard accustomed new or young Jewish residents to the incessant movement, raucousness, and changing consumption habits of city life. It made them aware of Warsaw's status as a European stage and metropolitan marketplace as they encountered performers from other parts of the continent and vendors from other districts in the city. Everyday observation of the courtyard and adjoining

Figure 5.1 "Music-Warsaw," watercolor by Lionel Reiss, 1921. YIVO, RG 1160 / ya-rg1160-101. Reproduced by permission of YIVO Institute for Jewish Research.

district streets also exposed the in-migrants to city types and potential role models they would never have known in the provinces. Their sociocultural horizons broadened as a result. For example, Jews relocated from the shtetl laid eyes on different types of Jews in Warsaw—not only the poor junk traders but also the Jewish porters, who could carry a week's goods for an entire household in baskets on their backs (see fig. 5.2). Hertz's portrait of these men, whom he distinguishes as "exceptional," glows with his boyhood awe at their fabled strength and gargantuan appetites:

> They were bearded strong men, dressed in short coats. When the athlete Christolf arrived at Salamoński's Circus and announced a prize for anyone who could knock him down, he had a lot of work fighting the porters from beyond the Iron Gate. I got to know one of them when he carried a fireproof safe (true, it had only one door) up to the second floor on his back. He was a giant of about fifty. He complained about a lack of appetite since he had only managed to consume a loaf of bread with cheese for breakfast. These Orthodox Jews were also unusual in that many worshipped Bacchus. They got thoroughly plastered at the saloon on Ptasia Street. Their guild was there.[15]

Isaac Bashevis Singer discovered a similarly exceptional Warsaw Jew in a close family friend, Reb Asher the dairyman, whose feats were so great that he merited his own story.[16] Reb Asher matched the strength of the porters, a "tall, broad, strong [man with] a black beard, black eyes, and the voice of lion." But he was also a pious, observant Jew and a bona fide hero who saved the entire Singer family when their apartment caught fire. Most impressive to the boy Singer, however, was Reb Asher's seeming command of the city due to his job, horse, and wagon. The dairyman regularly invited the boy to accompany him on his delivery runs, grand adventures that laid all of Warsaw (not just Nalewki district) at Singer's feet:

> The trip took several hours and I was overjoyed. I rode amid trolley cars, droshkies, delivery vans. Soldiers marched; policemen stood guard; fire engines, ambulances, even some of the automobiles that were just beginning to appear on the streets of Warsaw rushed past us. Nothing could harm me. I was protected by a friend with a whip, and beneath my feet I could feel the throbbing of the wheels. It seemed that all Warsaw must envy me. And indeed people stared in wonderment at the little Hasid with the velvet cap and the red earlocks who was riding in a milk wagon and surveying the city.[17]

In this passage, Singer—protected by a physically imposing, city-bred Jew "with a whip" and transported by "private" cart through the city—

Z TYPÓW WARSZAWSKICH.
Pankiewicz
Tragarz. Rysunek oryginalny I. Pankiewicza.

Figure 5.2 Porter, original drawing by Józef Pankiewicz. *Tygodnik Illustrowany* 10, no. 237 (July 16, 1887): 37. Mazowiecka Biblioteka Cyfrowa. https://mbc.cyfrowemazowsze.pl/dlibra/publication/64303/edition/59224. Public domain.

exults in feelings of power, freedom, movement, sweeping vision, and trespassing that would be unattainable in the shtetl. For the duration of these milk runs, the young Singer is electrified by the sights of so many vehicles and uniformed functionaries engaged in their important work for the big city. Singer is acutely aware that keeping company with Reb Asher has transformed him from a poor "little Hasid" into the envy of "all Warsaw."

From the late nineteenth century through the first decades of the twentieth century, in-migrants encountered "different" Jews in the city who impressed them as crossover artists—specifically, musicians whose choice of instrument or repertoire was recognized and valued by gentile-majority culture. As early as 1867, Polish journalist Wacław Szymanowski sketched one of the supposed "Jewish types" of the Warsaw street in the popular newspaper *Tygodnik Illustrowany* (The illustrated weekly), claiming that Mordko Fajerman, mentioned in chapter 4, was "the last hammer dulcimer player in Warsaw." In so doing, Szymanowski sought to satisfy his Polish readers' taste for the pleasant picturesque and to validate a real-life incarnation of the most benign, beloved, expressly "Polish" Jew in Polish literature, Jankiel, the tavernkeeper and maestro of the hammer dulcimer in Adam Mickiewicz's long narrative poem, *Pan Tadeusz* (1834). Szymanowski accompanies the visual sketch of the musician, shown in figure 5.3, with his verbal equivalent, carefully endowing Fajerman (whom he mainly addresses as Jankiel) with the majesty befitting the reincarnation of a Mickiewicz hero:

> There is no instrument, he says, like the hammer dulcimer. Everything is contained in it and it expresses everything. . . . He performs an expansive repertoire, though local specialties above all. He is incomparable in playing *mazurkas*, and most likes to perform them. When he enters a courtyard and children surround him, he gives them a dulcimer hammer and has them try the instrument. He seems pleased with their unsuccessful efforts. Once he is asked to show them how it is done, he begins with chromatic scales, trills, and an entire labyrinth of musical passages which would seem impossible to render on a hammer dulcimer. . . . The hammers fly in Jankiel's fingers as if they are enchanted, as if they had grown wings.

It is strange that this simple man appears to be so old and frail, yet when he picks up his hammers and strikes the dulcimer, his movements are sure, elastic, youthful. The old man is reborn and becomes an artist sure of his artistry and tireless in his play.[18]

By chance or design (either the musician's or the journalist's), Fajerman in this sketch echoes the ennobled fictional Jankiel in several ways—playing only when he is asked to do so (signaling modesty and graciousness), specializing in Polish music (proof of his "national" attachment), dazzling his listeners with his winged hammers, and literally rejuvenated by his performance (the manifestation of his implicitly transformative Romantic artistry). It is improbable that most Jewish newcomers to Warsaw (the great majority of whom were Yiddish speakers) would draw the connection between an itinerant Jewish hammer dulcimer player and a famed character in a work of Polish classic literature. But these observers must have noted that a musician like Fajerman attracted both Jewish and gentile listeners/clienteles. Such an artist crossed borders with ease, likely evoking nostalgia from Jews, who had sentimentalized their memories of the

Figure 5.3 Mordko Fajerman, woodcut, based on a photograph by Karol Beyer, 1867. Artist unknown. *Tygodnik Illustrowany* 16, no. 407 (July 13, 1867): 16. The National Digital Library Polona. https://polona.pl/item-view/b0fc7e82-0ed9-48cf-bbfc-aa90679afd15?page=3. Public domain.

shtetl, and rousing national pride among gentile Poles who embraced this "Jankiel" for his fine manners, superb artistry, "Polish" patriotism, and association with their subversive national bard.

With less fanfare, other Jewish performers crossed from gentile-majority Warsaw districts in the south to Nalewki in the northwest as they made their rounds. The writer Józef Henryk Cukier (pen name Józef Hen [1923–]), who lived in Nalewki between the wars, remembers many of the same sorts of courtyard entertainers as those who enliven the accounts of Hertz, Galewski, and others.[19] According to popular historian Marian Fuks, however, itinerant Jewish musicians in the interwar period preferred to frequent courtyards where at least 50 percent of the residents were Yiddish-speaking Jews.[20] Their circumscribed busking may have been due to the preponderance of Yiddish-language songs in their repertoire or increased antisemitism in gentile-majority districts. In his memoir, Fuks points out that some touring duos—singers who accompanied themselves on mandolin and guitar—performed Yiddish songs focused on themes and characters then popular in the Jewish community: the burden of heavy taxes, the horrors of the economic crises of the 1930s, and the once-rich Jews who went bankrupt and committed suicide by jumping off tall buildings.[21]

Yet, at least during the interwar years, the repertoire favored by most Jewish musicians reflected Jewish *success* in creating the best of modern Polish popular culture. Itinerant Jewish musicians liked to perform the many mainstream hits written by acculturated Jewish composers/conductors and recorded by almost exclusively Jewish dance bands in the 1920s and 1930s.[22] The street musicians' live performances of these hits were inferior to those recorded—Fuks recalls a shrill-voiced little girl being accompanied by a "one-man band"—but this pair's repertoire included such songs as the 1930 Andrzej Włast / Artur Gold love song "Nie odchodź ode mnie" (Don't step away) and the 1932 Włast / Zygmunt Białostocki "Rebeka" (Rebecca), which tells the story of a provincial Jewish girl who falls for a city slicker. People too poor to own gramophones paid a little for the privilege of listening to a homegrown rendition. Fuks remarks that another enterprising busker simply affixed a gramophone atop a baby carriage and played his recordings for those who would pay to listen, pioneering an early version of a jukebox.[23]

In an interesting complement to the courtyard's everyday use, which tended to secularize and citify the locals, some courtyards in the Nalewki district were also outfitted for religious purposes. Józef Hen attests that "the rhythm of life in our courtyard was determined by the [Jewish] holidays" until regular religious observance faded in the 1930s. He remembers most fondly the courtyard's great transformation during the autumn holidays of Sukkot. For Jews living in overcrowded Nalewki, the courtyard proved indispensable for the erection of each family's outdoor booth, where they reenacted their ancestors' experience by eating some meals outside and viewing the stars through their makeshift roofs. Hen loved celebrating Sukkot in Nalewki, where "[f]or eight days the courtyard was crammed with wooden booths with roofs made of rushes. The courtyard looked picturesque and the children made the most of it, playing hide and seek."[24]

According to Polish city guides and local historians today, more affluent Jewish residents attached permanent Sukkot booths, or *kuczki*, to their tenement apartments, even though a year-round booth, complete with roof, could not be considered kosher.[25] These structures resembled wooden porches, sometimes rather ornately carved, which hung above the courtyard; the walls might be made of inset glass. Fortunately, a number of these structures survived the Shoah in Łódź.[26] Such customized alterations indicate that the Jews who settled in these big-city tenements still asserted their religious identity regardless of the street's daily demonstration of city life as broadly diverse, secular, and market-driven. The Jewish kuczki can be read as nods to both God and the market—as a permanent public marker of one's faith and a time-saving convenience.

Downtown Warsaw and Nalewki Cafés: Congregating, Caffeinating, Debating

In late nineteenth-century Warsaw, as in other Central European cities with a growing middle class, businesses scrambled to provide eating and drinking locales suitable for more affluent patrons. While the inn was the lone stopping place for customers in the provinces and on the road, cafés and patisseries particularly attracted Warsaw's professional intelligentsia—a group that encompassed both gentiles and assimilated Jews. Despite the alleged dangers of caffeine addiction, coffee figured as the moral antidote to alcohol and was widely believed to stimulate intellectual acuity and rational discussion.[27] Jürgen Habermas famously argued that the coffeehouse enabled its patrons to conceive of themselves as a universal community bound by sobriety and common sense. It should be noted, however, that this universal community was exclusively made up of Polish-speaking and Polish-identifying male professionals, including assimilated Jews.[28] Warsaw cafés, like all European cafés, first served men alone, admitting women in the last decades of the nineteenth century only after the owners had redecorated the premises to be cleaner, prettier, and comfortably padded. Even then, well-bred ladies were expected to order lemonade or orangeade lest a caffeinated beverage stimulate them to lapse into unladylike behavior.[29]

Cafés in Polish-majority districts regularly encouraged conspicuous consumption and tolerated social and political grandstanding, in large part because they catered to a literate, politically homogeneous clientele for whom the Russian Empire posed the greatest threat. The café's patrons were generally preoccupied with the sorry state of their tsarist-ruled city and partitioned (Polish) nation. No one plotted conspiratorial activities in public; such work was to be carried out at home. But it was common for customers to debate assorted social issues, criticize rival political camps among the Poles, and generally let off steam. The Semadeni café and patisserie located in Warsaw's Great Theater complex was renowned as an impromptu political theater and an ever-flowing source of the latest news. It was patronized by famed journalists, lawyers, doctors, and, given its location, actors—men accustomed to holding forth on current events so that everyone in the establishment could hear them.[30] The poet and journalist Antoni Słonimski remembers that his assimilated Jewish father, Stanisław Słonimski (1853–1916), one of those famed Warsaw doctors, frequented this café to see and be seen and to star as one of its greatest wits.[31]

The well-appointed café and, by extension, certain fine dining establishments also came to function as extensions of city newsrooms. The Polish-language press and "gentlemen" of that press—the chief molders of gentile Varsovians' conceptions of their city's heroes, villains, and picturesque types—preferred to put together their issues out of the office and "on the town," preferably at good restaurants with well-stocked wine cellars. The staff of *Kurjer Warszawski* often met at Simon and Stecki, next to their office on Krakowskie Przedmieście, or moved down the street to Lijewski's, across from the Church of the Holy Cross. *Kurjer Poranny*'s editorial board (and friends of the board) held many a meeting at various cafés as well as in A. Stępkowski's restaurant, located at Theater Square not far from Semadeni's.[32] Café owners, in turn, shrewdly returned the favor, satisfying patrons' twinned pleasures of drinking coffee while reading the newspaper by stocking the latest issues of popular city dailies in their establishments. In Warsaw, as in other European capitals, the symbiosis between imbibing coffee and sweets and catching up on the news in print or in conversation evolved rapidly. The informal exchange facilitated by the provincial inns was transformed into a lucrative industry and an addictive, respectable daily pursuit for the professional strata of the big city—a not-quite-defined middle class that included a sizable number of assimilated Jews.

Jewish residents of Nalewki traveled south to downtown Warsaw to sample these cafés in the early 1900s, gaining admission only if they spoke Polish and did not wear traditional Orthodox clothing. These visitors included such renowned figures as the writer Y. L. Peretz (1852–1915) and journalist Avrom Reyzn (1876–1953), who occasionally frequented the elegant

Café Bristol (in the famous hotel Bristol) and the spacious Café Ostrowski located on the corner of Marszałkowska and Złota Streets. One of the most amazing accounts of Polish-language Warsaw café touring appears in the memoirs of the journalist Bernard Singer (1893–1966). In his teens, this Nalewki-born acculturated and multilingual Jew was hired by a rich Hasidic merchant to tutor his sons in Polish, a job Bernard approached with curiosity, prepared to be appalled by the household's extreme piety and insularity. Instead, the boy developed a tremendous crush on the merchant's much younger, beautiful, educated wife. To Bernard's astonishment, this enterprising woman took him out for coffee all over Polish-language Warsaw: "Until that time I'd never had the occasion to discover so many cafés and hidden treasures."[33] Their peregrinations took them to Trojanowski's café on Miodowa Street, Botta and Clotina (now known as Telimena) opposite the statue of Mickiewicz on Krakowskie Przedmieście, Blikle on Nowy Świat, and Anczewski's near Warsaw's Summer Theater in the Saxon Gardens.[34] Clearly, the woman whom Singer had presumed would be sheltered and parochial proved worldly in her knowledge of and comportment in a modern secular metropolis.

Yet many Jewish observers complained about Yiddish writers' patronage of Polish Warsaw's cafés as elitist; the critics disliked the fact that someone like Peretz wanted to mingle with or at least observe his Polish-language favorites up close.[35] What rankled them most was that these Jewish luminaries *belonged in* Nalewki, not swanky Polish establishments downtown, despite the fact that Nalewki cafés were literally buried in this overbuilt, physically unappealing district. Nalewki could not spare the space for a grand café, in the main because it was the first and last destination for traditional and poor Jews moving to the city. Hemmed in on its northern boundary by the Citadel, a fortress and prison built by the tsarist authorities, Nalewki was the most densely packed district in Warsaw. It absorbed newcomers not by expanding its boundaries but by subdividing extant properties and adding annex after annex in available in-between spaces to carve out new residential and retail quarters.[36] In consequence, Nalewki cafés tended to be cramped and smoke-filled, tucked away inside courtyards and consisting of a series of ever-tinier rooms burrowing deep inside the tenement. As Pinsker notes, these establishments "tended to be small, simple, and without much [*sic*] decoration or amenities."[37] This modesty was on display in a café that opened during the 1920s on 18 Karmelicka Street in the Jewish district, advertising to its Yiddish-speaking patrons hearty and inexpensive dishes rather than elegance and luxury (see fig. 5.4).

Already by the 1890s, the avid patrons of these new cafés combined always stimulating and sometimes explosive groups of newcomers and regular visitors. In addition to the locals and the Polish Jews who had just come from the provinces were Jews from the tsarist Pale of Settlement, who had fled increasing antisemitism in their hometowns and headed to the cities in the Kingdom of Poland as the few desirable places left them, given the restrictions mandated by the 1881 May Laws. Tensions immediately arose between Polish Jews and the so-called *Litwacy* due to the latter's proficiency in Russian, audacious entrepreneurship, strong attraction to Zionism and secular socialist ideologies, and disdain for the Hasidim, who made up the vast majority of Polish Jewry in Warsaw.

In terms of airing new political agendas, Kotik's café, like Sholem's café on Gęsia Street, Glotser's café on Dzika Street, and the Zionist café on Dzielna Street, hosted nonstop partisan debates between Zionists, Bundists, and socialists. The grandstanding at the Semadeni patisserie resembled dinner theater in comparison with the shouting matches that regularly erupted in Nalewki. According to the description of activist Abraham Teitelbaum, the atmosphere progressed from raucous to intensely conspiratorial as patrons passed through the sequence of rooms making up Sholem's café: "One ascended a few steps to enter the not too big room with tables, which were always packed with young men and women, who would lose their temper and discuss [*sic*], laugh and be loudly angry. . . . The same held true in the smaller rooms further off. But the very last room was given to our group, when we used to . . . listen to the talks of our leader, comrade Lampert, or to the leaders of other groups that would come to us."[38]

Avrom Reyzn opined that the Zionist café he frequented was perfectly situated in the building, since the voices and screams of its customers could not reach the street. While Kotik himself made sure that he stocked all the right newspapers for his ideologically diverse clientele, his wife hushed all the arguing parties, trying to keep the Russian police away.

In contrast to the Polish-language cafés further south, the few women present in Nalewki cafés were owners' wives or, more often, waitresses. Citing early twentieth-century Hebrew and Yiddish fiction as evidence, Pinsker underscores the dangers that young women faced in the intense homosociality of the Nalewki establishments: "As a server who did not participate in social and cultural masculine exchange, a woman was often an object of male desire and could easily be seen as a sexually available courtesan."[39] The memoir of Puah Rakovsky, a self-identified "radical Jewish woman" who moved to Warsaw in 1891 to teach in a girls' *kheyder* (Jewish

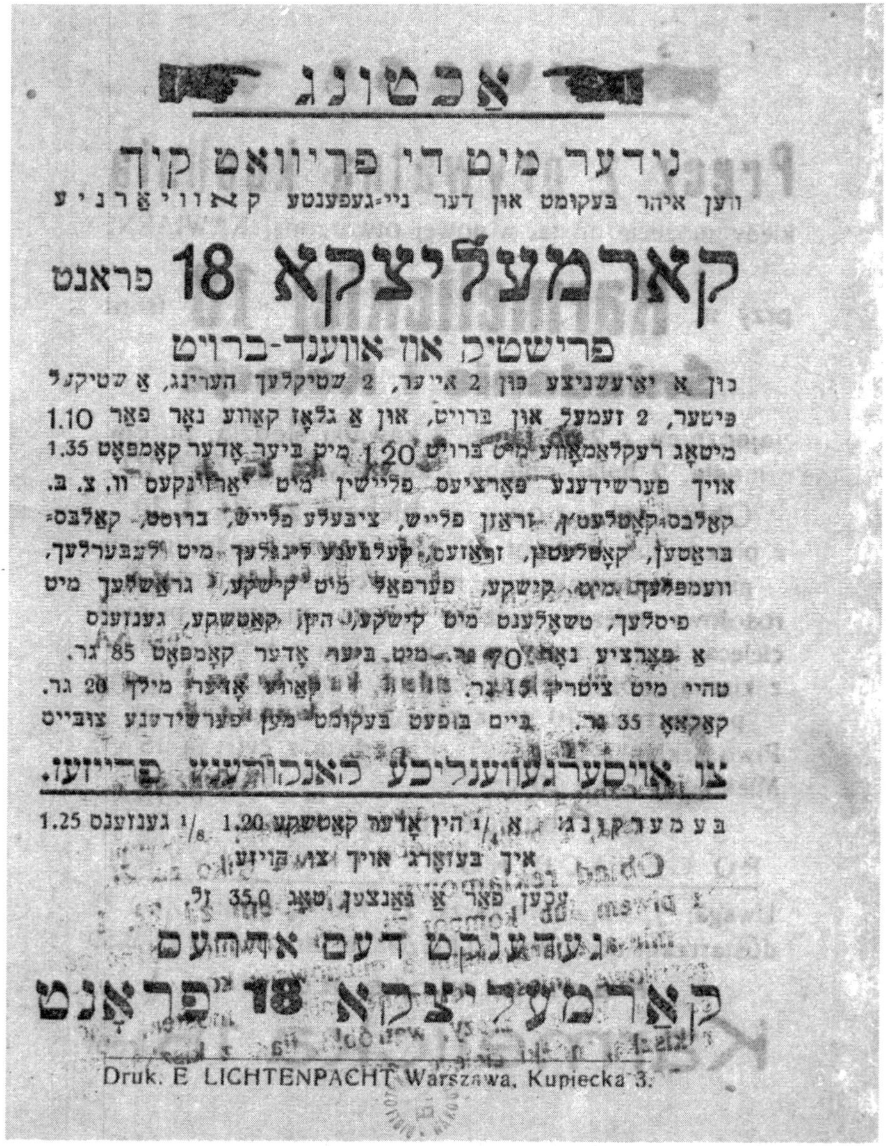
אכטונג
נידער מיט די פריוואט קיך
ווען איהר בעקומט און דער ניי-געפענטע קאוויארניע
קארמעליצקא 18 פראנט
פרישטיק און אווענד-ברויט
געדענקט דעם אדרעס
קארמעליצקא 18 פראנט
Druk. E LICHTENPACHT Warszawa, Kupiecka 3.

Figures 5.4a and 5.4b Flyer advertising the newly opened café on 18 Karmelicka Street (Warsaw: E. Lichtenpacht, 1920s). Warsaw, Biblioteka Narodowa, DŻS IK 2f. The National Digital Library Polona. https://polona.pl/item-view/25bde93d-1bb0-48c7-9de9-0df97b614141?page=0. Public domain.

Figures 5.4a and 5.4b *Continued*

religious elementary school) and later directed a gymnasium (secondary school) for girls, implicitly corroborates these perils. She repeatedly interjects that those young women who escaped the provinces to live, study, and work in Warsaw gathered in the safe spaces of her home and school.[40] Even in the early 1900s, Rakovsky remarks, female friends and acquaintances spent their "few free hours in our house, since, in those years, it wasn't the fashion to meet in coffeehouses, as it is today."[41]

The same Bernard Singer who had toured sumptuous Polish-language cafés with his patroness experienced the most thrilling political adventures in Nalewki cafés during the civil unrest in 1905–6, when Jewish and gentile socialists were preparing to rebel against the tsarist regime. Singer's journey with his father from south Polish-speaking Warsaw to north Yiddish-speaking Warsaw interestingly reversed his Polish-language café tour in the company of the lovely wife of a Hasidic merchant. Singer's father, an acculturated Jew proficient in Yiddish, Polish, and Russian, first paid a visit to Semadeni's for the latest news. Dissatisfied with the little he learned there, he steered himself and his son to the Café Ostrowski, which, while outside Nalewki, was strategically located next to a newspaper kiosk where the vendor sold illegal publications on the quiet (see fig. 5.5).

Ultimately, Singer and his father quit Polish-speaking Warsaw altogether, tracing the action to pop-up teahouses in Nalewki, which opened in shops after these had closed for the day: "There tea colored by flavored soda water was being drunk at little tables. Rarely was any pastry ordered. An indescribable din filled the space, passionate discussions mixed with bitter negotiations. There guns were purchased illegally, books from an illegal library were exchanged, and political leaflets smuggled in. . . . I learned what a 'gat' meant and that a Colt revolver was cheaper than a Browning. New revolutionary songs were being sung so loudly that the leaders had to shut up the choir."[42]

When the police did carry out a raid, the customers escaped through a convenient back door. These teahouses realized Singer's wildest boyhood dreams, directly connecting the Jewish café with the Jewish street and a radical working-class Nalewki with daring leftist political action.

Conclusion

In sum, Warsaw's tenement courtyards and cafés, which together fulfilled certain functions of the Jewish tavern for migrants to the city (refreshment, entertainment, broader socialization, and assorted secular transactions), differently affected Jewish self-perception in the metropolis. The courtyard

Figure 5.5 Early twentieth-century picture postcard of the Café Ostrowski (Warsaw: Zakł. Graf. B. Wierzbicki i S-ka, 1913). Warsaw, Biblioteka Narodowa, DŻS XII 8b/p.19/23. The National Digital Library Polona. https://polona.pl/preview/94334b44-7ac6-444a-b56f-093d369e22b5. Public domain.

helped newcomers acclimatize to the city: its fast pace, chaotic workings, terrible noise, urban (as opposed to small town) filth, tremendous array of goods and services, and city folks who were far more diverse in type than what newcomers had known in the provinces. The courtyard served to initiate new residents into city life, even if this initiation only enabled them to enter the ranks of the semiskilled or working-class laborers they saw on the street. It primarily conditioned migrants from the provinces to become self-aware Varsovians, though, as the evidence of attached Sukkot porches indicates, those rich and settled enough dared to advertise that they were observant *Jewish* Varsovians. In some cases, the "exceptional" Jews (mighty porters, mobile dairymen, touring musicians) and Jewish achievements (popular "Polish" interwar dance music) that the newcomers encountered close to home proved to be inspiring and empowering, literally enabling their broader view of the metropolis and demonstrating the impressive feats, both physical and creative, of which Jews were capable.

The owners and patrons of late nineteenth-century Nalewki cafés, however, purposefully distinguished their establishments from Warsaw's downtown cafés, intentionally separating a Yiddish-speaking Warsaw from a Polish-speaking Warsaw. Rejecting the paths of assimilation and acculturation that they felt had tempted too many Jews to the south, café owners and regular customers dug in in an impoverished, overcrowded Nalewki as the lone city base for building Jewish Yiddish-language culture and trying out new sociopolitical programs to improve Jewish lives. Owners provided and customers avidly consumed Yiddish-language mass-circulation newspapers, and cafés courted the patronage of the great writers who strived to elevate Yiddish to the status of a respected literary language and to produce a rich transnational literature. By the early interwar period, a new generation of Yiddish writers was already flourishing because of such devoted mentoring of a new readership.

Nalewki cafés welcomed the many single male migrants from the provinces who were seeking a larger, better home in this big bicultural city. Once these newcomers stepped inside the door, owners and regulars were eager to educate them through recommended newspapers, pamphlets, and passionate debates over conflicting, but always uplifting, ideologies designed to help modern, self-respecting Jews work together toward some higher collective good for all—be they folkists, socialists, Zionists, or Bundists. Whereas provincial Jewish inns adhered to traditional hierarchies of faith, class, and gender to keep the peace and serve the gentiles, Nalewki cafés functioned as pockets of concentrated opposition to all such hierarchies. The energy they generated—through fierce debate and public events—was primarily productive, fueling the emergence of different exclusively Jewish organizations that began operating and growing aboveground in the interwar period. Nalewki cafés helped engender an independent diverse Jewish community prepared from the outset to defend its existence in a violently nationalist Second Republic of Poland. As the growing membership of these organizations gathered for conventions in the Polish capital soon after World War I, the tiny, cramped rooms of the Nalewki cafés gave way to enormous halls filled with modern, proud, forward-looking Jews, who continued to debate over and advance their organizations' policies, services, recruitment, and activism.

Beth Holmgren, Professor Emerita of Slavic and Eurasian Studies at Duke University, has published ten monographs and edited volumes, including the award-winning *Starring Madame Modjeska: On Tour in Poland and America* (2012) and, most recently, *Polish Cinema Today: A Bold New Era in Film* (2021), which she authored with Helena Goscilo. Her scholarship in Polish Jewish studies encompasses the biography of a sixteen-year-old Jewish orderly in the Warsaw Uprising (*Warsaw Is My Country: The Story of Krystyna Bierzyńska*, 1928–1945 [2018]); representations of Jewish-gentile relations in late twentieth- and early twenty-first-century film; and analyses of the Jewish foundations of Polish-language cabaret and popular music in interwar Warsaw and the traveling diaspora of Anders Army during World War II.

Notes

If not stated otherwise, all translations are mine, B.H.

1. Glenn Dynner, *Yankel's Tavern: Jews, Liquor, & Life in the Kingdom of Poland* (Oxford: Oxford University Press, 2014); Judith Kalik, "The Inn as a Focal Point for Jewish Relations with the Catholic Church in the Polish-Lithuanian Commonwealth," in *Jews and Slavs*, vol. 21, ed. Wolf Moskovich and Irena Fijałkowska-Janiak (Jerusalem and Gdańsk, 2008), 381–90; Yohanan Petrovsky-Shtern, *The Golden Age Shtetl: A New History of Jewish Life in East Europe* (Princeton, NJ: Princeton University Press, 2015).

2. Dynner, *Yankel's Tavern*, 20.

3. Kalik, "Inn as a Focal Point for Jewish Relations," 387.

4. Petrovsky-Shtern, *Golden Age Shtetl*, 130.

5. Dynner, *Yankel's Tavern*, 18.

6. Scott Ury, *Barricades and Banners: The Revolution of 1905 and the Transformation of Warsaw Jewry* (Stanford, CA: Stanford University Press, 2012), 141–71; Shachar M. Pinsker, *A Rich Brew: How Cafés Created Modern Jewish Culture* (New York: New York University Press, 2018), 9–10, 55–72.

7. Isaac Bashevis Singer, *A Day of Pleasure: Stories of a Boy Growing Up in Warsaw*, with photos by Roman Vishniac (New York: Farrar, Straus and Giroux, 1969), 17–18.

8. Cf. Aleksander Łupienko, "Mikroświat kamienicy czynszowej doby zaborów. Funkcjonowanie i życie w warszawskich kamienicach w źródłach z lat 1864–1914," *Journal of Urban Ethnology* 11 (2013): 117, 125. For a fuller history of tenement life, see Łupienko's *Kamienice czynszowe Warszawy* (Warsaw: Polska Akademia Nauk, 2015).

9. Singer, *Day of Pleasure*, 19.

10. Isaac Bashevis Singer, "The Suicide," in *In My Father's Court* (New York: Farrar, Straus and Giroux, 1966), 77.

11. Józef Galewski and Ludwik B. Grzeniewski, *Warszawa zapamiętana. Ostatnie lata XIX stulecia* (Warsaw: Państwowy Instytut Wydawniczy, 1961), 13.

12. In chapter 4, Benjamin Vogel describes at length the Jewish musicians who performed in the provincial taverns.

13. Benedykt Hertz, *Na taśmie 70-lecia*, ed. Ludwik B. Grzeniewski (Warsaw: Państwowy Instytut Wydawniczy, 1966), 36.

14. Dynner, *Yankel's Tavern*, 18.

15. Hertz, *Na taśmie 70-lecia*, 36–37.

16. Singer, "Reb Asher the Dairyman," in *Day of Pleasure*, 47–58.

17. Singer, "Reb Asher," 53–54.

18. Wacław Szymanowski, "Ostatni cymbalista warszawski," *Tygodnik Illustrowany* 16, no. 407 (July 13, 1867): 16.

19. Józef Hen, *Nowolipie Street*, trans. Krystyna Boron (Bethesda, MD: DL, 2012).

20. Marian Fuks, *Muzyka ocalona: judaica polskie* (Warsaw: Wydawnictwa Radia i Telewizji, 1989), 3–32.

21. Fuks, *Muzyka ocalona*, 31.

22. For more on this success, see Beth Holmgren, "Cabaret Nation: The Jewish Foundations of the Polish-Language Literary Cabaret," in *Polin: Studies in Polish Jewry*, vol. 31, *Poland and Hungary: Jewish Realities Compared* (Littman Library of Jewish Civilization, 2019), 273–88. See also the essays by Hanno Loewy, Tomasz Lerski, and Ryszard Wołański in *Szafa grająca! Żydowskie stulecie na szelaku i winylu*, ed. Tamara Sztyma and Magdalena Prokopowicz (Warsaw: POLIN Museum of the History of Polish Jews, 2017).

23. Fuks, *Muzyka ocalona*, 31–32.

24. Hen, *Nowolipie Street*, 26.

25. Radosław Kożuszek explains that most Jews in the diaspora who had these structures built made sure that their roofs could be dismantled after the holiday, and that some affluent Jews even installed movable roofs. See "Kuczki," *Wiedza i życie*, no. 6 (June 1, 2019): 30.

26. See, for example, saper1390, "Kuczka z podwórza przy ul. Piotrkowskiej 88," PolskaNiezwykla, last modified March 16, 2013, last accessed December 27, 2023, http://www.polskaniezwykla.pl/web/place/31721,lodz-kuczka-z-podworza-przy-ul—piotrkowskiej-88.html; Matylda Witkowska, "Historia i obyczaje: Wiszące szałasy Łodzi," *Dziennik Łódzki*, last modified October 2, 2007, last accessed July 6, 2020, https://dziennikilodzki.pl/historia-i-obyczaje-wiszace-szalasy-lodzi/ar/168844; and Emilia Twardowska, "Rzecz o kuczkach," Miastol, last modified October 11, 2015, last accessed July 6, 2020, http://miastol.pl/rzecz-o-kuczkach/.

27. For a good general study of the rise of coffee drinking and the social functions of the coffeehouse, see Markman Ellis, *The Coffee House: A Cultural History* (London: Orion, 2004).

28. Jakob Norberg, "No Coffee," Eurozine, last modified August 8, 2007, last accessed July 6, 2020, https://www.eurozine.com/authors/jakob-norberg/.

29. Wojciech Herbaczyński, *W dawnych cukierniach i kawiarniach warszawskich* (Warsaw: Państowy Instytut Wydawniczy, 1988), 32.

30. Bernard Singer, *Moje Nalewki*, ed. Eugeniusz Szrojt (Warsaw: Czytelnik, 1959), 78.

31. Antoni Słonimski, *Wspomnienia warszawskie* (Warsaw: Czytelnik, 1957), 25.

32. Jadwiga Waydel Dmochowska, *Jeszcze o dawnej Warszawie: Wspomnienia* (Warsaw: Państwowy Instytut Wydawniczy, 1960), 14–16.

33. Singer, *Moje Nalewki*, 138.

34. Singer, *Moje Nalewki*, 139.

35. Pinsker, *Rich Brew*, 70–72.

36. Jerzy S. Majewski, *Warszawa nieodbudowana: Muranów i okolice* (Warsaw: Agora, 2012), 15.

37. Pinsker, *Rich Brew*, 61.

38. Pinsker, *Rich Brew*, 63.

39. Pinsker, *Rich Brew*, 68.

40. Puah Rakovsky, *My Life as a Radical Jewish Woman*, ed. Paula E. Hyman, trans. Barbara Harshav with Paula E. Hyman (Bloomington: Indiana University Press, 2002), 55, 59–60.

41. Rakovsky, *My Life as a Radical Jewish Woman*, 74.

42. Bernard Singer, *Moje Nalewki*, 79–80.

PART IV

Innkeepers' Daughters

6

Jula's Diary

A Hasidic Tavernkeeper's Daughter during the First World War

Glenn Dynner

Rachela, the sophisticated Jewish tavernkeeper's daughter in Stanisław Wyspiański's dramatic masterpiece "The Wedding" (*Wesele*, 1901), represented a familiar type in fin de siècle Kraków. "There were in Kraków many of these Rachelas: they filled the women's reading rooms, the book-lending facilities, the theaters, and concerts," wrote Tadeusz Boy-Żeleński.[1] The real-life model for Wyspiański's Rachela, Józefa "Pepa" Singer, converted to Christianity in 1919.[2] Such tavernkeepers' daughters were probably so intriguing to Christian audiences because their induction into avant-garde society seemed to symbolically redeem their fathers—emblems of daily encountered Jewish difference and ostensible backwardness.[3]

Rachel Manekin has identified several tavernkeepers' daughters among the three hundred registered female converts between 1887 and 1902.[4] She cautions, "Of the different forms of alienation from Judaism that one finds among Jewish women at the turn of the century, conversion was the extreme."[5] Wyspiański himself appears circumspect: his Rachela retains her biblical name and oscillates between European high culture and her *heimish* Jewish world. "As soon as books come, she reads them, but still rolls out dough herself, / at Vienna she's been to the Opera, / but at home she still plucks chickens," her father reassures the audience. Rachela's romance with the Polish Christian poet remains ambiguous. "And the music of my heart- / true love for my lord, nearly-?" she asks hopefully. "That would be devoted most sincerely—in verse," he deflects.[6] Significantly, the cross-cultural romance is never consummated.[7]

Most "Rachelas" acquired their unrequited love for Polish culture in Polish schools, a consequence of the traditional Jewish neglect of female *Jewish* education. Critics pointed out that such young women could hardly be expected to relate to their pious parents and preselected grooms anymore. "The father is a complete Hasid, he educates his son in the ways of Hasidism, and none of them knows the language of the land or secular knowledge; but the daughter often speaks only in Polish, thinks in Polish, and is interested only in Polish issues," warned Tzvi Scharfstein in 1910. "She looks upon the Jewish youth dressed in long clothes with scorn in her heart and does not want his crude conversation." The tragedy was manifested at the hour of their engagement: "The father wants to 'bestow' to his daughter a young man with sidelocks, a bit learned, a Hasid; in short: someone like him. The daughter rebels and fights—but in vain."[8] The writer Y. L. Peretz blamed the daughters themselves. "Hasidic girls—leave them be!" he quipped. "They all read Przybyszewski and Żeromski and are all in love with [the actor] Osterwa."[9]

Historians would at least agree with Peretz about the importance of the new reading practices. The scholar of Hebrew literature Iris Parush argues that many such women turned their educational neglect to their advantage, immersing themselves in non-Jewish fiction and becoming agents of enlightenment and social change.[10] Novels were especially transformative since, as the literary historian Ian Watt has argued, novels produce deep identification between the reader and the characters, whose romantic yearnings are on full display.[11] The reading of novels inevitably generated romantic expectations. Love should be the basis of marriage, which should therefore be "a free choice by the individuals concerned" rather than arranged by parents, many readers began to insist.[12] As a result, explains historian of Jewish culture Naomi Seidman, "Jews adopted European gender models alongside and through European genre conventions, learning the choreography of modern courtship and its attendant gender roles from the characters, plot, pacing, and conventions of romantic novels."[13]

Jewish tavernkeepers' daughters were particularly well-positioned for the transformation, since they benefited from extended leisure time for reading while minding the family tavern and, especially in the case of taverns located near major cities, conversations with well-read Polish Christian and Polonized Jewish men. Many left their traditional Jewish communities or abandoned Judaism altogether, but many more agreed to parental arranged marriages in the end. As traditionalist Jewish culture discouraged self-writing, the latter "Rachelas" left little record.[14] Our perception of female Jewish modernity in Poland is thus heavily prone to data bias, warped in such a way that universalizes the experiences of a prolific fringe.[15] Fortunately, the YIVO archives have preserved a rare 418-page diary of a Hasidic tavernkeeper's daughter named Jula Wald who, like most such women, ultimately remained within the Hasidic community.[16]

Jula's diary begins on August 10, 1917, and extends through the early 1920s, unveiling the rare perspective of a self-declared Hasidic woman (*chusyta*) at a watershed moment in Polish history. Much of the diary was written while Jula minded her family's tavern in a small town outside of Kraków ("El.," possibly Liszki). The tavern emerges as a complex setting of Jewish-Christian and secular-traditionalist encounter, constantly morphing: now a raucous bar, now a genteel salon, now a mundane workplace, now a space of physical or moral danger. Adding to its dynamism was the ongoing exchange with nearby Kraków, which emitted travelers and drew in young women like Jula like a magnet. Throughout much of the diary, the First World War raged in the background, followed by bursts of pogroms accompanying Poland's rebirth.[17]

These tumultuous years surrounding the First World War saw the crystallization of several Jewish secularist currents, including politics (Zionism, Jewish socialism, diaspora nationalism); the Hebrew, Yiddish, and Polish-Jewish press; modern Jewish literature; the establishment of secularist Jewish schools; and the breakdown of conventions like arranged marriages. But the secularization process was less inexorable among the traditionalist majority, who usually wished above all to preserve their familial and business networks and, in some instances, retain custody of their children. The experience of the formerly Hasidic memoirist Ita Kalish is cautionary: when she left the Hasidic court for Warsaw and was forbidden to take her infant son, she felt compelled to resort to kidnapping him and fleeing abroad.[18] Most Hasidic daughters understandably considered the price of exit too high.

Nevertheless, Jula's diary reflects the emergence of unmistakably new attitudes among Hasidic women as well. The very act of keeping a diary for six years in the Polish language was itself unusual.[19] Moreover, Jula attended a Polish public school, read modern Polish literature, frequented the theater, and moved comfortably between Jewish and Polish Christian circles. She dressed in the latest fashions, exchanged photographs with dashing Polish officers, held séances with Christian and Jewish friends to predict the war's end, received invitations to Christian weddings (which she, however, felt it prudent to refuse), and repeatedly fended off advances and romantic confessions by Christian men, including a marriage proposal while a pogrom raged nearby.[20]

Jula's decision to remain within her familial orbit was not a forgone conclusion. She was extremely restless, suffered from her parents' constant criticisms and recriminations, and bitterly resented having to deal with the tavern's "rowdy peasants," even more so when she had a headache. More distressingly, the tavern could be a place of real danger. Unpredictable soldiers were quartered there.[21] The tavern had to be closed up during times of "riot" and "plunder" by nearby villagers or during one of the several postwar pogroms or near-pogroms in Kraków.[22] Christian customers moreover constantly flirted with Jula, trying to get her to drink with them and sometimes grabbing her and attempting to kiss her. One drunk Christian regular loved to chat about pornography while Jula was forced to "stand in the tavern like a martyr." The harassment was mortifying. "What kind of company I have to keep!" Jula exclaimed.[23]

But the tavern also afforded ample opportunities for discussion with the more charming Christian patrons—Jula discussed politics "seriously" with Pan Kolski for about three hours one afternoon, though he eventually fell in love with her and proposed (it pained Jula to think that he was suffering on her account).[24] The tavern could unite enemies—amid the war Jula sat joking and singing with an Austrian sergeant major and "several heroes from the Russian army."[25] On quieter days, the tavern afforded an opportunity to read, including a "very fine book by Reymont called *Fermenty*," and romantic poems by Andrew Lang.[26] It also afforded opportunities to write, though her parents screamed whenever they caught her.[27] By the summer of 1919, a local "intelligentsia" composed of students and officers from the recently reestablished university had emerged. Now, the tavern gave "the impression of a private salon in which fine guests gather, sparring with words, flirting on the highest scale by means of attempts to dance to songs from a set repertoire . . . every evening."[28]

Another powerfully formative setting was Kraków. Jula constantly devised ways of escaping the small-town tavern life by visiting the nearby city, which was for her the very embodiment of freedom. Kraków was where she could enroll in a bookkeeping course and hope to establish a better career, if only her parents would agree to it. Best of all, she could attend the theater or cinema, or just walk around the market square and people watch. But Kraków held its own palpable dangers. At one point, Jula had to flee a group of soldiers who were following her with catcalls.[29]

Jula related to her Hasidic identity with ambivalence. She was at one point deeply inspired by a blessing pronounced over the wine (*Kiddush*) by the B[obover] Rebbe, who was visiting in honor of her father. She was genuinely surprised that the "vision of Jews gathered respectfully around a single rabbi could so awaken my dormant feelings." She began to "tremble involuntarily, recalling the numerous times I had been urged to get baptized, and might have voluntarily deprived myself of this vision that so moves me. Oh no, never!"[30] These entries disclose an ongoing spiritual conflict: Jula's apparent religious apathy and temptations to leave the faith altogether were, for the moment at least, overwhelmed by the reverence and spiritual exhilaration generated by the presence of the charismatic "rebbe" and his devotees.

More often, Jula experienced her Hasidic identity as a burden. Her parents chastised her for her religious apathy, "lightmindedness," and interest in fashion. She felt like she was "enclosed by a 'Chinese wall' of Hasidic superstitions." Her Hasidic identity prevented her from going on excursions to Zakopane with friends and receiving male visitors. She lamented that she was "known as a *Hasidah* who doesn't care about boys." Was she really "such a Hasidic girl?" she chided herself when her sense of modesty got in the way of fun. Sometimes it amused Jula that she was "generally known as a Hasidic girl" and thus uninterested in boys, and that her Christian suitors dared not try to kiss her on account of her being Hasidic. "She is such a *Hasidah* that she would rather have her head chopped off than permit herself to give a kiss," one of her friends warned his buddy. Jula was annoyed that *this* was the reason for their restraint, rather than their respect for her refinement.[31]

Jula sometimes felt sure that she would have had a better life if she did not have to dress so markedly Jewish and had not been born into such a "fanatical home." All that awaited her after the war's end was marriage to "some fanatical Hasid" at the insistence of her parents, yet she wanted to "marry for love and not to some fanatic who in my parents' eyes will be 'ideal' and in mine worse than a 'demon.' . . . Would it not be better to die?" A Hasidic man would inevitably fail to understand her emotional needs and would treat her merely as someone to help with his businesses and prepare his meals ("Is this the life I am consigned to? How can I not despair? But what can possibly help?!!!").[32] She was stunned at how quickly her friend Tosia, who was Hasidic yet progressive, had just two days after her wedding "become completely indistinguishable from a fanatical little Hasidic woman."[33]

Nevertheless, Jula resolved to try to find a Hasidic husband. In one of her most pensive moments, she mused: "I am strangely not sure what I want, I do not want a Hasid due to several considerations yet due to other considerations I do, of course, but I more or less want someone with qualifications like: older than me, a Hasid yet acquainted with the contemporary world, handsome, not necessarily gorgeous, but polite and kind, with a character and spirit to my taste, which I cannot yet define. Is this obtainable? Big question mark."[34] As it turned out, Jula's eventual groom did essentially meet these conditions, even if he was as much her parents' choice as her own.

Jula was unusually expressive, even for an adolescent, describing states of moodiness, loneliness, boredom, restlessness, and despair, as well as irritation, anger, passion, and awakenings of love.[35] She loved her friend Tosia so much as to exclaim "actually I am in love with her, a shame she is not a boy; we would be happy together."[36] Yet she felt increasingly powerful romantic yearnings for her Hasidic cousin, Szmulek. Their tragic love affair emerges as the diary's central theme. At first, Jula dismissed the notion that Szmulek could be in love with her; it actually made her laugh: How could this fanatical Hasid really love her? Besides, he was always mocking her, teasing her about her close female friendships because he was obviously too young and stupid to understand women.[37] Nevertheless, while minding the tavern one evening, Jula could barely sit due to the terrible pain over the long-anticipated arrival of her "love," Szmulek.[38]

Though he may have been a Hasid, Szmulek was at least progressive in his manners, Jula reassured herself. When a secularist Jewish friend asked her friend teasingly how Jula could plan to marry such a "Hasidic barbarian," she refrained from responding so as not to offend him. But she would have liked to let him know that she wanted a Hasid and never one of these "progressive boys." She would sooner agree to a "Goy,"[39] who could at least be forgiven for having such an attitude.[40] Nevertheless, she sometimes did test Szmulek by holding out her hand to see whether he was too fanatical to take it.[41]

Jula often referred to male Hasidic identity as "fanatical." Yet the Hasidic youths she encountered usually seemed to defy the label. Earlier in her diary, for example, she described one of her travel companions to Kraków as a Hasid who "flirted like a pro" throughout the entire journey. "Too bad he is a Hasid," Jula lamented, "for he might otherwise have personally introduced himself." All that she could gather was that his name was Josek and that he was on his way to "arrange his affairs" with his rebbe. Jula would have found the whole incident amusing were it not for her splitting headache.[42]

Soon, her romance with Szmulek grew complicated. She puzzled over Szmulek's complete silence as he sat in her busy tavern. He was slow in answering her letters. When they were together, they quarreled. But she always seemed to miss him, and she soon found she could no longer even speak with other men, let alone flirt with them. Jula became so lovesick that some of the tavern customers inquired if she was ill.[43] Other times she wavered. She did not care about Szmulek at all, he only got on her nerves, she hated him; yet she could not wait for him to visit, and she was sure she loved him. "Does every girl suffer like this for love?" she wondered.[44]

And then, like a thunderclap, the news reached Jula that Szmulek was engaged, the betrothal arranged by his parents. At first, Jula was sympathetic: "My poor, poor Szmulek!" she writes. Then she tended to her own sorrow: "A terrible pain pierces my heart. . . . Szmulek my Szmulek, is it possible that I have lost you forever?" She tried to convince herself that she felt "happy that I loved and was loved without limit."[45] But her regret quickly turned to anger. Why didn't Szmulek fight for her? Must he always play the role of a good Hasidic son?[46] It might not have made much difference. Jula admitted that her mother had opposed the match all along, proclaiming that "as long as I live, you will not have Szmulek."[47] There was some bitter solace when Jula's friends reported that Szmulek "looks awful" now despite his pretty young bride, for it was a sign that he must really love Jula. He asked to talk to her, but she thought better of it.[48]

Resigned to the situation, Jula agreed to meet with prospective grooms proposed by her parents. The ultimate choice among her parents' nominees was apparently hers, however. After a few indignant rejections of candidates, who were too young, too pious, or too physically awkward, Jula agreed to marry a Hasidic lawyer named Szymon. He was nice, intelligent, and "although completely religious not a fanatic." Most importantly, he did not run a tavern. Szymon fit Jula's earlier description of the ideal groom so well that one suspects that her parents were, in the end, quite receptive to her stipulations.[49] But Szymon was not Szmulek. During the betrothal process, Jula cried "like a little child." The betrothal proceedings were uneventful—in typical Hasidic fashion, only finances and dowry were discussed. The groom's sister kindly assured Jula that she would be a satisfied wife. Nevertheless, she cried and cried.[50]

After a few weeks, Jula began to reconcile herself to the situation. The family tavern had come to feel like a prison more than ever, and marriage to Szymon promised the freedom of a new life. Now Jula "played the role of a happy fiancée better than the best artist."[51] She felt frustrated that she could not meet with Szymon, noting sardonically that the Hasidic custom of not allowing couples to meet before the wedding must be designed to avoid shattering the illusion of an ideal match. She insisted only that the couple be permitted to live in Kraków. By the last entry, on December 15, 1924, she had resigned herself to living in her husband's town, "Ka," perhaps Kazimierz, and thought only about having children.

Conclusion

Jula's fate may seem to confirm notions about the retrograde nature of Hasidic marriage practices during this period, in contrast to the more liberated, romance-based unions espoused in the novels she had been reading. However, Jula's betrothal forms a striking contrast with earlier marital practices, which were almost entirely under the parents' control. Parents during the prior century virtually assumed the role of suitors, seeking out scholarly young men on their daughters' behalf and attempting to outbid each other with offers of dowry and years of room and board that would enable the groom's future studies. The bride seemed like an afterthought. The most common concern in petitions to the anomalous non-Hasidic miracle worker Rabbi Eliyahu Guttmacher (d. 1874), for example, was whether the young woman had sufficient money for a dowry. These petitions do not tell the whole story, since petitioners would have likely concealed their romantic longings from Rabbi Guttmacher. But their economic-based concerns may reflect the limited opportunities for Jewish couples throughout the pre-emancipation Polish lands, particularly in the late nineteenth century. As most married couples worked together as business partners in an enterprise like a tavern, or augmented each other's income in other ways, the inability to secure a match would have been a severe economic disadvantage.[52]

By Jula's generation, thanks to the relative economic diversification in what would become the Second Polish Republic, such marital functionalism seems to have declined. While Jula worked in the family tavern just like her ancestors and nourished a strong Hasidic identity, she also read novels and poetry, attended public school, formed genuine friendships with non-Jews, and could more easily imagine a future life beyond the tavern (at one point she and her friends attempted to enroll in a bookkeeping course in Kraków, but the plan did not apparently materialize). Though denied her Szmulek, Jula still had much say in the selection of her eventual match, a

Hasidic lawyer who seemed to satisfy all the qualities Jula demanded in a groom, aside from not being Szmulek.

Jula, as well as the other Hasidic women mentioned in her diary, differed from the more transgressive "Rachelas" encountered throughout the scholarly literature. Jula and her friends ultimately refused to allow their romantic yearnings to prevail and cause their secession from the traditionalist Jewish community. Unbeknownst to Jula, moreover, at this time another Hasidic woman named Sarah Schenirer was beginning to create a network of schools for Hasidic girls in Kraków and environs to help stem the tide of female defections from Hasidic and Orthodox society. Schenirer's school system, known as Bais Yaakov, would come to include as many as 250 branches throughout Galicia and Central Poland, instructing around thirty-eight thousand students by the late 1930s.[53] Even without such a school, however, loyalty to parents and community remained paramount for most Hasidic girls and women. Jula may have had to give up on Szmulek, who felt similarly bound by filial obligation. Yet, she did manage to escape the tavern life.

Glenn Dynner is the Jay Berkowitz Professor of Jewish History at the University of Virginia, editor of the journal *Shofar: An Interdisciplinary Journal of Jewish Studies*, and a recent Guggenheim Fellow. He is author of *"Men of Silk": The Hasidic Conquest of Polish Jewish Society* and *Yankel's Tavern: Jews, Liquor, & Life in the Kingdom of Poland.* His new book is entitled *The Light of Learning: Hasidism in Poland on the Eve of the Holocaust.*

Notes

If not stated otherwise, all translations are mine, G.D.

1. Tadeusz Boy-Żeleński, "Plotka o Weselu Wyspiańskiego," *Ludzie żywi* (Warsaw: Państwowy Instytut Wydawniczy, 1956), 102.

2. Eva Plach, "'Botticelli Woman': Rachel Singer and the Jewish Theme in Stanisław Wyspiański's *The Wedding*," *Polish Review* 41, no. 3 (1996): 321, 324. See also Larry Wolff, "Dynastic Conservatism and Poetic Violence in Fin-de-Siècle Cracow: The Habsburg Matrix of Polish Modernism," *American Historical Review* 106, no. 3 (June 2001): 735–64, esp. 759–63.

3. As Eliza Rose notes in chapter 7 of this volume, "This Jew will not transcend his type—that potential belongs to his daughter." On the Polish Jewish tavernkeeper, see Glenn Dynner, *Yankel's Tavern: Jews, Liquor, & Life in the Kingdom of Poland* (New York: Oxford University Press, 2014), chap. 1.

4. Rachel Manekin, "The *Lost Generation*: Education and Female Conversion in Fin-de-Siècle Cracow," *Polin: Studies in Polish Jewry* 18 (2005): 189–219. Manekin highlights the case of Deborah Lewkowicz, a tavernkeeper's daughter who fell in love with a Polish Catholic and took refuge in a convent, but ultimately returned. On conversions of Jewish tavernkeepers'

daughters in tsarist Russia during an earlier period, more a result of daily socializing, see Ellie R. Schainker, *Confessions of the Shtetl: Converts from Judaism in Imperial Russia, 1817–1906* (Stanford, CA: Stanford University Press, 2017), chap. 3.

5. Manekin, "*Lost Generation,*" 219.

6. Stanisław Wyspiański, *Wesele* (1901), act 3, scene 6, 114; Plach, "'Botticelli Woman.'" On the hybridized, negotiated nature of acculturated East European Jews, see Naomi Seidman, *The Marriage Plot: Or, How Jews Fell in Love with Love, and with Literature* (Stanford, CA: Stanford University Press, 2016), 9–10.

7. On hybridity as a more accurate term than "assimilation," see *Marriage Plot*, e.g., 66.

8. Tzvi Scharfstein, "Mehayei aheinu be-Galiẓiyah: Hinukh habanot," *Ha'olam*, September 29, 1910. See also Shaul Stampfer, "Gender Differentiation and the Education of the Jewish Woman in Nineteenth-Century Eastern Europe," *Polin* 7 (1992): 53–85; Manekin, "*Lost Generation,*" 218.

9. Y. L. Peretz, "In My Little Corner," *Haynt* 210 (November 1, 1912): 3. According to Florian Sokolow, "Polish culture was very attractive, and the women were especially influenced by it. Even affluent Hasidic women and their daughters spoke fluent Polish and dressed according to the new fashions." See Florian Sokolow, *Avi Nahum Sokolov* (Jerusalem: Hasefriyah haẓiyonit, 1970), 45.

10. Iris Parush, *Reading Jewish Women: Marginality and Modernization in Nineteenth-Century Eastern European Jewish Society* (Waltham, MA: Brandeis University Press, 2004), esp. 245.

11. Ian Watt, *The Rise of the Novel: Studies in Defoe, Richardson and Fielding* (London: Chatto and Windus, 1957), e.g., 201.

12. Watt, *Rise of the Novel*, 138. See also Seidman, *Marriage Plot*, 59.

13. Seidman, *Marriage Plot*, 35.

14. For evidence of such a sentiment, see "Esther," in Jeffrey Shandler, ed., *Awakening Lives: Autobiographies of Jewish Youth in Poland before the Holocaust* (New Haven, CT: Yale University Press, 2002), 331.

15. On autobiography in Eastern and East Central Europe, see Paula Hyman, *Gender and Assimilation in Modern Jewish History* (Seattle: University of Washington Press, 1995); Marcus Moseley, *Being for Myself Alone: Origins of Jewish Autobiography* (Stanford, CA: Stanford University Press, 2005); Gershon Bacon, "Woman? Youth? Jew?: The Search for Identity of Jewish Young Women in Interwar Poland," in *Gender, Place and Memory in the Modern Jewish Experience: Re-placing Ourselves*, ed. Judith Tydor Baumel and Tova Cohen (London: Vallentine Mitchell, 2003), 3–28; Shulamit Magnes, "Sins of Youth, Guilt of a Grandmother: M. L. Lilienblum, Pauline Wengeroff, and the Telling of Jewish Modernity in Eastern Europe," *Polin: Studies in Polish Jewry* 18 (2005): 87–120. See also Karen Auerbach, "Bibliography: Jewish Women in Eastern Europe," in *Polin: Studies in Polish Jewry*, 273–306.

16. Jula Wald, YIVO Youth Autobiographies, YIVO Archives, RG 4, RG 3838, e.g., 78. Excerpts of this diary appear in Alina Cała, "The Social Consciousness of Young Jews in Interwar Poland," *Polin* 8 (1994): 43–65.

17. Wald, YIVO Youth Autobiographies. On pogroms in reborn Poland, see William W. Hagen, *Anti-Jewish Violence in Poland, 1914–1920* (Cambridge: Cambridge University Press, 2018); Anna Cichopek-Gajraj and Glenn Dynner, "Pogroms in Modern Poland, 1918–20 and 1935–7," in *Pogroms: A Documentary History*, ed. Elissa Bemporad and Eugene Avrutin (New York: Oxford University Press, 2021).

18. Ita Kalish, *Etmoli* (Israel: Ha-kibbutz ha-meyuhad, 1970), 92–100. See also Barbara Alpern Engel, "Gesia Gelfman: A Jewish Woman on the Left in Imperial Russia," in *Jews and Leftist Politics: Judaism, Israel, Antisemitism, and Gender*, ed. Jack Jacobs (New York: Cambridge University Press, 2017), 189; ChaeRan Y. Freeze, *Jewish Marriage and Divorce in Imperial Russia* (Hanover, NH: Brandeis University Press, 2001), 17.

19. Other self-narratives by Hasidic women include the writings of Sarah Schenirer (in Yiddish) and Bronia Baum (in Russian). See Naomi Seidman, *Sarah Schenirer and the Bais Yaakov Movement: A Revolution in the Name of Tradition* (Liverpool: Liverpool University Press, 2019); Joanna Lisek, "'To Write? What's This Torture For?': Bronia Baum's Manuscripts as a Testimony of the Formation of a Writer, Activist, Journalist," *Jewish History* 33 (2020). See also Bernard Singer's memoir, *Moje Nalewki* (Warsaw: Czytelnik, 1959), e.g., 65–66.

20. Wald, YIVO Youth Autobiographies, 213. Another Christian man thought he could have Jula just because he was rich, prompting her to write "among Jews there are rarely such stupid people." See 302.

21. Wald, YIVO Youth Autobiographies, 184.

22. Wald, YIVO Youth Autobiographies, 114. The riots occurred on February 20, 1918; the Kraków pogroms referenced here occurred on June 10, 1919. Jula also witnesses the more well-known Kraków pogrom of April 16 while at school in the Podgórze District. In Kraków, a rabbinically endorsed self-defense initiative led by former Jewish soldiers helped avert another one, but that was rather exceptional. On the Kraków pogroms, see Hagen, *Anti-Jewish Violence*, 94–100, which also mentions attacks, theft, and plunder by armed gangs against "Jewish tavern keepers in villages near Kraków." See Wald, YIVO Youth Autobiographies, 135–42.

23. Wald, YIVO Youth Autobiographies, 41, 57, 59, 385.

24. Wald, YIVO Youth Autobiographies, 82.

25. Wald, YIVO Youth Autobiographies, 8.

26. Wald, YIVO Youth Autobiographies, 87. Władysław Stanisław Reymont (1867–1925) was a Polish novelist who in 1924 received the Nobel Prize. Andrew Lang (1844–1912) was a Scottish poet, novelist, and amateur anthropologist.

27. Wald, YIVO Youth Autobiographies, 197.

28. Wald, YIVO Youth Autobiographies, 209, 236, 349.

29. Wald, YIVO Youth Autobiographies, 16–17.

30. Wald, YIVO Youth Autobiographies, 145, recorded June 1918. See also Cała, "Social Consciousness of Young Jews," 56. The rebbe is called the rabbi from "Be.," likely Rabbi Ben Tziyon Halberstam of Bobov (1874–1941). "Be." could also stand for Belz; however, the Belzer Rebbe was in Munkacz at this time.

31. Wald, YIVO Youth Autobiographies, 315, 323–24, 331, 347.

32. Wald, YIVO Youth Autobiographies, 71, 79, 85, 133.

33. Wald, YIVO Youth Autobiographies, 299.

34. Wald, YIVO Youth Autobiographies, 98.

35. Wald, YIVO Youth Autobiographies, 5. Compare with the numerous YIVO Autobiographies in RG 4, for example.

36. Wald, YIVO Youth Autobiographies, 6.

37. Wald, YIVO Youth Autobiographies, 29–31, 41.

38. Wald, YIVO Youth Autobiographies, 126.

39. *Goy*, a non-Jewish person, often pejorative.

40. Wald, YIVO Youth Autobiographies, 250–51.

41. Wald, YIVO Youth Autobiographies, 128.

42. Wald, YIVO Youth Autobiographies, 5. Jula tells her friends about him later (18), and he turns out to be related to one of them.

43. Wald, YIVO Youth Autobiographies, 128, 135, 137, 141, 191, 200, 225.

44. Wald, YIVO Youth Autobiographies, 257, 279, 280, 314, 316.

45. Wald, YIVO Youth Autobiographies, 325.

46. Wald, YIVO Youth Autobiographies, 341.

47. Wald, YIVO Youth Autobiographies, 338.

48. Wald, YIVO Youth Autobiographies, 365, 367.

49. Wald, YIVO Youth Autobiographies, 369.

50. Wald, YIVO Youth Autobiographies, 375–76.

51. Wald, YIVO Youth Autobiographies, 408.

52. Glenn Dynner, "Those Who Stayed: Women and Jewish Traditionalism in East Central Europe," in *New Directions in the History of the Jews in the Polish Lands*, ed. Antony Polonsky, Hanna Węgrzynek, and Andrzej Żbikowski (Brighton, MA: Academic Studies Press. 2018), 295–312.

53. See Seidman, *Sarah Schenirer*, 549.

7

Writing for Hay

Wyspiański's Rachela as Arbiter of Speculative Value

Eliza Rose

Money, wrote Karl Marx, is the "fraternization of impossibilities. It makes contradictions embrace."[1] This claim lifts the object described from the economic sphere to the poetic one. Money becomes the mechanism by which one thing becomes another, objects disappear while others materialize, factories burn to the ground and new ones are erected. The affinity between monetary exchange and figurative transference of meaning resonates in the lines of a Jewish innkeeper and his debtor in Stanisław Wyspiański's play *The Wedding* (*Wesele*, 1901): "I take, I pay / I give, I take / mine, yours / yours, mine."[2] The lyric's rhyme in the original Polish (moje, twoje / twoje, moje) gives formal expression to the alternation of value and meaning that transpires when money changes hands. The innkeeper is the town's moneylender, and it is in this capacity that he occupies a significant place in Wyspiański's major work of Polish modernism.

The innkeeper can, counterintuitively, be construed as a fictional double of the playwright himself who, as leader of the Young Poland movement, was "speculating" on a sovereign Poland still to come. Included in this speculation was his assessment of Polish Jews' place in the incipient Polish national community. This essay traces transactions throughout *The Wedding* for which value is not material but speculative. I posit as their arbiter Rachela—the innkeeper's daughter—who combines the circulation of money and meaning into one modality of speculative poetics.

Rachela's speculative poetics, I argue, reflect three dynamics outside the diegetic space of the play: the first is the notion of Polish Jews' candidacy as constituents of a future autonomous Poland. The second pertains to the futurity of that Poland, which remained "dormant" during the century's first years, when Poland was still partitioned between Austria-Hungary, Prussia, and Russia. The third lies in Wyspiański's male perception of a female subjectivity paradoxically constituted by desire and its denial: Rachela, *The Wedding*'s sole agentive female protagonist, is a strongly desirous subject whose force as a character rests on future possibilities postulated through poetry rather than present-tense possession or consummation of value. In all three scenarios, value exists in a state of conjecture. Since all three potentialities are embedded in the person of Rachela, we can access the above-named dynamics shaping Wyspiański's world through a close reading of her character.

In and around Rachela, Wyspiański stacks figures of dormant or proxy value: her father's tavern, for instance, is a provisional hearth—not a true home but a transitory shelter. Rachela has a special kinship with the *chochoł*—a symbol central to the play that shares the inn's function of provisional shelter. The Chochoł (pictured in fig. 7.1) is a sheath of hay that insulates shrubs to protect them through the winter. It is the chosen addressee of Rachela's poetry, as she declares, "Before that mannequin of straw / I confess my poetry."[3] Wyspiański anthropomorphizes the figure and aligns it with both Rachela and fin de siècle Poland, which (in his symbolic system) will only bloom when its long winter of subjugation has passed.

To describe the straw sheath, Wyspiański uses the words *chochoł* and *pałuba*. With its connotations of feminine witchery,[4] pałuba aligns the hay with the enigma of femininity as beheld by the male gaze. The uniquely Polish term *chochoł* carries connotations of pseudo-animacy, tawdry materiality, and liminal proximity to the natural and constructed worlds. Given its lack of an English-language equivalent, I leave the Polish term intact throughout this text.

Wrapped always in her signature shawl, Rachela is likened to the straw-wrapped shrub by a Polish Poet who courts her:

> So, as you go your way, my dear,
> If your shawl should brush a shrub,
> then may your yearning sorrows seep
> into its wintery livery
> and, in return, the sadness creep
> from shrouded bush, subconsciously,
> into your heart.[5]

„Idź precz! . . idź precz na pole
huś ha! . . hulaj, chochole!“
45148 Nakładem S. W. Niemojowskiego we Lwowie.

Figure 7.1 Rachela and the Chochoł. Postcard published on the occasion of the premiere of Wyspiański's *The Wedding*. Lwów: Nakładem S. W. Niemojowskiego, [1901]. Warsaw, Biblioteka Narodowa, Poczt. Z.261/Poczt. The National Digital Library Polona. https://polona.pl/preview/f11dad20-4a4d-4ff9-9a11-2d9c67bc977e. Public domain.

These verses envision a reciprocal transmission of feeling between Rachela and the shrub. Their mutual wrappings are permeable membranes through which woman and plant share in one another's grief. These lines, addressed to a woman whose charm rests on her identification as a poet, set up a compelling image for figurative language as fleeting contact between two entities' outer shells. Rachela is linked to the shrub not by internal essential equivalence. Instead, their kinship is the product of partial contact—an accidental skimming or brushing-against.

This analogy is premised on action rather than essence. The poet's language here is effective not due to its descriptive accuracy or fidelity to reality but to its ability to precipitate change in the objects it describes. Rachela's connection to the shrub has little to do with their shared inherent properties. It is the product of a speech act: the male Poet's soft but suggestive command (in Polish: "*więc jak* . . . ," "so if . . ."). His words activate the described empathic exchange between person and plant.[6]

If the above reading injects too much meaning into these lines, it is because Rachela's evasive flirtation with her poet-suitor invites the reader to overinvest in their playful, mutually generated garland of images. They communicate on a lofty, figurative plane from which they never touch ground. Such is their lot, given the illicit nature of their union (which forces them to speak in code) and their shared vocation as poets, which predisposes them to the figurative register. Yet the "contact analogy" of Rachela skimming the shrub seems to exceed typical figurative language, belonging instead to a category I call speculative poetics. The analogy estimates inchoate values and even wills these values into being through efficacious speech. It corresponds to the scholar of rhetoric Noah Roderick's definition of analogy as a "productive distortion of predicates."[7] The symmetry produced when objects interact through analogy is, for Roderick, not sameness but similarity, which he describes as "an emergent state":[8]

> The experience of superficial similarity (i.e., analogy) is neither an indicator of some deeper commonality nor a mere illusion; it is the effect of objects translating or conforming to the forms of other objects. And wherever there is translation or conformation, there are new objects entirely. There is emergence.[9]

What is the brushing of straw against shawl—the rubbing of surfaces occasioned by the poet's analogy—but an "experience of *superficial* similarity" that activates a state of emergence? Wyspiański uses the perfective verb *muśnie* (skim; dab), which onomatopoeically sounds out the predicted soft rustling between fabric and plant. The perfective mode suggests a near-future action that will surely come to pass. The words themselves precipitate the action they describe.

Rachela does not submissively oblige the Poet's fantasy. She proactively self-affiliates with the Chochoł: "You needn't fear I'll come to harm," she assures. "The sharpest frost no problem poses / for one who breathes the scent of roses."[10] She also responds to her alleged alliance with the shrub by projecting it back onto the poet. In their flirtatious contest of wit, each rival bests the other by retaining the symbolism already generated and contributing a new layer. Rachela assigns the rose bush the pronoun *he/it*, thus implicating her male suitor, just as he implicated her. Noel Clark's translation goes so far as to use the pronoun *you* in this next line, linking the rose bush explicitly to Rachela's addressee. The line's literal translation preserves the ambiguity: "Clad him/it in straw / and unwind him/it in spring / so he/it can bloom at will."[11]

Just what does Rachela's suitor have in common with the straw-clad shrub? Is it his Polishness, which aligns him with a dormant sovereignty? Is it his vocation as poet, which makes him, like her, an arbiter of figurative speculation? Could it be their rapport of hesitant courtship, which makes them both objects of potential value to each other? The Chochoł has traditionally been taken for granted as a male-coded symbol for the Polish nation. Andrzej Wajda's film adaptation of *The Wedding* reinforces the Chochoł's assigned masculinity with Czesław Niemen's iconic performance as its voice. However, once dissociated from Niemen's voice, the straw persona can become an intensely fertile figure for femininity, Jewishness, and the elasticity of value and meaning inherent to what I call speculative poetics.

The Chochoł's symbolic capaciousness may explain its primacy as the play's narrative fulcrum. Its encounter with Rachela and the Poet is the sole catalyst advancing the storyline. Without it, the narrative arc would flatten to the progression of nightlong bacchanalia through which the titular wedding is celebrated. Indulging her suitor, Rachela offers herself not to him but to the Chochoł by inviting the latter to the wedding, thus setting into motion the play's climax and expanding its scope from the interpersonal to the national and political, for the chochoł's arrival coincides with an attempted uprising. In what follows, I read into the triangular coalition among Rachela, Poet, and Chochoł to map the play's overlapping speculative threads.

This triad's prime mover is Rachela herself. To understand the speculative claims staked in the play, we must first contend with her unique subjectivity. In a manner consistent with male-authored portraits of agentive femininity, Rachela's subjecthood is equated with desire. She remains, however, always one degree removed from visceral pleasure, which she fathoms as unrealized value glimpsed on a never-nearing horizon. In this regard, she is aligned with her moneylender father, who, by vocation, skims profit by transacting between past capital and future interest. The film scholar Paul Coates has observed how the innkeeper's financial speculations parallel his daughter's poetic ones. Speculations, he writes, "bestow a form on airy nothing,"[12] just as Rachela's poetic speech elides the potential with the real. Her power is clear when she addresses the frozen mass of hay: her invitation to the Chochoł wakens life dormant within it.

Structuring Rachela's romantic triangle with the Poet and Chochoł is a dynamic of displaced desire. Their flirtatious banter requires three parties in lieu of the usual two—an example of what the literary critic René Girard called mimetic or displaced desire.[13] Girard proposed the triangle as desire's ahistorical configuration. By his argument, we learn how to want and what to want from others, who model and mediate our desire. His theory is supported by the behavior of *The Wedding*'s male characters, who pass Rachela back and forth, gauging their own interest by measuring her appeal to others. She first appears as a fleeting fascination for the play's Groom and is only then passed onward to the Poet. The titular marriage between the groom and his peasant bride may also be motivated by mimetic desire given the ongoing trend of "chłopomania" (peasant-mania) and the fad among gentry of taking peasant wives. Girard's concept of mimetic desire is, at bottom, cynical in that it expresses deep distrust of human nature, which it presumes to be innately competitive and conflict prone. For Girard, desire is not the emotional cousin of affection or respect. Rather, it arises from an innate competitive reflex to covet what others seek or possess.

Looking beyond mimetic desire, I propose two alternative explanations for the triadic courtship between Rachela, Poet, and Chochoł: the first pertains to their poetic vocation, the second to cultural difference. Let us begin with the first: as poets, Rachela and her suitor are unwilling to state their love plainly and instead diffuse it through a shared figurative code. The Poet takes pleasure from displacing the idea of intercourse with Rachela onto a third party: "With pleasure I will watch you [. . .] / inclined over the *chochoł*."[14] Meanwhile, his own seduction goes unconsummated.

Suggestion without satisfaction is also a driving dynamic of Rachela's "unconsummated" poetry, for she does not write anything down. Rachela lives what her male gentile counterpart, the Poet, puts down in words—

roles she delegates: "You write it, I feel it,"[15] she explains. She represents art sublimated into life and, paradoxically, permanent deferral of the passage from the symbolic to the real: a pen poised to write that never touches paper. This paradox may expose the limits of Wyspiański's ability to write agentive female (or Jewish) characters. Indeed, his philosemitic elevation of Rachela as Jewess parallels his tempered respect for her as a woman. On both counts, Rachela is endowed with qualified agency and a subjectivity wrought with internal contradiction. She is erotic but virginal, desirable but ineligible, always desiring and always deferring the thing desired.

Rachela is attended by figures of botched or just-missed contact not unlike the brushing of a shrub discussed above. She likens the prospect of finding love to a clap of lightning that misses its target.[16] She stages her verbal foreplay with the Poet at a physical remove: "Stand here in the window," she commands, "and I'll imagine you from far away."[17] Similarly, the Groom remembers calling on Rachela but just missing her: "I meant to seek her out / Called once, but she was not about."[18] Wyspiański emphasizes through repetition the desire preceding this missed contact: "I wanted to, I wanted to" ("Chciałem, chciałem").[19]

Rachela's coquetries do not indicate a deficit of desire. When the Poet asks her what she really wants, her reply is hedonistic: "Pleasure, honey, joy and laughter, sweets of love and passion's bliss, happiness."[20] Yet when asked how she might satiate this desire ("Free love . . . ?"), she retreats into past tense: "Ach, I always dreamt of it!"[21] It seems Rachela's variant of desire and, by extension, love can only be realized in (unwritten) verse. In the third act, Rachela nearly declares her love: "The music of my heart— / the love—or nearly—which I feel / for you—most dearly—?" This staccato would-be confession is riddled with qualifiers ("or nearly"; the closing question mark). The Poet finishes her thought: "Would find its outlet most sincere, most real— / in verses—clearly."[22] Wajda's filmic adaptation underscores the subtext of Rachela's deferred gratification. Played by the stately Maja Komorowska, the character suffers public humiliation after attempting to join the wedding's dancing. For her one attempt to lurch from verbal speculation to embodied experience, she is punished. A circle of disapproving guests widens around her. Rachela's pleasure proves to be the "wrong kind" for the party.

A second factor may explain Rachela and the Poet's use of the Chochoł in their three-sided courtship. Perhaps it is due to the Poet's Polishness and Rachela's Jewishness, which make the two uncertain prospects for each other and require them to launder their avowals through a third party. Who better than an enigmatic Chochoł aligned with a Poland soon to bloom, whose economic and demographic fertility may well depend on alliances between its constituent ethnic groups? Such mixing could be an antidote to the stagnation polemicized in the play. *The Wedding* ends with an abortive uprising: yet another instance of missed contact. Rachela's prominence in the plot suggests the possibility that the intermixing of social classes represented by the play's peasant-gentry marriage (and its real-world reference point—Lucjan Rydel's marriage to Jadwiga Mikołajczyk) could be proof of concept for an even fuller commitment to demographic diversity. In devising the flirtation between Rachela and the Poet, Wyspiański created for himself the opportunity to extrapolate from the cross-class union to the intermarrying of gentiles and Jews. His lack of follow-through suggests that he perceived the Jew as a less assimilable Other than the peasant.

As literary scholar Eva Plach has suggested, Wyspiański meditates on the role of Polish Jews in the nation-to-come through the character of Rachela.[23] I would go further to say that he uses Rachela to assess the potential value of gentile-Jewish integration, as one might appraise a promising new industry or economic deal. Plach argues that Rachela's character is colored by a particularly Polish understanding of Jewish women as mediators "between two worlds" (the religious and secular, Polish and Jewish, numinous and banal). This belief has its origins in the legend of Esterka—the Jewish mistress of King Casimir III the Great and model for the modern Jewish woman who finds her place in the Polish world. According to Plach, Rachela serves the play as an "indispensable intermediary between the Polish past and present."[24] My focus lies instead on her future-facing poetics. Rachela's postponement of gratification links her to the multiethnic nation, which exists only as hypothesis. If the state of indebtedness can be defined as the postponement of obligation to reap immediate benefits, then Rachela (as creditor's daughter) lives in an inverted state, postponing not the cost but the reward. I will return to this below, when I argue that Rachela transposes her father's moneylending from finance to language in the form of speculative poetics.

The play offers telling commentary on the prospect of Jewish participation in a future Poland. While the Polish men gathered at the wedding are intrigued by Rachela, they court her evasively. The Groom is fond of Jewish women but does not take them seriously as reproductive partners for demographic reasons: "I like the Botticelli type, / but wouldn't choose to fill the land / with girls of that exclusive brand."[25] Ultimately, the Groom is unprepared to stake real investment in a Jewish wife or, by extension, in the prospect of a multiethnic Poland. Perhaps, then, Wyspiański's reluctance to write Rachela and the Poet's union into the play more definitively implies his own skepticism on this front.

Rachela is a hybrid personage informed by several reference points from Jewish reality and scripture alike. Most famously, she is based on the real-world Józefa (née Perel) Singer, daughter of innkeeper Hirsz Singer. A second precursor not yet explored in scholarship may be the biblical Rachel, who protects the Jewish nation during its period of exile. The insatiable desire of Wyspiański's Rachela can be seen to parallel her biblical forebear's unyielding drive to bear offspring. Rachel shares her husband, Jacob, with her sister and co-wife Leah. Leah and the handmaid-surrogates Zilpah and Bilhah bear Jacob eleven children before Rachel conceives on her own. This prolific procreation does not satisfy Rachel's urge to be a mother. When she finally brings her own child, Joseph, to term, she demands more: "May the Lord add to me another son!" (Genesis 30:22–24). The moment of satisfaction coincides with the moment of desiring anew.

Rachela and the biblical Rachel have a shared plight: they are both uncertain heiresses to their fathers' estates. Indeed, they expose an internal paradox of inheritance, be it of wealth or genes. The socially accepted link of inheritance from father to son is an unreliable guarantor of genetic continuity, as Jewish law reminds us with its emphasis on matrilineal descent. All inheritance relations, paternal and maternal, are mutually contingent: the bond between father and son must pass through the mother. Conversely, a daughter's birthright must be socially ratified by an associate male heir. In the story of biblical Rachel, this role falls to Jacob, who becomes a conduit through which Rachel and Leah can access their father's wealth. This process is long and indirect: to earn Rachel and Leah's bridewealth, Jacob labors in Laban's service for fourteen years. At the end of this tenure, Laban repudiates his twice-over son-in-law. Rachel, a tenacious figure like her counterpart in Wyspiański's play, retaliates by stealing her father's teraphim. To conceal her loot, Rachel turns the handicap of her womanhood to her advantage. Sitting on the teraphim to hide them, she refuses to stand on the pretense that she is menstruating (Genesis 31:33–35). Like Rachela, Rachel has qualified agency: her femininity is her asset and her burden.

Rachela, meanwhile, occupies *The Wedding* as a liaison and potential marital link between her Jewish father and their gentile neighbors. One might take Rachel and Leah's dynamic as jealous yet cooperative co-wives as biblical precedent for demographic coexistence between Polish, Jewish, and other cultural groups, represented here by Rachela and her father's integration into their social and economic milieu—pointed toward yet left incomplete in Wyspiański's play. Despite their rivalry, Rachel and Leah accept each other. Leah prays for her sister's fertility. Even the strong-willed Rachel has sympathy for her sister. The midrashim suggest an unexpected alliance between the two sisters. In one midrash, Rachel and Jacob devise secret signs so that he will always be able to distinguish her from Leah. Yet later, Rachel takes pity on her sister and teaches her the signs: "I did this out of my compassion and kindness to her. And I wasn't jealous of her. I would not allow her to be disgraced."[26] The sisters coexist in compassionate competition—perhaps a less violent, sororal counterpart to fraternal mimetic desire. Recall the scene in Wajda's adaptation of *The Wedding* in which Rachela is humiliated after dancing with gentiles. Observing the faces of the women watching her, one might wonder: Could Rachela and her gentile peers demographically coexist in "compassionate competition"? Clearly, this wedding ensemble is not yet ready for this arrangement.

The scene calls to mind a famous portrayal of humiliation through dance from the Polish-Jewish literary canon. In I. J. Singer's *The Brothers Ashkenazi* (1934–35), gentile officers force the eponymous brothers to perform a self-mocking dance. The brother who resists is fatally shot. In an article devoted to this scene, Sonia Gollance, a scholar of Yiddish Studies whose work focuses on dance, theatre, and gender, shows how dance scenes in this novel serve to "juxtapose nineteenth-century dreams of embourgeoisement with the reality of twentieth-century antisemitism."[27] The gap between the two is on acute display in Rachela's public humiliation, at the century's turn. Her tentative sense of belonging, encouraged by the flirtatious Poet and Groom, is unreciprocated by the Polish society represented in microcosm by the wedding guests, who hail from both peasant and gentry classes. As Gollance argues, participating in mixed-sex dancing was equivalent to displaying one's membership in the convened social milieu (by performing correct etiquette and comportment) and sometimes also one's eligibility for marriage.[28] The wedding guests dramatically reject Rachela's bodily comportment and, by implication, her suitability to join their ranks through marriage. The gap between the speculative prospect of mixed marriage and the ugly reality of antisemitism is succinctly, spectacularly conveyed through Rachela's solitude as wedding guests recoil from her, repulsed by her dancing but also fixated on it, unable to look away.

The biblical Rachel's tale reminds us that all returns from exile raise demographic questions. To lay claim to land is to repopulate that land. In the Book of Jeremiah, the children of Israel, in exile from Egypt, pass Rachel's grave. Their predicament wakes the dead woman, who then negotiates with God on behalf of her children to demand their safe passage homeward. Her petitions contain the cryptic clause "a woman shall encompass a man" (Jeremiah 31:22b), which is interpreted by some to align the return from exile with the resumption of procreation by alluding to heterosexual intercourse[29] and to the female womb encompassing future progeny. If, at the break of a new century, Wyspiański and his generation were to invest in the prospect of a Polish-Jewish polis, the question remains: What would this look like in demographic terms? Who would encompass whom? How would a shared land be seeded? Recall the Groom's disinclination to take a Jewish wife due to his skepticism about Jewish population growth: "[I] wouldn't choose to fill the land / with girls of that exclusive brand."

Scholarship on *The Wedding* tends to undertake a forensic game of mapping the play's real-world reference points from Wyspiański's Kraków milieu. The established fact that the play followed the actual wedding between Lucjan Rydel and Jadwiga Mikołajczyk invites scholars to indulge a temptation we must otherwise distrust: the urge to read a text through the biography of its author, as if literature were linked to reality by one traceable cord, and as if the sum of an author's life provided an adequate key for unraveling a text's mysteries. Getting down to the bottom of *The Wedding* then becomes a matter of diligently investigating Wyspiański's life and times. Rachela (based on Józefa Singer) is bait for this fantasy, for an ample paper trail links the character on the page to her real-world referent.[30]

Wyspiański's play had material benefits for Józefa Singer, whose social status on the Kraków scene was elevated by her affiliation with the play to the extent that she was even eclipsed by her fictional counterpart: Tadeusz Boy-Żeleński wrote that she became "a walking shadow of her literary double . . . known only as Rachel."[31] One wonders, as we did of Rachela's unwritten poetry ("you write it, I feel it"), whether this is a case of poetry subsuming life or life giving body to poetry. Yet Rachela's speculative poetics seem to discredit any straightforward identification of her character with Józefa or, for that matter, any single point of reference. She embodies a relation of sign to referent that is always displaced before coming into its meaning. The one-to-one correspondence of characters to historic personae is confounded by Rachela, who cannot be reduced to any one person or idea. Instead, she is a conduit for symbolic production. In her transformative poetics, reified forms can be melted and reforged. This process may include the dissolution of demographic (class and ethnic) categories. In the Poet's words: "Everything melts into poetry for you: the father, peasants."[32] Poetic language *melts* the boundaries separating social classes.

Any interrogation of Rachela as arbiter of speculative value is incomplete without reference to her father. The innkeeper of *The Wedding* reproduces the Jewish moneylender stereotype, which has long been weaponized in antisemitic rhetoric. However, the archetype also reflects the historic reality of Jewish innkeepers who sold goods to Polish peasants on credit and the practice of private moneylending common in Jewish Galicia.[33] Granting credit established a relationship between creditor and debtor that extended beyond monetary transactions to favors, gifts, and a general interest in mutual welfare. The social anthropologist Rosa Lehmann has explored gentile-Jewish business relations as forms of interdependency; the Jewish innkeeper was emblematic of an intertwined economic and cultural rapport along these lines, just as his inn was a locus of integrated life. The tavern was never a purely Jewish space, for it was the site of intricate socioeconomic relations between Jews and gentiles. By naming the innkeeper "The Jew" (Żyd), Wyspiański invokes his full suite of archetypal attributes. This Jew will not transcend his type—that potential belongs to his daughter.

As Glenn Dynner argues in this volume, innkeepers' daughters in fin de siècle Kraków may have offered inspiration for literary representation in part "because their induction into avant-garde society seemed to symbolically redeem their fathers—emblems of daily encountered Jewish difference."[34] Rachela, in accordance with this description, decoheres her archetypal father and recombines his traits into something new. She inherits but also refunctions her father's moneylending, adapting it as speculative poetics: a mode for which value exists not as recuperated losses but as affirmative exploration of realities to come—among them, a future in which Rachela and her gentile suitor could consummate their courtship, their ability to make value together now ratified by their peers. Rachela, thus, does not duplicate her father's role; she renders it anew. She is not his double but his satellite—an image assigned to her by the Groom.[35] She also disaggregates and recombines the genetic codes of her real and fictional precursors, becoming something saturated with past precedents but uncannily new. Since Wyspiański's repeated allusions to the swaddled rosebush on the brink of blooming link Rachela to the maternal womb, she also represents a temporary shelter where the genetic material of the past can be recoded into something yet unknown.

Would the Polish sovereignty yearned for in *The Wedding* be a restoration of the past? Alternatively, could it be the birth of something new? The literary historian Colleen McQuillen has noted how the reincarnation of Christ and the reclamation of the Polish nation are linguistically joined in the Polish word *powstanie*, which translates to resurrection and insurrection ("rising up" and "uprising").[36] A nation that would include Polish Jews as full-fledged constituents would require a different kind of resurrection or return. A Poland where Polish and Jewish narratives of meaning and value are fairly and productively joined would require scrambling the pieces of both cultures' real and mythologized pasts into a new story.

To revive the past is to cash in on dormant value. Subject to the passing of time, value is never stable: it diminishes or grows. Speculative poetics, like moneylending, require a readiness to predict that value will grow over time and to set stake in this outcome. Through his writing of Rachela, Wyspiański seems to survey Jewish eligibility for a Poland held in common without ever putting money down. He does, however, give his readers a character who models speculative poetics—the mode of meaning-making needed to invest in a new and not entirely Polish Poland. By addressing her poetry to the Chochoł—by writing for hay—Rachela invests in a future that has not yet come to pass.

Her futurity can also be understood as a messianic attribute. After all, prolonged expectation and deferred gratification are the building blocks of Jewish eschatology.[37] This specifically Jewish temporality of deferral can be linked to a broader modernist "now-time" (Walter Benjamin's phrase).[38] Wyspiański's modernism and Jewish modernism are, in this light, sympathetic ways of waiting. *The Wedding* was written at the century's turn, when expectancy and postponement were by no means proprietary features of Jewish thought. Its dramatic fabula has the peculiar structure of a parade-like procession. The brevity of its scenes intensifies the sense it imparts of hyphenated yet protracted time. The crescendo building up to marital consummation is prolonged over three acts. Rachela's deferred gratification is not unique, for it mirrors the deferred consummation embedded in *The Wedding*'s plot and structure.

Rachela's speculations take on new shades when viewed in hindsight, through the dual catastrophes of the Holocaust and antisemitic campaigns of 1968—two foreclosures on the prospect of a Polish-Jewish state. Coates has noted that in Wajda's film, Rachela and her father have otherworldly blue and orange hues.[39] This "other world," I suggest, may be the future, or one possible future—in hindsight, a future that never came to be.

The pluralistic Poland that existed as potential for Wyspiański and his peers has since weathered over a century of assaults from many sides, with the prospect of an integrated Jewish community lingering like phantom limb pain.[40] Revisiting Rachela's speculative poetics today, we may feel remorse, as if we regret a good bet that was not placed. If we take seriously Rachela's link to the biblical Rachel, we might even think of her as an advocate negotiating for her people. Like Rachel's petitionary weeping, perhaps Rachela's speculative banter is an intercession. Perhaps she is bargaining on behalf of her "children"—future generations of Polish Jews. We might then recall Benjamin's reminder that the present moment, like all those preceding it, is "endowed with a *weak* messianic power, a power on which the past has a claim" that "cannot be settled cheaply."[41] Rachela, who speculated on a future that has not yet come to pass, has a claim on the present that has not expired. This impression is acute in Wajda's film, produced mere years after thirteen thousand Jews emigrated from Poland following the 1968 anti-Zionist campaign.[42] Could the blue-lit Komorowska of 1972 evoke Rachel risen from her grave, petitioning for her children to come home?

The recent film cycle *And Europe Will Be Stunned*, by Israeli-born artist Yael Bartana, envisions precisely this—a Jewish mass return to contemporary Poland. The trilogy tells the story of the semifictional Jewish revival movement, which enjoins Jews to make their home in Poland once more. The cycle meditates on Poland's loneliness as a monoculture, as the movement's slogans attest: "With one culture we cannot feel"; "With one color we cannot see." The movement's leader is played by the leftist public intellectual Sławomir Sierakowski. While the films are inflected with irony, Sierakowski's participation seems earnest. He shares a name with his character. The cycle opens with a speech outlining the movement's mission authored by Sierakowski himself. Unlike Wyspiański's Groom, who is reluctant to increase Poland's Jewish population ("I wouldn't choose to fill the land / with girls of that exclusive brand"), Sierakowski takes a Jewish wife and measures Jewish absence in Poland in rectifiable statistics: "3,000,000 Jews can change the life of 40,000,000 Poles."[43] His rationale for Jewish return accounts for how Poles, too, will benefit from this goal.

Mixing metaphors of financial speculation into the imagining of a multiethnic state may seem a crude approach to cultural pluralism. Why should Jewish inclusion in a diverse Poland be justified as a good investment? The Russian Jewish author Lev Levanda, advocate for Jewish assimilation (until the 1881–82 pogroms), once envisioned Jewish-gentile integration as "the reconciliation of equals . . . not in the name of some archaic tendencies or illusions, but in the name of a more rational economic modus vivendi."[44] Can we envision a form of Jewish-gentile coexistence that draws stability from a commitment to mutual welfare based on converging interests that, over time, turn into an intuitive feeling of a shared common good? Recall Rachel and Leah's compassionate competition: the glue binding their complicated family was sororal solidarity and a commitment to fair exchange. Lamenting her barrenness, Rachel strikes a bargain with her sister, temporarily ceding her right to Jacob's bed. In exchange, Leah gives her a mandrake root for fertility. Leah takes her extra night with Jacob but in turn prays that her sister will conceive. Sharing the world with others—sisters, rivals, strangers, neighbors—means sharing resources and negotiating the ethics of exchange.

ELIZA ROSE is Assistant Professor and Laszlo Birinyi Senior Fellow of Central European Studies at University of North Carolina at Chapel Hill. She received her PhD in Slavic languages at Columbia University. Her current research investigates interactions between art and industry in late-socialist Poland. Her articles have been published in *Slavic Review*, *Studies in Eastern European Cinema*, *View: Theories and Practices of Visual Culture*, *Journal of the Fantastic in the Arts*, and *Science Fiction Studies*. Her translations of Polish scholarly and art writing have been published widely.

NOTES

1. Karl Marx, "Economic and Philosophical Manuscripts of 1844," in *Karl Marx-Frederick Engels Collected Works, Volume 3, 1843–1844* (London: Lawrence & Wishart, 1975), 324.

2. Stanisław Wyspiański, *The Wedding*, trans. Noel Clark (London: Oberon, 1998), 52. "Bierę, płacę / daję, bierę / moje, twoje / twoje, moje." Stanisław Wyspiański, *Wesele* (Kraków: Zakład Narodowy im. Ossolińskich, 1977), 69.

3. Wyspiański, *The Wedding*, 60. "Przed tą pałubą słomianą poskarżę się mej poezji." Wyspiański, *Wesele*, 84.

4. The word *pałuba* has long puzzled translators of Polish literature. It appears frequently in the stories of Bruno Schulz and was assigned different English equivalents each time by translator Celina Wieniewska, as David Goldfarb notes in his introduction to the stories. See David Goldfarb, introduction to *The Street of Crocodiles and Other Stories*, by Bruno Schulz, trans. Celina Wieniewska (New York: Penguin, 2008). *Pałuba* has several meanings—an effigy or doll, a hag, or the covering of a cart. The former meanings capture the humanlike animacy of Wyspiański's figure, while the last evokes the chochoł's literal function as a protective sheath.

5. Wyspiański, *The Wedding*, 59. "[W]ięc jak pójdzie panienka, / a muśnie jej szal który krzew, / to jej tęsknota i żal / udzieli się przyciętej słomie, / a z krzaka smutek i cień / udzieli się nieświadomie / panience." Wyspiański, *Wesele*, 83.

6. Paul Coates suggests that the Chochoł eventually replaces Rachela. Shunned by the carousers, Rachela flees the party. Coates writes: "Rejected, Rachel in essence reappears as the Straw Man; and as such, she has the last word." See Paul Coates, "Revolutionary Spirits: *The Wedding* of Wajda and Wyspiański," *Literature/Film Quarterly* 20, no. 2 (1992): 132.

7. Noah Roderick, *The Being of Analogy* (London: Open Humanities, 2015), 24.

8. Roderick, *Being of Analogy*, 25.

9. Roderick, *Being of Analogy*, 28.

10. Wyspiański, *The Wedding*, 59. "[N]ie przeziębi najgorszy mróz, / jeźli kto ma zapach róż [. . .]" Wyspiański, *Wesele*, 84.

11. Wyspiański, *The Wedding*, 59. "[O]winą go w słomę zbóż, / a na wiosnę go odwiążą / I sam odkwitnie." Wyspiański, *Wesele*, 84.

12. Coates, "Revolutionary Spirits," 132.

13. See René Girard, "Triangular Desire" and "The Goodness of Mimetic Desire," in *The Girard Reader*, ed. James G. Williams (New York: Crossroad, 2000), 33–44, 62–65.

14. This is my literal translation to retain the explicit mention of the Chochoł: "[U]jrzę panią rad . . . pochyloną nad chochołem." Wyspiański, *Wesele*, 84.

15. "Pan to pisze, ja to czuję." Wyspiański, *Wesele*, 49.

16. "POET: A lightning bolt — / RACHEL: can go astray." Wyspiański, *The Wedding*, 39. "Trzask gromu / spudłować można." Wyspiański, *Wesele*, 47.

17. "RACHELA: [I] będę sobie wyobrażać pana / z daleka [. . .]." And later: "[A] pan niech tu w oknie stoi." Wyspiański, *Wesele*, 83.

18. Wyspiański, *The Wedding*, 36.

19. "Chciałem, chciałem. / Raz byłem, to nie zastałem." Wyspiański, *Wesele*, 42.

20. Wyspiański, *The Wedding*, 40. "Miodu, rozkoszy, słodyczy, miłości, roznamiętnienia i szczęścia." Wyspiański, *Wesele*, 49.

21. This is my literal translation. Noel Clark brings the phrase into present tense, thus losing the original's sense of unattainability: "Ach, marzyłam o tym zawsze!" Wyspiański, *Wesele*, 49.

22. Wyspiański, *The Wedding*, 115. "RACHELA: A moja muzyka / serca—prawie miłość do pana / najszczersza — —? POETA: Ta będzie najszczerzej oddana, co do wiersza." Wyspiański, *Wesele*, 194.

23. Eva Plach, "'Botticelli Woman': Rachel Singer and the Jewish Theme in Stanisław Wyspiański's *The Wedding*," *Polish Review* 41, no. 3 (1996): 310.

24. Plach, "'Botticelli Woman,'" 317.

25. Wyspiański, *The Wedding*, 36–37. "Kocham te z Botticellego, lecz nie chcę zapychać niemi każdej piędzi naszej ziemi." Wyspiański, *Wesele*, 43.

26. Wendy Doniger, *The Bedtrick: Tales of Sex and Masquerade* (Chicago: University of Chicago Press, 2000), 163.

27. Sonia Gollance, "Dance as a Tool of Pleasure and Humiliation in I. J. Singer's *The Brothers Ashkenazi*," *Prooftexts* 39, no. 3 (2022): 422–53.

28. Gollance, "Dance as a Tool," 427–28.

29. Robert P. Carroll interprets the phrase to mean "the vagina envelops the penis." Robert P. Carroll, *Jeremiah: A Commentary* (Philadelphia: Westminster, 1986), 601, 605.

30. Roman Brandstaetter's *Ja jestem Żyd z "Wesela"* (Poznań: Wydawnictwo Poznańskie, 1972) continues this investigative game. The book tells the story of Hirsz Singer—father of Józefa and basis for the Jewish innkeeper in Wyspiański's play. The first-person title invites speculations: does Brandstaetter, a Catholic convert with a religious Jewish upbringing, identify with the Jewish community represented in *The Wedding*?

31. Tadeusz Boy-Żeleński, "Plotka o *Weselu*," in *Tadeusz Boy-Żeleński, O Wyspiańskim*, ed. Stanisław Witold Balicki (Kraków: Wydawnictwo Literackie, 1973), 118, cited in Plach, "'Botticelli Woman,'" 320.

32. This is my literal translation to retain the verb *melt* (topić się): "wszystko się w poezji topi u pani, ojciec i chłopi." Wyspiański, *Wesele*, 81.

33. See Rosa Lehmann, "Jewish Patrons and Polish Clients: Patronage in a Small Galician Town," in *Polin: Studies in Polish Jewry*, vol. 17, *The Shtetl: Myth and Reality*, ed. Antony Polonsky (Oxford: Littman Library of Jewish Civilization, 2004), 160.

34. See Glenn Dynner, "Jula's Diary: A Hasidic Tavernkeeper's Daughter during the First World War" in this volume. On the Jewish innkeeper, see Dynner, *Yankel's Tavern: Jews, Liquor, & Life in the Kingdom of Poland* (New York: Oxford University Press, 2014), chap. 1.

35. "ŻYD: [M]oja córka, to kobita, [. . .] jak gwiazda. PAN MŁODY: Więc satelita?" Wyspiański, *Wesele*, 41.

36. Colleen McQuillen, "Sanctity or Sanctimony in Stanisław Wyspiański's *Akropolis*: On Boundary Oppositions, Subverted Expectations, and Irony," *Sarmatian Review* 29, no. 2 (2009): 1471.

37. Temporalities of deferral and delay in Jewish modernism are most extensively theorized in Harriet Murav's book *David Bergelson's Strange New World: Untimeliness and Futurity* (Bloomington: Indiana University Press, 2019).

38. Explicating the concept of now-time (*Jetztzeit*), Benjamin wrote that a moment's revolutionary ripeness is perceptible as a "messianic arrest of happening." Walter Benjamin, "On the Concept of History," in *Selected Writings, Vol. 4, 1938–1940*, ed. Howard Eiland and Michael W. Jennings, trans. Edmund Jephcott et al. (Cambridge, MA: Belknap, 1996), 396.

39. Coates, "Revolutionary Spirits," 130.

40. Geneviève Zubrzycki uses this metaphor in her article "Nationalism, 'Philosemitism,' and Symbolic Boundary-Making in Contemporary Poland," *Comparative Studies in Society and History* 58, no. 1 (January 2016): 86.

41. Benjamin, "On the Concept of History," 390.

42. For an account of these events, see, for instance, Dariusz Stola, "Jewish Emigration from Communist Poland: The Decline of Polish Jewry in the Aftermath of the Holocaust," *East European Jewish Affairs* 47, nos. 2–3 (2017): 169–88.

43. Yael Bartana, *Nightmares* (2008), last accessed May 17, 2020, https://artmuseum.pl/en/filmoteka/praca/bartana-yael-mary-koszmary-2.

44. These words appear in his positive review of Eliza Orzeszkowa's novel *Eli Makower*. Lev Levanda cited in Brian Horowitz, "A Jewish Russifier in Despair: Lev Levanda's Polish Question," in *Polin*, vol. 17, *The Shtetl: Myth and Reality*, ed. Antony Polonsky (Oxford: Littman Library of Jewish Civilization, 2004), 288.

PART V

The Voided Austeria

8

From Lost Center to Not-Knowing

On the Use of the Jewish Inn in Julian Stryjkowski's *The Inn* and Piotr Szewc's *Annihilation*

Alexander Lindskog

In a Poland where only few Jews now live, the memory, representation, interpretation, and lingering traces of historical Jews and Jewish life have been and remain an object of (sometimes contentious) discourse—both for their own sakes and as part of Polish national historical imagination.[1] And the question of how to connect these proximate and intertwined histories is one of the cruxes of this discussion.[2] With this historical and cultural debate in mind, this chapter examines the role of the inn as a (lost) unifying center and a meeting space for Jews and gentiles within the broad Polish postwar literary context using two post-Holocaust works that take place in a prewar world, Julian Stryjkowski's *The Inn* (Pol. *Austeria*, 1966) and Piotr Szewc's *Annihilation* (Pol. *Zagłada*, 1987). It argues that the trope serves several functions: it articulates a relatively acceptable prosthetic phantom pain within the belated writing of a phantasy body politic, adding to a complex hope for mourning, exculpation, and self-reckoning; and expresses an intra-Polish longing for others as well as for order in the postmodern condition.

The Polish People's Republic generally repressed discussions of the relationship between Jewish history and the Polish national idea by, among other things, officially enforcing nonethnic epistemologies of class; however, such discussions have made an uncanny return since the 1980s and have only grown during the Third Polish Republic, with a mushrooming academic as well as nonacademic literature—to name only two, albeit important, signs of that growth, the Jewish Culture Festival in Kraków has been ongoing since 1988 and the POLIN Museum of the History of Polish Jews opened in 2013.[3] While the most-noticed debates have centered around national self-image and culpability in the Holocaust—such as the case of Jan Tomasz Gross's *Neighbors: The Destruction of the Jewish Community in Jedwabne, Poland* or debates around the film *Aftermath* (Pol. *Pokłosie*)—there has also been a growing Polish interest in Jewish life beside and before the Holocaust, which many works of literature, an interest in Polish-Jewish memoirs, and many Poles' search for their Jewish roots bear witness to. Renewed interest in Jewish aspects of history is also evident in the larger intellectual trends of exploring and uncovering Jewish traces of Polish culture, such as that which has yielded shelves of books on Jewish aspects of the works of the writer Bruno Schulz, to name but one example.[4] Elements of antisemitic bigotry and conspiratorial obsessions also appear.[5] In contrast to this seemingly vibrant picture, the indifference of the general population to these matters should not be underestimated—which nevertheless does not exclude the possibility that a wider public could be affected passively by such discussions.

Some people conscious of tensions between different understandings of Jewish and Polish histories—such as some Marxists or those maintaining an assimilationist or post-assimilationist stance—may find them irrelevant. It is more common, at least for those who have found the issue pressing enough to take up their pens, that the matter is perceived to be more complicated and that the reductiveness and tensions of the fixed categories of Poles and Jews was and is a source of conflict and something yet to overcome, which, for all that, perversely, bespeaks their pervasiveness. For many eschewing the divisions reified in the categories of Poles and Jews—not least those for whom aesthetics or subjectivity transcend them, such as for many modernists—the Holocaust and subsequent antisemitic campaigns forced these categories upon them, as when Julian Tuwim felt compelled to write his Jewish pledge of allegiance "We, the Polish Jews . . ." in 1944.[6]

The Inn

The Poland emerging after the Second World War was in tatters: its decimated population was governed by socialists and locked in a civil war. Only a fraction of its Jewry survived the Holocaust.[7] In its traumas to work through—with a past to repress, to be haunted by, and to mourn, but also to mythologize—this lost minority would keep returning. Historically, perspectives on gentile-Jewish relations, a coexistence spanning nearly a millennium, have never been unified. From at least the mid-nineteenth century onward, gentiles and Jews held a multitude of different viewpoints, visions, and political positions on assimilation, on such Jewish nationalisms as Zionism, and on "the Jewish question" in general. This conversation continued after the war, and diverse Polish and Jewish actors found macro- and micropolitical power through various processes of memory work and mythologization in which the pre-Holocaust world figured prominently. While much has been said about the politics and strictures of Holocaust representation, this ideologically charged minor genre of literary reimaginations of Polish-Jewish coexistence in the precatastrophe world is, however, less discussed. Similarly, traumatic upheavals and imaginations of an arcadian past are integral to Polish national mythology, as this narrative structure also forms the core of the enduring Romantic mythos of the lost Poland in Polish messianism. To see how lively the debate on the politics of the Romantic view of the past is even today, one can look at Ewa Thompson's and Jan Sowa's dramatically different readings of Poland's attitude toward the loss of the First Polish Republic opening the anthology *Being Poland: A New History of Polish Literature and Culture since 1918*.[8]

A locus useful for engaging with interaction, shared experience, and gray zones, often for that reason used synecdochically, is the inn: owned by noblemen and visited by gentiles and Jews of different classes, inns in the nobility-dominated prepartition economy had come to be leased to and run by Jews.[9] The most famous such image is no doubt Jankiel's tavern in the 1834 Polish national epos *Pan Tadeusz*, where it serves as a center and frame, an anchoring point and image of harmony and coexistence among the different social groups of the lost world, in which the Jew naturally has a place. (For the genealogy and aporias of this image, see chap. 2.) The inn appears in countless other works of literature and art, too many to list. An example complicating the image is Władysław Reymont's *The Peasants* (Pol. *Chłopi*, 1904–9), in which the inn also serves as a cross-cultural meeting place, but the peasants frequenting the inn spout antisemitic slurs and feel guilty for supporting the Jews—Reymont's inn is still a unifying center, but one in which the Jew is not included in the category of Poles.[10]

Sublimation of the Lost World

Julian Stryjkowski was born Pesach Stark in 1905 in the town of Stryj (today Ukr. Stryi; Yid. Stri), which had Magdeburg rights from 1341 and an ethnically mixed population. Over one-third of the inhabitants were Jewish, lending it a shtetl character at the time.[11] Born into a nonassimilated Jewish family, Stryjkowski was sent to a Polish-language school and later received a PhD in Polish literature. He was involved with both a Zionist organization and communism before the war.[12] He was in Moscow in 1943 when he began writing his first novel *Głosy w ciemności* (*Voices in the Dark*).[13] Published in 1956 (although finished a decade earlier), it formed the first part of what ultimately became his so-called Galician Tetralogy, the second part of which is *Austeria* (1966, Eng. title *The Inn*).[14] By the time of his return to Stryj, the Jewish population had been murdered and the town had fallen on the Soviet side of the redrawn borders (and lies in Ukraine today). He took the name Julian Stryjkowski—a missive from the lost prewar, borderland world to a new Poland. As the philosopher Katarzyna Kornacka-Sareło puts it: "He could not return home, because his 'previous world' had vanished, was in ruins: after the Second World War his 'Stryj[. . .]' was no longer a Jewish shtetl; neither has it been a Polish town since then. So, the only solution available to the writer was to become an émigré who tried not to forget any details of his previous life and who wanted to save 'the old world' from a complete oblivion."[15]

The tetralogy is built around conflicts of modernization in small-town Jewish life: secularization, assimilation, interethnic relationships, modern ideologies, the weakening authority of religion, and the like; while the novels have some central conflicts and characters, they are polyphonic and sometimes oneiric. Only the first and final novels have an overlapping cast of characters. All are set before the First World War, except *The Inn*, which takes place during its onset. Arguably, however, the most important aspect of the book—and the tetralogy—is the writing of the lost Jewish world in Polish. A Yiddish-speaking child's confrontation and entry into a broader Polish and Polonophone world is thematized (in Polish) in *Echo*,[16] but the interplay of Polish and Jewish life-worlds also extends to the language of the novel itself, which is imbued with Yiddishisms. In the literary critic Ida Pizem-Karczag's words, the work "actually reads like a translation from Yiddish."[17]

The titular inn lies on the outskirts of an unnamed Galician town. The book begins by setting up various dramas and intrigues of town life. When the town is attacked by the Russian army, several thematic aspects of the overdetermined inn come to the fore: the inn becomes a space of safety, of exception, of difference, and of meeting. A variety of people of different ethnicities and religions—including a girl that has been shot by the Cossacks, the local *tsadik* (Hasidic spiritual leader) and his followers, and a

Hungarian soldier—seek shelter at the inn. The people's internal conflicts come to the fore in the crowded space. After one of those seeking shelter in the inn is killed by the Russian occupants after sneaking out, the innkeeper, Tag, and a priest go into town in the vain hope of getting justice from the new authorities. All this is cadenced by the chants of the Hasidim.

The book is not divided into chapters, and at times, it is hard to follow its many voices and gazes. The preamble emphasizes the (still modest) modernization of the shtetl and the effects of new technologies. However, the deeper tension of the book lies in the dissonance between these conflicts that define people's lives and the war, as the modernization of the diaspora was a sprawling process that was arrested by the coming of the war. All the while, the songs of the Hasidim facing away from the modern world become a tragic chorus of sorts, reminding the reader of what is going to happen. The inn—and *The Inn*—becomes an ark where this prewar world is going to be permanently put up, sublimated into language by (no-longer-Stark) Stryjkowski.[18]

Annihilation—Suspicions of Remembering

Like *The Inn*, Piotr Szewc's short novel *Zagłada* (1987, Eng. title *Annihilation*) is also written without chapter breaks, as one continuous text.[19] It follows a day in interwar Zamość, the author's birthplace (as well as that of such luminaries as Rosa Luxemburg and Yitskhok Leybush Peretz). Zamość was planned and realized as a *città ideale*, an "ideal city," in accordance with humanistic Renaissance ideals of comfort and safety, which granted the city a geometric character and a preponderance of open spaces.[20]

In the novel, we see the everyday dramas of the prostitute Kazimiera M., the local policemen, and the innkeeper Rosenzweig—the latter portrayed against the background of his tavern, where most of the townspeople converge. The long text has an even more sweeping yet deconstructed gaze than that of *The Inn*, briefly following one character, then another one, with minute detail. Its tone is that of a stillness tinged with apprehension; it is written in the present tense interspersed with the future tense—the future tense of what will happen, and, for the reader, of what will have happened. The novel's Zamość is as sleepy, sunny, and hazy as Bruno Schulz's Drohobycz, and the conceit of the novel rests on the contrast between this sleepiness and the title—the original Polish "zagłada" (extinction) is also the word used for the Holocaust.

The contextless, camera-like poetics are, however, sometimes subtly interrupted by foreboding images. Several characters have reveries of destruction, and a painting in the inn appears to show the likeness of the town and its inhabitants "wrapped in flames." A "fiery ball, followed by a smoke and a tail of sparks, rolls on a narrow street." The painting also depicts people soaring "over the town, among white clouds" in a Chagall-like image that evokes a post-Holocaust frame of reference. The image seems so out of place that the narrator adds that the "scene is like a snapshot from an improbable dream."[21] The fiery ball, however, reappears throughout the novel, primarily on photographs but sometimes outside them, as a "second sun" or "the eye of the town," and it is easy to miss that it is the "the dome of the town hall."[22] Moreover, the narrative flow is interspersed with a clicking camera, and photographs of the town appear outside the text, as the novel's endpapers enwrap it in photographs of Zamość's prewar market square. It is only at one point—the reader could easily overlook it—that the painting and town merge, as the fiery ball falls out of the picture as a diegetically concrete object, breaking into sparkles, and is suggested to set the town on fire.[23] It is as if nobody takes notice of the risk of imminent destruction.

The palpable summer haziness lingers, matched by a postmodern breaking of genre and the ontological instability of the difference between fiction and reality that the indexicality of the photographs and their blending into the book make for. With a similar ambiguity, the Renaissance dome of the town hall, which "sees everything,"[24] is suggested to double as a watchtower.

Renegotiations of the Phantom Body Politic: "We Long for You, Jews!"

According to the literary historian Przemysław Czapliński, postwar Polish literature was characterized overall by a shift from geopolitics to geopoetics.[25] As Poland's borders shifted and the war, the Holocaust, Soviet domination, and repatriations created a new smaller and ethnically homogenous Poland, an imaginary *Heimat*-ification (Pol. "mała ojczyzna") of the lost borderlands emerged. Czapliński places *The Inn*'s author among a group of writers who write the borderlands as "an arcadia of tolerance, a homeland of agreeable differences, a space of harmony on Europe's margins, a victim of modernity."[26] But in the case of *The Inn*, this idyll is shown as locked up in an inn, a metaphorical ark—sublimated into imagination, but betraying that its refugees are from a world that no longer exists.

Piotr Szewc no longer has his own memory of prewar Poland or of the war, instead having postmemory, or memories of memories.[27] For him, the borderlands and Jews who inhabited them were mobilized again,

Czapliński argues, as one of the strategies of "multiplying the center," a reaction to the homogeneity of "anti-socialist realism" of the early 1980s. I quote Czapliński: "It is *ghosts* that are the most real content of these novels [of multiplying the center]; they represent what 1980s Poland was missing the most, social difference. At a time when communism was waning in Poland, Polish culture was in danger of becoming excessively undifferentiated; these novels called on the ghosts of past differences for help."[28]

In addition to their interactions with Polish Romanticism and the negotiation of the phantom borderlands, *The Inn* and *Annihilation* also interact with the strictures and politics of Holocaust representation, not least the demand for authenticity and the reluctance to speculate that suffuse them.[29] While the Holocaust is diegetically absent from both *The Inn* and *Annihilation*, they both have a sense of rehearsal for it—in the former, the destruction of the shtetl and the Austro-Hungarian order foreshadow the destruction of Central Europe's Jews, and in the latter, the sense of looming catastrophe and anterior futurity anticipate it. This could also be seen as one way of answering the demands of Holocaust representation—pointing at the event but remaining silent before it.

The Inn and *Annihilation* also interact with the specificity of Jewish-gentile relations and Polish/Jewish postwar negotiations of the imaginary, which include different and sometimes competing martyrologies. While these relations are in both cases shown in a favorable light, it should be noted that this negotiation nevertheless is in several respects an intra-Polish dialogue on the memory of Jews. An image of coexistence on the one hand, the novels also play into what the philosopher Andrzej Leder has called the "transpassive enjoyment" of the Holocaust, which in his account was a class revolution that helped to create the Polish middle class, a class revolution that Poles as a collective nevertheless "slept through."[30] Leder's analysis is Lacanian, arguing that until Polish discourse takes responsibility for this unacknowledged desiring, it will collectively be locked up in a complex. Even if one does not follow this analysis to its full consequences, one can still note how ghosts of a different past sometimes intermingle uncomfortably with a present haunting of sameness.

Besides the obfuscatory and compensatory discourse this complex would engender, perhaps we can see the attempt to write a belated phantom pain—a groping to affix a limb lost or never quite connected: an image of what could have been, in the worst-case scenario a sanitizing nostalgia and screen memory, but possibly also the sublimated realization of a fantasy of suffering with and for the other. Taking a longer perspective, the attempt to write a Polish-Jewish world places itself in the tradition and negotiations of the writing of an imaginary body politic, which has characterized Polish culture since Poland's territorial loss—but according to the sociologist Jan Sowa has been going on much longer—here looking to include Jews in that phantom image.[31] If these images seem drastic or compensatory, it is perhaps only in seeing the discrepancies of such a retrospective fantasy image that responsibility for what actually came to pass can be accepted, and mourning can take place. However that may be, it is interesting to note that the imaginary body politic here seems more whole with Jews anatomically integrated.

In a more recent example of working to attach a like prosthetic hurting limb, in Rafał Betlejewski's performative street art of the mid-2000s, the slogan "I long for you, Jew!" (Pol. "Tęsknię za tobą, Żydzie!") was painted across Poland. For him, this was an explicitly intra-Polish endeavor: "I want to retrieve the word 'Jew,' take it from the [Polish] antisemites, who are the only ones who feel that they can use this word uninhibitedly in this country."[32]

Why Does the Gentile Long for the Jew? Postmodernity and the Jew as *Sinthome*

The figure of the Jewish tavern takes on a particular role in this Polish writing of a prosthetic phantom pain. The tavern is the image where Jews and gentiles meet and, sometimes, intermix; it is a shelter during wartime; it is where Jew becomes Polish. If it is not quite a carnival, then it is perhaps something of a heterotopia, a space integrated into and part of society, but where norms are excepted—until the space is co-opted or erased.[33] Another potential way to think about the tavern trope is as a search for an image of heterotopia, and perhaps a nostalgia for it. And perhaps a heterotopia, for it can function as a redeeming image in this prosthetic limb. A heterotopia relies on an outside (of sameness, of capitalism, of repression), and perhaps also for this reason it is mobilized as a wish for difference as well as for norms. This could be read in light of the epistemological insecurity of the postmodern condition and its "incredulity toward metanarratives" and "pragmatics of language particles" in which historical and epistemological foundations, but also difference or outside, are annihilated.[34] Iwona Kurz, in chapter 9 of the present volume, observes something similar in responses to the film adaptation of *The Inn*—a subtext to the effect that "the 'lost continent' did not mean just the Jewish world but a broader cultural whole in which there still existed (on equal footing) the sacred and the profane."[35]

The trope betrays a fantasy image of ontological stability in more ways than one. If the image of the Jew functions as an othering that holds a group—such as the Poles—together, then the tavern might function as a more palatable version of it. If this reading holds, then, more importantly, the image of the Jew functions as an obsession that creates meaning out of chaos or relativism: in the worst case, paranoia and othering, as for example in antisemitism; in better cases, a pattern that can lead to a meaning based in responsibility. In either case, an image betraying the fantasy of exiting the postmodern condition can be deduced.

From a psychoanalytic point of view, the problem of the postmodern condition can be expressed as a lack of fathers (to kill). Following Lacanian theory, this lack of a father renders everyone in the postmodern era borderline psychotic, as there is no name-of-the-father to repress and therefore no repression through which to enter the symbolic.[36] Thus, the postmodern subject is reduced to picking strawman fights in order to ground a center, and an entry into symbolic structures. A similar condition existed in Poland in the nineteenth century, when the fatherland was lost and needed to be maintained in imagination.[37] Psychotic structures can, however, be compensated by what Jacques Lacan calls *sinthome*, a structural obsession that ultimately is meaningless but allows what could be a conspiracy merely to remain a set of patterns and provide an opening for meaning: a structural substitute for the paternal metaphor.[38] If the Jewish inn—and the Jew himself—functioned for Poles as one of these sinthomes, it would explain how each can work as an image uniting Poles and, when the image's unifying and meaning-giving function breaks down, can turn into a conspiratorial othering. It also would explain how the postwar (re)incorporation of the Jew and the Jewish inn into Polish literature interplays with a nostalgia for an easier meaning in addition to and in conjunction with the affixed phantom pain. Furthermore, it explains in what way such cultural-psychological memory work can be pursued as an intra-Polish conversation.

The trope of the Jewish tavern thus serves several functions—a succinct synecdoche for the tolerant yet sprawling image of multiethnic coexistence, an image of which helps add to a fantasy of the possibility of mourning, compensatory imagery for violence and antisemitism, but also potentially redeemable images for coexistence; it is also mobilized against the postmodern condition, which reinforces the connection between the Holocaust and postmodernity. It cuts both ways—it offers both potential exculpation and self-reckoning, both a fragment of something good that can be recycled and a blurring of one's own violent desires, a wish to inhabit Poland with others and simultaneously a wish for order in postmodernity.

Coda, or Toward Not-Knowing

In the pre-postmodern universe of *The Inn*, the innkeeper, Tag, considers Judaism something he simply has and cannot lose; similarly convinced of the substance of his faith, the priest has secretly baptized him in—from his point of view—a considerate gesture, saving his soul. As the Hasidim sing the names of God in the morning, and the priest and innkeeper walk together to the town in a vain search for justice for the young man shot by the Cossacks, it is ultimately the justification of the law that is lost, a predicament that resonates with the postmodern condition, as there is no way to meaningfully be inscribed in this new symbolic order.

Annihilation is more self-aware in its poetics, inscribing processes of reality- and memory-construction into the text itself. A metacommentary appears on its final page: "For its own sake our memory determines the hierarchies of what is or isn't worth remembering. Those hierarchies are illusory, and our knowledge of their meaning is never complete. Yet the pain is always the same because we have managed to save barely a fraction of events simultaneously."[39]

This postmodernist, *nouveau roman*–like view of poetics emphasizes that we are lost in language. More so than do the poetics of *The Inn*, it cuts close to the nonmemory that the attempt to relive or re-member no doubt will produce, underscoring that this effort will end in guesses and simulacra. This humbles expectations about the authenticity of memory, but for the same reason, decoupled from such ambition but holding on to the pain of being unable to speak it, the continued attempt to do so may be able to formulate what a language more capacious of alterity can look like within the premises of Polish cultural and memory negotiation. While the index of the event may slip away amid fragmentariness and nominalism, these may suggest more sensitized ways of writing in the future.

Alexander Lindskog is Assistant Instructional Professor of Polish at the University of Chicago and a PhD candidate at the University of Illinois, Chicago. His dissertation looks at the later work of Witkacy (Stanisław Ignacy Witkiewicz). He has published "The Subversion of Sexuality: A Comment on Sexual Difference in Bruno Schulz's Work in the Context of Modern Heterosexuality" in *Przed i po. Bruno Schulz* (in Polish, 2018).

Notes

If not stated otherwise, all translations are mine, A.L.

1. Geneviève Zubrzycki estimates that there were "between 4,500 and 13,000" Jews living in Poland in 2022; the variation "hing[es] on how Jewishness is determined: halacha

[Jewish law], formal membership in Jewish organizations, meeting the criteria for Israel's Law of Return, or self-identification in the 2011 census." See Zubrzycki, *Resurrecting the Jew: Nationalism, Philosemitism, and Poland's Jewish Revival* (Princeton, NJ: Princeton University Press, 2022), 12. Thus, while small numbers of Jews continue to live in Poland, in comparison with the pre-Holocaust estimate of 3.5 million, one can speak of a virtual Jewish absence.

2. Mirroring this, discussions on how to view the period of Jewish-gentile coexistence abound in the post-Polish-Jewish diasporas and in Israel.

3. It is beyond the scope and intentions of this section, and chapter, to give a full picture of Polish discourse on gentile-Jewish relations; I intend merely to sketch a few large trends and events.

4. Jan Tomasz Gross, *Neighbors: The Destruction of the Jewish Community in Jedwabne, Poland* (New York: Penguin, 2002); *Aftermath*, directed by Władysław Pasikowski (Apple Film Productions, 2012). For a substantial but incomplete bibliography of Schulzology, see "Bibliografia przedmiotowa," Schulz Forum, last accessed June 15, 2019, https://schulzforum.pl/pl/bibliografia/przedmiotowa.

5. See the film *Hi, Tereska*, directed by Robert Gliński (Telewizja Polska, Propaganda Film, 2001), for instance, for gratuitous and ubiquitous use of antisemitic slurs in a context devoid of Jews or of any memory of their presence.

6. Julian Tuwim, "We the Polish Jews . . . ," trans. Madeline G. Levine, *Polish Review* 17, no. 4 (1972): 82–89.

7. To a smaller extent, wartime and postwar emigration as well as the antisemitic purges of 1968 added to the overall disappearance of Jews in Poland.

8. Ewa Thompson, "Sarmatism, or the Secrets of Polish Essentialism"; Jan Sowa, "Spectres of Sarmatism," in *Being Poland: A New History of Polish Literature and Culture since 1918*, ed. Tamara Trojanowska, Joanna Niżyńska, and Przemysław Czapliński, with the assistance of Agnieszka Polakowska (Toronto: University of Toronto Press, 2018), 3–29, 30–47.

9. See Glenn Dynner, *Yankel's Tavern: Jews, Liquor, & Life in the Kingdom of Poland* (New York: Oxford University Press, 2014).

10. Władysław Reymont, *Chłopi*, 2 vols. (Wrocław: Zakład Narodowy im. Ossolińskich, 1999), passim.

11. Some controversy surrounds Stryjkowski's birth name, as he used several allonyms and gave different accounts. According to Ireneusz Piekarski, his father's family name was Rosenmann, whereas Stark was his mother's, but as his parents only had a religious marriage and not a civil one, he had been officially recorded under his mother's name. See Ireneusz Piekarski, *Z ciemności: O twórczości Juliana Stryjkowskiego* (Wrocław: Wydawnictwo Uniwersytetu Wrocławskiego, 2010), 15–42. According to the 1931 census, Stryj was 35.6 percent Jewish.

12. Julian Stryjkowski came out as a homosexual at the end of 1988. While I will not pursue this line of inquiry in this article, Grażyna Borkowska has argued for the centrality of unenunciated homosexuality in his work. See "The Homelessness of the Other: The Homosexual Experience in the Prose of Julian Stryjkowski," in *Framing the Polish Home: Postwar Cultural Constructions of Hearth, Nation, and Self*, ed. Bożena Shallcross (Athens: Ohio University Press, 2002), 54–67.

13. Julian Stryjkowski, *Głosy w ciemności* (Warsaw: Czytelnik, 1956). This was the first novel he wrote. However, by the time it was published, he had already published the novel *Bieg do Fragalà* (*Race to Fragalà*) (Warsaw: Czytelnik, 1951).

14. Julian Stryjkowski, *Austeria* (Warsaw: Czytelnik, 1966); *The Inn*, trans. Celina Wieniewska (New York: Harcourt Brace Jovanovich, 1972). The other two novels in the series are *Sen Azrila* (*Azril's Dream*) (Warsaw: Czytelnik, 1975) and *Echo* (Warsaw: Czytelnik, 1988).

15. Katarzyna Kornacka-Sareło, "Where Is the World of Ours? Assimilation, Acculturation, and Emancipation Process of the Galician Jews in the Prose by Julian Stryjkowski (Pesach Jakob Stark)," in *Jews in Eastern Europe*, ed. Waldemar Szerbiński and Katarzyna Kornacka-Sareło (Newcastle upon Tyne: Cambridge Scholars, 2016), 177.

16. See Kornacka-Sareło, "Where Is the World," 177.

17. Ida Pizem-Karczag, "The 'Jewish' Trilogy of Julian Stryjkowski," *Polish Review* 28, no. 4 (1983): 93. While she is writing about the first book in the series, the statement applies just as well to *The Inn*. See Pizem-Karczag, "'Jewish' Trilogy," 92–93, for examples.

18. Andrzej Zieniewicz similarly ponders autobiographical writing about a place that is always already not yet formed in "The Already-Non-Existence as a Category of Autobiographical Memory: Galician Places of Timelessness in the Prose of Bruno Schulz, Artur Sandauer, and Julian Stryjkowski," in *Galician Polyphony: Places and Voices*, ed. Alina Molisak and Jagoda Wierzejska (Warsaw: Dom Wydawniczy ELIPSA, 2015), 81–91.

19. Piotr Szewc, *Zagłada* (Warsaw: Czytelnik, 1987); trans. Ewa Hryniewicz-Yarbrough, *Annihilation* (Normal, IL: Dalkey Archive Press, 1993). Szewc and Stryjkowski were friends, but Szewc is of a different generation, born in 1961.

20. See Helena Kozakiewiczowa and Stefan Kozakiewicz, *Renesans w Polsce* (Warsaw: Arkady, 1976), 230–39.

21. Szewc, *Annihilation*, 37.

22. Szewc, *Annihilation*, 72.

23. Szewc, *Annihilation*, 102.

24. Szewc, *Annihilation*, 72.

25. Przemysław Czapliński, "Shifting Sands: History of Polish Prose 1945–2015," in *Being Poland: A New History of Polish Literature and Culture since 1918*, ed. Tamara Trojanowska, Joanna Niżyńska, and Przemysław Czapliński, with the assistance of Agnieszka Polakowska (Toronto: University of Toronto Press, 2018), 373–80.

26. Czapliński, "Shifting Sands," 375.

27. For this generation of Polish literature's engagement with the Holocaust in particular, see Alina Molisak, "Figures of Memory: Polish Holocaust Literature of the 'Second Generation,'" in *Imaginary Neighbors: Mediating Polish-Jewish Relations after the Holocaust*, ed. Dorota Głowacka and Joanna Żylinska (Lincoln: University of Nebraska Press, 2010), 205–22; for Szewc in particular, see 209–15.

28. Czapliński, "Shifting Sands," 390.

29. For general background, see Berel Lang, *Holocaust Representation: Art within the Limits of History and Ethics* (Baltimore, MD: Johns Hopkins University Press, 2000).

30. Andrzej Leder, *Prześniona rewolucja* (Warsaw: Wydawnictwo Krytyki Politycznej, 2013), 20–25 and passim.

31. Sowa has argued that part of the particularity of Polish romanticism comes from the fact that Poland as a true body politic stopped existing much earlier, as it did not really have a head (i.e., a sovereign king) and was ruled by the nobility, who in actuality acted as its sovereign and even considered themselves to be a different ethnos (i.e., Sarmatians). According to Sowa, Poland had been an imaginary, phantom body already since the sixteenth century and in some ways earlier—the partitions had merely been the symbolic fulfillment of a truth in the real. This predicament keeps shaping Polish imaginary "form" to this day. *Fantomowe ciało króla: Peryferyjne zmagania z nowoczesną formą* (Kraków: Universitas, 2011). Another thinker who was preoccupied with the lack of solid foundation to Polish Romanticism was Stanisław Brzozowski, famously calling it "a flower's revolt against its roots." *Legenda Młodej Polski: Studya o strukturze duszy kulturalnej* (Lwów: Nakładem Księgarni Polskiej Bernarda Połonieckiego, 1910), 34.

32. Quoted in Piotr Pacewicz, "Płonie stodoła," *Gazeta Wyborcza: Duży Format*, last modified May 22, 2010, last accessed June 15, 2019, http://wyborcza.pl/1,76842,7899683,Plonie_stodola.html?as=1&startsz=x.

33. See Michel Foucault, "Of Other Spaces: Utopias and Heterotopias," trans. Jay Miskowiec, in *Facing Value: Radical Perspectives from the Arts* (Amsterdam, Stroom Den Haag: Valiz, 2017), 164–71.

34. Jean-François Lyotard, *The Postmodern Condition: A Report on Knowledge*, trans. Geoff Bennington (Minneapolis: University of Minnesota Press, 1984), xxiv.

35. See chapter 9 of the present volume. The film version of *Austeria* was directed by Jerzy Kawalerowicz (Zespół Filmowy "Kadr," 1982).

36. Jacques Lacan, *The Psychoses: The Seminar of Jacques Lacan, Book III*, trans. Russell Grigg (New York: W. W. Norton, 1993). For a brief account, see Dylan Evans, *An Introductory Dictionary to Lacanian Psychoanalysis* (London: Routledge, 1996), 156–59, 195–97.

37. As Filip Mazurkiewicz puts it, this lack of a Polish *signifié* "takes away fathers from their sons, which in turn leads to them not being able to kill them in symbolic patricide, and—as this inability generates further inabilities—it deprives them of the possibility to form full, and so to speak, 'healthy' subjectivities. From this perspective [. . .] the nineteenth century becomes a procession of successive generations of castrated males condemned to a hereditary *identification-not-yet* and the types of troubles it creates in the symbolic sphere." "Męskość dziewiętnastowieczna—prolegomena," *Teksty Drugie*, no. 2 (2015): 41–42.

38. Jacques Lacan, *The Sinthome: The Seminar of Jacques Lacan, Book XXIII*, trans. A. R. Price (Cambridge: Polity, 2016). For a brief account, see Evans, *Introductory*, 191–92.

39. Szewc, *Annihilation*, 107.

9

Austeria and the Inn

Kawalerowicz's Movie and Its Reception in Poland

Iwona Kurz

The Jews it was who brought it here to us.
It's shaped like a ship in front, a temple behind;
The ship part is a Noah's Ark on land,
Or, as the vulgar say, a barn—a house
For sundry creatures (horses, oxen, cows,
Billy goats); while flocks of poultry dwell upstairs
With crawling insects too, and snakes in pairs.
The oddly formed rear section brings to mind
The Temple of Solomon on the Mount, designed
By Hiram's carpenters—who for their part
Had been first to learn the builder's art.[1]

Noah's Ark (or Rather Not)

The inn represented in Jerzy Kawalerowicz's *Austeria* (*The Inn*, prod. 1982)—the first film in postwar Poland, forty years after the Second World War, that focused entirely on Jewish life in Polish lands—does not resemble the above-cited description by Mickiewicz (which is discussed in chap. 2). It is instead a wooden building, of course, built to a plan that connects living and farm rooms, a building with an inviting facade, whose style remains plain, bearing almost no decorations, just simple carvings. Kawalerowicz does not analyze the inn's space regarding its religious meanings and symbols; rather, he treats it from an anthropological perspective as a space of hospitality, open for human activity.

Still, the comparison to Noah's Ark appears here directly, in dialogue.[2] The film, an adaptation of Julian Stryjkowski's novel *Austeria* (Pol. *The Inn*, 1966), is set during one day and in one place (apart from the characters' flashbacks and a few scenes in the town). We watch a group of people, mostly Jewish, finding shelter from the threat of possible battle and from Cossack pogroms in an inn at the edge of a town somewhere in Galicia. As the subtitle at the movie's beginning states directly, it is the first day of the Great War.

Thus, the biblical comparison concerns not only the function of the ark but also the diversity of the entities that inhabit the metaphorical "vessel." They are various Jews and non-Jews. All bring to the inn their individual worlds: their philosophies, ways of life, appearances, and emotions. The Jewish townspeople who stop there are more or less religious, more or less progressive.[3] The Jews include a group of Hasidim gathered around the great *tsadik* and led by a hyperactive Josełe (Wojciech Pszoniak), and they are joined by two visitors—one, a lost Hungarian hussar hiding in the inn, and the other, a troubled Catholic priest, a childhood friend of the innkeeper. The owner, Tag (Franciszek Pieczka), is a central figure of this world, trying to organize the chaos and comment on it from a distance. He lives in the inn with his daughter, granddaughter, and a Ukrainian maid, Jewdocha (Lilianna Głąbczyńska), who is also his lover. The local "baroness" and the "emperor" himself also appear in body and flashbacks, respectively. They fill out the image of the full social structure of the "liberal" Austro-Hungarian Empire. The inn, as the shelter for any person of goodwill, is a part and an emanation of this image. The structure of the film's cast of characters is an inversion of most Polish literary and filmic works. Jews used to be an "addition," a folkloristic or episodic element appended to the main theme—here, the construction is reversed, as the authors introduce one Polish and Hungarian man and one Ukrainian and Austrian woman as "types" into a complex Jewish community.

The compound construction of the film allows for encounters not only between different characters, ethnicities, and social classes but also between different symbols and languages. As Daria Mazur wrote, "The features attributed in the Judaic topic to the shtetl space—provincialism, 'a refuge of tradition,' 'substitute of Eretz Israel' in the community dimension of the chosen nation, the neighbourhood of the sacred and the profane—have been transferred to the tavern."[4]

However, this shelter—both physical and symbolic—is only temporary. The film structure—the unity of time and place proper for Greek tragedy—

emphasizes the fate that will eventually meet the characters. The first day of the war is the last day of the world in which they lived.

Here the "ark" analogy fails. The ensuing world-engulfing war will be totally fatal, and the universe destroyed in the catastrophe is not going to be re-created. The final scene of the morning ablution of the Hasidim closes with the image of the river flowing down with blood. The shot evokes not only the Great War but also the Second World War and the Shoah—the association well recognized by contemporary reviewers and the audience. The story thus becomes not a parallel of the creation but rather its antithesis, and the ark turns out to be a pontoon boat. Does it head toward the heavens, Sheol, or perhaps again toward the earth?

At the Crossroads of History (Or, Rather, Politics)

> If a man is not safe in his own bed, then where can he be safe?[5]
>
> (from a dialogue in *Austeria*)

Such a complex structure builds the tension between myth and history.[6] A specific historical event and a specific space saturated with history—a village inn at the outbreak of the Great War—transform into a mythical space of eternity that gives hope for salvation. But it is also a form of escape from any aspect of history that is untouchable, unspoken, tabooed, or censored in any way; it reveals class, ethnic, gender, and other conflicts. It matters what the "ark" takes, but it also matters what it leaves behind.

Paradoxically, the historical events to which the story refers—that is, the outbreak of the First World War—are politically less important than the movie's contemporaneity. In Stryjkowski's novel, historical events are, on the one hand, narratively concentrated, and on the other, the story about them subtly differentiates in the attitudes, views, and opinions of the characters. In Kawalerowicz's movie, the process of condensation is still progressing, and is enhanced by the visual form of film narration confined to a single day and night and built around a main character.

However, the production of the movie took place in a specific context, which greatly influenced the immediate reading of it. The script based on the *Austeria* novel was created by Julian Stryjkowski and Tadeusz Konwicki in cooperation with Jerzy Kawalerowicz directly after the novel's publication in 1967. Probably for the sake of clarity, they decided to organize the story more around Tag's character, silencing the chorus of the novel's "many voices and gazes." (On the inn's meaning in Stryjkowski's novel, see chap. 8.)

Nevertheless, like many other projects related to Polish-Jewish history, the film could not be realized then. Israel's victory over Egypt in the Six-Day War had unexpected consequences for Poland's internal policy.[7] It provoked an outbreak of antisemitic, xenophobic, and anti-intelligentsia attitudes. The authorities' official actions, combined with the social atmosphere of resentment, resulted in the forced emigration of many people of Jewish descent. An estimated thirteen thousand or even as many as twenty thousand people left Poland at that time. In the world of Polish film, the antisemitic purges led to emigration of many artists and the suspension of all projects touching on Jewish themes.[8] The background for this process was, of course, the memory of the Second World War or, to speak precisely, forgetfulness about it, because the unspeakable experience of the Holocaust was at issue.[9] More than twenty years after the war, this event remained unnamed in Polish public discussion, the catastrophe of the Jewish world was indescribable, and the role of gentiles as witnesses, sometimes as co-perpetrators, and above all as those who silently remained at the crime scene could not be discussed.

In the 1980s, the new generation with a "hole in the head" emerged in Polish public life. The writer Tadeusz Konwicki proposed the "hole" metaphor to describe Polish problems with communal memory, including forgetfulness about Jewish, Lithuanian, Belarusian, and other minorities' Polish past.[10] However, political circumstances changed. In 1982, after the imposition of martial law, the authorities were more worried about possible criticism of the current political situation. New films were not supposed to be "anti-party" or anti-Soviet. The decade of the 1980s, sometimes described as the period of mass "internal migration" (escaping into privacy), resulted in the breakdown of the cultural monopoly.[11] A binary division of Polish culture and society into "us" (society and the church) and "them" (the party and government) developed. Still, underneath this division, there emerged more initiatives, practices, and stories alternative to the party or to the "God and Fatherland" martyrology stories rooted in the nineteenth-century Polish imaginary—such as green and pacifist movements or non-Polish origin of Polish citizens. Amid such cultural and political developments, Kawalerowicz obtained permission to film *Austeria* based on the script from the 1960s and to tell the story of a Jewish people.[12]

The political change was not significant enough to protect the film and the director from accusations of anti-Russianness, however. This context was still politically problematic. War is portrayed as a total threat but also mostly unspecified in terms of motives and mechanisms taking place in August 1914. In the film, during a nervous discussion, men from the town notice that wars used to be different. There were battles supervised by generals from the hill, not such chaos. "Enter the town? This is rudeness," says the character Apfelgrun. The idealized vision of military conflicts from previous epochs serves to underline the new character of the Great War and the new focus on civilians, especially Jewish ones. Nevertheless, the inhabitants of the Galician town are afraid of an invasion by Russians—Cossacks, as the film refers to the special military units of the tsarist army. They are enemies of the Austro-Hungarian Empire, and reports of pogroms have preceded them for many years. This threat in the film remains implicit, but the people in the tavern know that the town is on fire, and the Cossacks may burst into the inn at any time. Thus, after the premiere, in March 1983, the Soviet Embassy intervened. Somewhat surprisingly, the diplomatic note issued by the embassy did not affect the distribution of the film.[13]

Still, the anti-Soviet or anti-Russian undertone of the film was not the most crucial issue. The picture of Jewish life was. The director, an important artistic and political figure of the Polish film world, aspired to become the discoverer of the "lost continent" of the Jewish world.[14] One may say that the lost continent of the film was triply lost: the pogrom reality of the Great War is superimposed on the afterimage of the Holocaust. Moreover, in the unspoken memory of the 1980s audience, there also lingered the memory of the 1968 antisemitic campaign.

Kawalerowicz himself had a memory of a shtetl like the one represented in the movie. He was born in 1922 in Gwoździec, a predominantly Jewish-Ukrainian town in independent Poland (nowadays Hvizdets in Ukraine). The famous synagogue there was destroyed by the Germans in the Second World War; its ornate roof was reconstructed in the POLIN Museum of the History of Polish Jews in Warsaw in 2012. Kawalerowicz intended to present visually a prewar Jewish world that was unknown to many viewers in Poland, and that to many was just a picture from childhood. This picture of Jewish (and Ukrainian) lives in Poland was latently present in old photographs, books, newspapers, films, things, buildings, and sometimes oral recollections, and undermined the postwar imaginary of a homogenously Polish past. Kawalerowicz said, "[In Poland] there are still people who remember this lost world, artists who still have the visual shape of the murdered civilization, who still hear the sounds and melodies of those times."[15]

To build this picture, Kawalerowicz reached out to the actors from the Jewish Theater in Warsaw, an institution with a special status in Polish culture because of its mission of supporting Yiddish culture.[16] It was also one of a few cultural organizations (besides several associations and their press titles) that were allowed to function as a proof of the Communist authorities' openness and the diversity of Polish society. These political circumstances and its role as the guardian of memory meant that the Jewish Theater did not focus on the search for new artistic languages but rather upheld a noble conservatism. The transfer of such a manner of acting to the film further strengthens the impression of an antiquated or even strange world. A distinctive Yiddish-inflected Polish pronunciation and the rhetoric of "wise men's disputes" played a role here, along with religious costumes and practices.

The role of the protagonist, Tag, came from a slightly different order. It brought associations from another film featuring Franciszek Pieczka, *Żywot Mateusza* by Witold Leszczyński (*Days of Matthew*, 1968). There Pieczka played a young boy, impaired in communication with the world of people but in harmony with nature and what it transcends. Tag touches the ground more firmly. He is a figure of a wise man who knows his place in the order of creation. On the one hand, he is continuously disputing with God, but he knows that he is too insignificant to offend God. He also recognizes that people update God's rules on earth, so caring for a single person may be more important than a formal ethical principle. After all, he also is a sinful man, at the least because of his debauchery: Jewdocha, the embodiment of unbridled folk sexuality, calls him an old *chort* (devil).

This "earthly" approach is of fundamental importance in the scenes about encounters with real death. The sound of the guns emphasizes the threat; young Asia becomes the first victim of the war, hit by a random bullet in the forest. The thread seems vital for at least three reasons. First, Asia was in love with Bum, who cannot come to terms with her death. Second, her body should rest somewhere before burial, but according to Jewish orthodoxy, the dead body is impure. Tag's decision to put Asia's corpse in his bedroom causes a stir among the Hasidim. There is also no prayer over the body, though this may also be due to the attitude of the girl's family. Above all, however, Tag's response to Asia's death emphasizes his earthly pragmatism. Finally, Asia's body is accidentally set on fire—one more image strikingly anticipating the Holocaust.

In the complex Jewish world, there is a conflict between the rigorous religious order and the human social order. This conflict is erased by its very cause: neither Asia and Bum nor the Hasidim would build a new Jewish future. The war first breaks the foundations and then destroys the entire building. The Jewish world of the film is losing both the future and its traditional ground.

Kawalerowicz's interpretation, however, stretches between the religious world and the earthly desires of most of his characters.[17] Tag's approach and choices, the sensual tension present in many of the film's scenes, confronting the characters with death and eroticism, make the tavern a temporary welcoming stop on earth.[18] The idealized past of the Galician town becomes "heaven."

"Estranged *Austeria*" (Or Crossroads of Interpretations)

The tavern is normal. *Austeria* is funny and estranged.

It is worth emphasizing once again that *Austeria* was the first film in postwar Poland—forty years after the Second World War—that focused entirely on Jewish life in Polish lands. Earlier, Jews appeared as characters in war movies, mostly as Holocaust victims or in episodic roles. *Austeria* hit a sensitive spot.[19] The film received the main award—the Golden Lion—of the Polish Feature Film Festival in Gdańsk in 1984.[20] The reception of the movie was three-dimensional—in the context of its inner structure and style, in the context of the "true" image of Jewish life in prewar Poland, and in the context of 1980s Poland.

The first reviewers (i.e., those who wrote prior to the jury's decision in Gdańsk) mentioned the aura of the masterpiece that surrounded the film from the beginning. *Austeria* was an event already during its production. Of course, the name of Kawalerowicz—Oscar nominee and Cannes awardee—had its significance. The authorities regarded this relatively large and spectacular historical production as presentable and worth publicizing amid the gray reality of Poland under martial law. The reviews, however, were symptomatic. They not only commented on the work itself but also referred to the reaction of the audience. Moreover, in passing, they revealed something essential and usually unspoken about the Polish memory of Jews.

First, the reviewers noticed that the film told the story of the catastrophe and the end of the Jewish world. They read a metaphor of World War II's events hidden in the final scene. There were phrases like "the world that is gone"[21] or "just before the moment of extermination."[22] One critic complained, however, about the quality of the final scene: "After what the

Nazis had done to the Jews, this is indeed a not very revealing metaphor."[23] Significantly, some of the reviews avoided the word *Jew* (there was even one review without any mention of the ethnic character of "micro-society" depicted in the film).[24] Others were strict about naming: "Kawalerowicz's film, regardless of the judgment of its values, is about Jews, and one needs to reflect on it in these categories without seeking escape into the streets of generalizations. Besides, it is the work of a goy (as the director confessed), which also has its meaning."[25]

The appreciative voices for the "fascinating" reconstruction of the Jewish world by Kawalerowicz prevailed, but there were also opposite opinions. One critic stated that the film is a "dead dummy," primarily because its dialogue was in Polish.

Another reviewer wrote, "In this film, only the austeria played a false role, too reminiscent of a mock-up, and by no means an old, noble tavern. Besides, the interior of the tavern was shown as extremely sterile, arranged in the highest order, which is in apparent contradiction to objects of this type and those years. The stage designer probably also forgot what a man traveling a rural cart had to look like, in the scorching sun and clouds of dust."[26]

This opinion weakens in comparison to the action of the film, where, for example, much attention is paid to the sore feet of Blanka. These statements express the tension resulting from expectations of authenticity, on the one hand, and deliberate theatricalization introduced by Kawalerowicz, on the other.[27]

More significantly, sometimes these opinions went hand in hand with the recollection of one's own memories or with the mention of postmemory knowledge passed down in the second generation and thus dependent on the reviewers' imagination. A reviewer of the *Trybuna Ludu* (*People's tribune*), an official journal of the Polish United Workers' Party, wrote in the context of the film and the image of Jewish society represented in it: "The strange habits of side-locked Hymies, the garlic, kosher food, the well-known adage 'your streets, our tenement houses.' I learned all about it well after the war."[28] For the reviewer, the film opened the thread anew, made the audience think about the latent past.

The title of this chapter came from the review "Karczma i austeria" (The Inn and Austeria).[29] Its author compared the film image of Jewish Austeria to the tavern Rzym (Rome) in Sucha Beskidzka, a small town in the mountain region of Poland where vodka, salmon (5 dkg for PLN 170), and *żurek* (sour rye soup) were served. (On the context for the name tavern Rome, see chap. 1.) The sarcastic description of the reality of the late Polish People's Republic also involved some men lying in front of the inn, presumably because of alcohol abuse. These men belonged to the same society that constituted a possible audience of *Austeria*. The film's Jewish inn seemed funny and foreign to them. The viewers' reaction, cited in the review, was an evident confirmation of this "estrangement," as they laughed, or even "croaked," in response to the film. Also, the review obliterated the intuition that the "lost continent" did not mean just the Jewish world but a broader cultural whole in which there still existed (on equal footing) the sacred and the profane.

Importantly, these reactions from viewers were not isolated. Another reviewer wrote that the film "takes over and raises emotions. . . . Even those like in the Palladium cinema. Let them be," he added, revealing that there was something uncomfortable about a loud and sometimes vulgar expression of emotions in the cinema room.[30]

Another critic, Oskar Sobański, develops this issue further in the review "Karczma na polskich rozstajach" (Inn at the Polish crossroads) for the *Film* weekly.[31] He writes from a certain temporal perspective, being cognizant of "the controversy" about *Austeria*—as some reviews called it—that swept through the media. The reviewer refrains from assessing faithfulness of the adaptation to the literary original and the Judaic tradition. He instead situates the world evoked by Kawalerowicz in the broader Polish cultural context—among other things, citing Mickiewicz's *Pan Tadeusz* (also cited here). Such a reading seems closer to the intention of the movie's creators. Sobański writes about the "ritual" reproduced in the film as a common denominator, which also "allows for everything that is the Ruthenian, Lithuanian, Belarusian, Jewish to be equally considered as 'Polish.'"[32]

At the end of his article, the author concludes, "Of course, not everyone feels this heritage, recognizing only the western component of our culture. They see in *Austeria* only a bizarre ethnographic reconstruction of an alien world. And they throw malicious comments into the darkness of the cinema room. By doing so, they demonstrate involuntary surprise and fear of the suddenly revealed, unknown side of their soul."[33]

The image of the lost culture forced *Austeria*'s audience members to confront the forgotten or repressed part of their culture. The film's reception testifies to an awakening of the moods that were soon to come alive fully, both through attempts to reconstruct the lost Jewish world and through the discussions about Polish-Jewish heritage and the Holocaust. From the perspective of the Polish inn of 1983, the Jewish Austeria seems funny. This laughter it provoked is a reaction to what is not only foreign but also disturbing, however. After all, Tag's house is open to every wanderer. The Polish audience of 1980 was cut off from this invitation; it lost its contact with Jewish culture and was consumed by guilt, thus a further estrangement.

IWONA KURZ is Professor at the Institute of Polish Culture at the University of Warsaw. Her main fields of interest include the visual history of European and Polish culture in the nineteenth and twentieth centuries, the visual memory of the Shoah, and the anthropology of body and gender. She is the coauthor of, among others, *Visual Culture in Poland* (in Polish; two volumes), *Displays of Modernity: Exhibitions and the Experience of Modernization Processes in Poland, 1821–1929* (in Polish), and *Traces of Holocaust in the Imaginary of Polish Culture* (in Polish).

NOTES

1. Adam Mickiewicz, *Pan Tadeusz*, book 4, "Diplomacy and the Chase," trans. Bill Johnston (Brooklyn, NY: Archipelago, 2018).

2. The other biblico-historical reference in the dialogue is the comparison of the first day of the war to the Destruction of the Temple.

3. However, the movie does not recall any specific political context. *Austeria* would not allow for the analysis that Yuri Slezkine proposes in his reading of Sholem Aleichem's tales of Tevye the Milkman as the essential story on Jewish choices at the beginning of the twentieth century. See Yuri Slezkine, *The Jewish Century* (Princeton, NJ: Princeton University Press, 2004).

4. Daria Mazur, "Paradoks i topika judajska. *Austeria* Jerzego Kawalerowicza," in *Gefilte film: Wątki żydowskie w kinie*, ed. Joanna Preizner (Kraków: Szolem Alejchem, 2008), 152.

5. Mickiewicz, *Pan Tadeusz*.

6. See Roland Barthes, *Mythologies*, trans. Annette Lavers (New York: Hill and Wang, 1972).

7. The Six-Day War (the June War, the 1967 Arab–Israeli War) was a military conflict fought June 5–10, 1967, between Israel and Egypt, Jordan, Syria, and a broader Arab coalition. As a result of the rapid campaign, Israel had seized the Gaza Strip, the Sinai Peninsula, the West Bank of the Jordan River (including East Jerusalem), and the Golan Heights, significantly increasing its territory. In response, Poland—along with the whole Socialist Bloc that was connected politically and economically with the Arab countries—took a pro-Egyptian position in opposition to Israel, which itself was allied with the United States.

8. See my article on such a case and its 1967 context: "'This Picture Is a Bit Horrifying': The Story of a Film or the Polish Nation Face to Face with the Jew," *Holocaust Studies and Materials* (2010): 422–38.

9. There is a vast and growing literature on the topic, just to recall works by Barbara Engelking, Jan Grabowski, Elżbieta Janicka, Justyna Kowalska-Leder, Jacek Leociak, Tomasz Żukowski, and many more.

10. "A man with a hole in his head" is a character in the novel *Wniebowstąpienie* (*Ascent*, 1967). The concept is developed in many of Konwicki's works and in the film *Jak daleko stąd, jak blisko* (*How Far From Here, How Close*, 1971).

11. Still, in the 1980s, about 1.3 million people left Poland out of lack of hope for political change.

12. Two other films that return to the mythological reality from before the Second World War and try to regain memory of the lost universe of the multicultural Eastern Borderlands, a manor house (*dworek*), and a shtetl, are the adaptations of Czesław Miłosz's *Dolina Issy* (*Issa Valley*) and Tadeusz Konwicki's *Kronika wypadków miłosnych* (*Chronicle of Amorous Accidents*). Konwicki filmed *The Issa Valley* (1982) as a nonfictional, poetic journey into childhood in Lithuania. In turn, Konwicki's *Kronika wypadków miłosnych*, also set in Lithuania just before the outbreak of the war and focused on the experience of adolescence, was made into a film by Andrzej Wajda (1985).

13. See Przemysław Kaniecki, "Z archiwum KC PZPR," in *Adaptacje, adaptacje*, ed. Sławomir Bobowski (Wrocław: Wydawnictwo Uniwersytetu Wrocławskiego, 2009), 203–10.

14. Mazur, "Paradoks i topika," 148.

15. Jerzy Kawalerowicz, "*Austeria* (1982)," in *Więcej niż kino*, ed. Seweryn Kuśmierczyk and Stanisław Zawiśliński (Warsaw: Skorpion, 2001), 75.

16. The theater still operates as The Ester Rachel and Ida Kaminska Jewish Theater of the Center for Yiddish Culture in Warsaw (http://www.teatr-zydowski.art.pl/en). Its director is Gołda Tencer, who played the role of Blanka, the unfaithful wife of a respected burgher in *Austeria*.

17. Michał Boni wrote, among other things, that the film misses internal truth. He argued that the director lacked understanding of the religious dimension as the deepest motivation of the characters' lives and that the movie was too hieratic in the context of the "last day" experience. Michał Boni, "Przed dniem ostatnim," *Kino*, no. 193 (April 1983): 7.

18. Mazur also notices that the river, coming back in three movie scenes, brings associations with criticism, not purity or salvation. Mazur, "Paradoks i topika . . . ," 153.

19. The discussion that took place in Poland after the Nobel Prize in Literature for Isaac Singer in 1978 probably played a certain role in the reception of the movie.

20. Still, some critics found the decision political, too, as they perceived Wajda's *Danton* as the better pretender to the award.

21. Ewa Moskalówna, "Austeria," *Głos Wybrzeża*, February 7, 1983.

22. Bogdan Knichowiecki, "Tuż przed chwilą zagłady," *Trybuna Robotnicza*, March 12, 1983.

23. Tomasz Śrutowski, "Pech Żyda Taga," *Gazeta Olsztyńska*, August 21, 1983.

24. There is one Jewish word in the review: *tsadik*. Moskalówna, "Austeria."

25. Śrutowski, "Pech Żyda Taga."

26. T. G., "Austeria," *Nowiny*, April 26, 1983.

27. The filmmakers certainly did not intend to create a naturalistic image. However, the cleanliness of the tavern may also be attributed to the execution of the Talmudic law ordering to keep clean the body, the interior of the house, and the environment (*Parashat Shoftim*): surround yourself with purity. I owe this comment to Bożena Shallcross.

28. Czesław Dondziłło, "Austeria," *Trybuna Ludu*, May 5, 1983.

29. W. I. K., "Karczma i austeria," *Tak i Nie*, no. 23 (September 1983).

30. Janusz Termer, "Głosy do *Austerii* Kawalerowicza," *Film*, no. 21 (1983): 9.

31. Oskar Sobański, "Karczma na polskich rozstajach," *Film*, no. 22 (1983): 8.

32. Sobański, "Karczma na polskich rozstajach."

33. Sobański, "Karczma na polskich rozstajach."

PART VI
After Nostalgia

10

Serving *Ciulim* in the Polish Countryside

Food and the Construction of a "Polish-Jewish Heritage"

Magdalena Zatorska

THE PHENOMENON OF THE JEWISH inn is strongly embedded in imaginaries of the history of social, cultural, and economic engagements involving Jewish and gentile Poles. Although historians argue that inns created an important and multilayered sphere for contacts between gentiles and Jews, in today's Poland a popularized image of an inn often serves to present an idealized and simplified story about the imagined "Polish-Jewish" past. In *People Love Dead Jews: Reports from a Haunted Present*, Dara Horn sensitizes the reader to the practice of defining and determining Jewish identity through the opinions and projections of others, taking a form of a "distorted public looking glass."[1]

The Jewish inn as a phantasm becomes a point of reference for restaurants serving meals advertised as "Jewish cuisine" in many cities and towns across Poland. For tourists, such "Jewish cuisine," reconstructed and invented by gentiles trying to build a local brand on Jewish history, has become a substitute for experiencing Jewish culture. It works well because cuisine, like folklore, is a safe ground for discussing cultural contacts—similarities and differences can be easily reduced to matters of aesthetics and taste. Then again, both aesthetics and taste are embodied and internalized. The practices accompanying the preparation and consumption of food reveal values, cultural norms, and ways of thinking. They also influence social relations and the collective imagination. By analyzing the tensions between new representations of food and their current cultural significance, we can learn about how collective and individual identities are produced and reproduced, and how they change. As the anthropologist Arjun Appadurai puts it, eating is a "highly condensed social fact."[2] On the one hand, it materializes social interactions; on the other, it cocreates these relations. Food "can serve to indicate and construct social relations characterized by equality, intimacy, or solidarity; or it can serve to sustain relations characterized by rank, distance, or segmentation."[3]

Considering both the context of the typical imaginaries of the past that involved Jews and Christians and the widespread food heritage practices, I would like to show how contemporary food practices—specifically, the local tradition of preparing *ciulim*—reveal the construction and creation of a perceived "Polish-Jewish heritage" in Lelów (Yid. Lelov). The local construction of a "Polish-Jewish heritage" in Lelów is embedded in the dichotomous thinking of two separate identities: Polish, associated with Christianity, and Jewish (in both ethnic and religious understanding). Such a dichotomous optics, widely shared by my interviewees from Lelów and many citizens of Poland, is prone to primordialism, stereotyping, objectification, commoditization, and other forms of violence built on the mechanism of exclusion. The chapter aims to show these mechanics in the Polish countryside's culinary and cultural activities, which, on the one hand, are built on the binarism of simplified images of "Jewishness" and "Polishness" and, on the other hand, are an attempt to find a link between contemporary inhabitants of Lelów (identifying themselves mostly as Polish and Christian) with Hasidic pilgrims who have been visiting the village since the 1980s.

Praxis: Ciulim

Ciulim is traditional local food prepared in Lelów (see fig. 10.1). The dish appears on the Polish list of traditional products under the name of "Lelowian ciulim" (*ciulim lelowski*). Ciulim is made of grated potatoes and pork ribs, with spices such as onion, salt, pepper, and marjoram. The most distinctive feature of the dish, which gives it its specific flavor, is the preparation process. Namely, ciulim is made in a big pot and placed in a bread oven for twelve to twenty-four hours and removed from the oven immediately before consumption.

The majority of Lelowians prepare and serve ciulim on holidays (for example, Easter or Christmas) as well as at special family events. Our interviewees find it completely natural to prepare ciulim when their child comes home after a long absence due to work or studies abroad. Preparing ciulim

Figure 10.1 Ciulim. Photo by Karolina Listoś, née Gmyz, 2015. Photo made during fieldwork of the research team under supervision of the author.

is always associated with a family togetherness—it is a dish served on occasions when the whole family comes home and meets at a common table. Therefore, ciulim is a sign of reinforced family bonds.

Cooking ciulim strengthens and maintains social relationships not only within the family but also within the local community. In the past, ciulim was baked for twelve to twenty-four hours in the bread oven at home. Nowadays, as bread ovens have become uncommon, Lelów inhabitants bring their ciulim to the local bakery, and for a small fee they leave their pots overnight in the bakery's oven. It is common for the inhabitants of Lelów to bring their ciulim to the baker before the most popular holidays, such as Christmas. However, some of Lelów's residents who have a bread oven at home (for example, one of my interlocutors, who is the former president of a local association of amateur historians) invite carefully selected guests to bake ciulim together. Each guest's pot has its place in the hosts' oven, and the very order in which the pots are placed inside the oven reflects the hierarchy and structure of social relationships.

Preparing and eating ciulim is a cultural practice important to local identity. During our fieldwork, we met only one person in Lelów who openly told us she does not like the dish. Lelowians emphasize that the inhabitants of the neighboring villages call them "ciulim-makers" or "ciulim-eaters" (*ciulimiarze*). Ciulim therefore serves as an identity label.

Discourses: Jewish Genealogy of Ciulim and Ciulim-Cholent Day

Jewish Genealogy of Ciulim

What makes ciulim stand out from the array of dishes prepared from grated potatoes in the Polish countryside is its unique genealogy. My interlocutors believe that ciulim derives from cholent (Pol. *czulent*), described as a traditional Jewish dish associated with the Sabbath dinner. One of the Lelów residents describes the origin of ciulim in the following way:

> The Jews were living in the same building with us. They were nice people. And there is a tradition . . . there is the Sabbath. A holiday. It starts at 4 p.m. and lasts till 10 p.m. And it is such an important holiday that you can't work at all; can't do anything. And I was little. And the Jewish woman was at home alone. She came to me; it was dark already, and it was the Sabbath; they can't switch on the light. Can't do anything. Even to switch on the light. And she came to me, and took me, and I had to do it, to switch on the light. And that's why ciulim began. Because it is a Jewish recipe. Because they were making this ciulim in order not to do anything, not even cook food. However, their ciulim was made with goose meat. Because pork isn't kosher. It wasn't kosher. And from them the ciulim derives. And we put in pork, ribs. And ciulim is good, it is.[4]

Ciulim functions therefore as an originally Jewish recipe, cholent, that was adapted by Lelowian women into non-Jewish cuisine. According to my interviewees from Lelów, during the transition, ingredients from the original recipe were substituted or left out: replacing the groats with potatoes or kosher meat with pork, and abandoning beans and huge amounts of garlic, as some Lelowians claim. Although the variety of cholent recipes in Jewish cuisines cover a much wider range of possible ingredients, including potatoes, the "original cholent recipe" reconstructed by my interviewees highlights differences between supposedly original and contemporary versions of the dish and invokes culinary stereotypes—that is, the belief among non-Jews that an excessive use of garlic is typical for Jewish cuisine.[5] The perceived consistent and "codified" recipe for cholent makes it easier to use it as a point of reference when discussing the alleged connection between the two dishes.

What complicates this discussion is the fact that we do not know what cholent looked like in the Jewish homes of Lelów before the Holocaust. We cannot even be sure whether the Jewish genealogy of ciulim claimed by Lelowians reflects the historical emergence of the dish, as the earliest documented mentions of ciulim are from the postwar period and they do not confirm this. This is not unusual for peasant culture, which is only partially documented in written sources, but this does not bring us any closer to knowing the history of the dish.

As a dish made of potatoes and pork, ciulim fits in perfectly with the traditional flavors of gentile Polish cuisine. A casserole made with grated potatoes could be found in many regions throughout Poland, and the most famous of them is *potato babka* (Pol. *babka ziemniaczana*). However, unlike potato babka, ciulim is not a widely recognized dish in Poland. The inhabitants of Lelów claim that its taste, due to the slow baking process, makes it unique. Therefore, on the culinary map of Poland, ciulim serves as one of many examples of local potato dishes, with its own distinctive features recognizable for connoisseurs. In comparison to dishes popularly considered as Jewish in contemporary Poland and as emblematic of Jewish cuisine yet satisfying the conditions of invented traditions (e.g., *gefilte fisz* [gefilte fish], *kugel* [kugel], or *cymes* [tzimmes]), ciulim is neither Jewish nor well known outside Lelów and its region.

The use of pork ribs for ciulim—a choice potentially insulting to Jews, given the purportedly Jewish origins of this dish—is embedded in gentile Polish culinary tradition, in which pork is considered very tasty. It is popular, cheap, and accessible, and it is especially favored in stew-like recipes. The fact that most Lelowians would not think of this as an offensive act shows that connecting Christian and Jewish cultures in Lelów through the narrative of ciulim's Jewish origins raises the question of cultural appropriation. This question becomes more explicit once we delve into the narratives and practices of Ciulim-Cholent Day, an event that is built around ciulim promoted as a "Polish" dish contrasted with supposed "Jewish" cholent.

Ciulim-Cholent Day / *Święto Ciulimu-Czulentu*

Both ciulim and cholent became the main features of a festival that is organized in Lelów in August of every year (see fig. 10.2). The Meeting of Cultures in Lelów—The Ciulim-Cholent Day has been taking place since the early 2000s. Today, the event is built around the two dishes: "the Lelowian ciulim and the Jewish cholent" (the latter expression has been recently replaced by "the Lelowian cholent"). Event participants consume food and drinks sitting at large outdoor tables. The atmosphere resembles one of a family picnic, combining food, music, and entertainment. The festival does not evoke any ideas of Jewish innkeeping either through its program or its marketing. Festival is built around an even more phantasmic concept of a "common table," at which imagined "Polishness and Jewishness" symbolically meet in a form of two dishes sharing a common genealogy. According to the organizers, one of the purposes of the festival is to commemorate the Jewish community of Lelów and the "Polish-Jewish" neighborhood. During the festival, the recently built *ohel* of Rabbi Dovid Biderman (1746–1814, the founder of the Lelów/Lelov Hasidic dynasty; also known as Reb Dovid Lelover) is opened for guided tours as a local "historical monument." For many years, a small Hasidic delegation from the Lelów group would come on the "Jewish Day" (Sunday) of the festival to prepare cholent and distribute it among the participants. While nowadays the visits of the Hasidic guests are limited to a short speech from the festival stage, the research we conducted shows that their presence is interpreted by the organizers and the local authorities as a sign of imagined good "Polish-Jewish" relations in Lelów, both today and in the past.

For my interviewees, religious and national identities are inseparable when discussing ciulim and cholent in Lelów. In their narratives, perceived Polishness is strongly associated with Christianity and differentiated from Jewishness seen as both a national and a religious characteristic. Also, Hasidism is not problematized by many of my interviewees as a distinctive religious practice, and Hasidic religious practices are projected onto Judaism as a whole.[6] Such associations are expressed also in the imagined microcosmos of Lelów societies of the past and present, in which ciulim, as a traditional local dish believed to derive from cholent, is supposed to be the binding element between the Hasidic pilgrims, the exterminated local Jewish community, and current inhabitants of Lelów.

Jerzy Szydłowski, an initiator of this festival and a former head of the village, explains that the main aim of organizing the event was to promote openness and tolerance among local inhabitants toward the Hasidim, who a few years earlier started to visit the tomb of Rabbi Biderman in Lelów. The festival, as an element of the strategy for regional development, was intended to stimulate tourism in Lelów and reinforce the local economy.

Ciulim is strongly present in the local micropolitics of history as local food heritage. It is a constant and widely advertised element of Lelów's image. In the central space of the village (because of its settlement history, the site resembles a market square and is more typical of a market town than a village), newcomers are informed about ciulim and its significance at almost

Figure 10.2 Serving ciulim and cholent during Ciulim-Cholent Day in Lelów. Photo by Jacek Wajszczak, 2015. Reproduced by permission of Jacek Wajszczak.

every turn. We could find information on ciulim on huge banners advertising two local restaurants serving regional cuisine, as well as on the storefront of the local bakery. Moreover, ciulim is served at almost all the ceremonies or galas organized by local authorities and at conferences on local history.

Contexts: The History of Lelów and Hasidic Pilgrimages

Lelów is a village located in Częstochowa County, Silesia Voivodeship, in southern Poland. It is a rural administrative center for nearly twenty villages and settlements. Although the current number of inhabitants in Lelów is about two thousand (or even less, due to migration to bigger towns and cities), it was an important urban center in the past, specifically since becoming a county town in the Kraków Voivodeship in the fourteenth century.

According to the historian Przemysław Zarubin, the first mention of Jews in Lelów dates to the sixteenth century. Although we do not know much about the Jewish population of Lelów at that time, the available information indicates that the Jewish community was initially small (six to eighteen people or families).[7] In the nineteenth century, Lelów had a rabbi and a kahal, which included congregants from twenty-nine villages in the region.[8]

Lelów became a Hasidic center as Rabbi Dovid Biderman developed a following and established a court there. In the mid-nineteenth century, the descendants of Rabbi Biderman moved to the Land of Israel, and thus Lelów Hasidism began to develop communities in cities such as Bnei Brak, Jerusalem, and later New York.[9] The number of Jewish residents in Lelów grew steadily until World War I. In the interwar period, according to data provided by the historian Edyta Gawron, Jews probably constituted about 50–60 percent of the town's population.[10] In 1942, almost all Lelów Jews were murdered in the extermination camp in Treblinka. Available statistics show that a dozen or so Jewish Lelowians survived in Poland.[11]

After World War II, the traces of Lelów Jewish history were systematically removed from the town's public space. Headquarters of the Communal Cooperative were built on top of the Jewish cemetery in the center of Lelów (the so-called Old Jewish Cemetery). The second Jewish cemetery located on the northeastern border of the village (the so-called New Jewish Cemetery) was transformed into a crop field. The synagogue was used as a grain store and later was handed over to the "Galmet" Cooperative for Handicapped Persons.[12]

With the discovery of Rabbi Biderman's tomb under the buildings of the Communal Cooperative in 1988, the Hasidim began their efforts to reclaim the cemetery. The long negotiation process lasted until 2008.[13] For years, the first ohel functioned in the back room of the Communal Cooperative building.[14] After the storehouse was demolished, the cemetery was fenced in and an ohel was built over the tomb of Rabbi Biderman. Nowadays, Lelów is a center of Hasidic pilgrimages, visited by about two hundred to three hundred pilgrims on *yortsayt*, the anniversary of Biderman's death (seventh of Shevat, in January or February of the Gregorian calendar). Smaller groups of pilgrims come to Lelów throughout the year. According to the data gathered by the historian Marcin Wodziński, Hasidic Jews of the Lelów group live in Israel, including the territory of the West Bank (c. 93%) as well as in North America (c. 4%) and Europe (3.6%).[15]

Interpretations: Food and Constructions of a "Polish-Jewish Heritage"

Ciulim as a Mediator

What does it mean that an imagined "Polish-Jewish" coexistence—an imagined "Polish-Jewish" past, but also an imagined "Polish-Jewish" present and future in the context of contemporary Hasidic pilgrimages to

Lelów—is described by a narrative centered on food and performed by collectively preparing and consuming food during the Ciulim-Cholent Day?

As anthropologists Ronda Brulotte and Michael Di Giovine explain in the book *Edible Identities*, "The consumption of food is the practice in commensality; it brings people together . . . it emphasizes in both discourse and practice the aspect of togetherness, of social exchange."[16] This idea of food as an agent that unifies people is reflected in the festival organizers' narrative on the perceived "Polish-Jewish" past and the origins of ciulim. The genealogy of ciulim promoted both by the festival organizers and the residents of Lelów presents an image of a peaceful coexistence of gentiles and Jews in the past, understood as a well-being of these two communities living together. The organizers extensively use descriptors such as "the meeting of the two cultures," "common history of Poles and Jews," "cultural influence," "intermingling," "coexistence," "communities living next to each other, but at the same time—with each other," and so on. The evidence of this "Polish-Jewish" coexistence imagined by my interviewees is the simple dish of ciulim whose name derives from Jewish cholent. This belief is present in the name of the festival, Ciulim-Cholent Day (*Święto Ciulimu-Czulentu*), and the words *ciulim* and *cholent* in this expression are linked by a hyphen, which in the Polish language implicates a strong ontic bond and equality.

As cuisine can both unite and divide people, the narrative on ciulim and cholent is also used to denote cultural differences. Food brings people together, yet it is also "a powerful device for the articulation and negotiation of individual and group identity."[17] What surely attracts tourists to the festival in Lelów is the commodified Jewishness and "Lelówness," sold in the form of food and alcohol. But such commodification works only because it creates and essentializes—in this case—two distinctive ethnicities. As one of my interviewees put it: "You know what? I will tell you the truth. Yes, Ciulim Day . . . ciulim derives from Jews in a way, but it is being made from potatoes. . . . Maybe they [the Jews] made it this way some time ago, but they have their cholent! Their own! These are two separate things! Two separate things!"[18]

The interviewee recognizes the claim of the Jewish origins of ciulim ("ciulim derives from Jews") but immediately undermines this claim by adding "in a way" and explaining such features of ciulim that in her opinion make the dish different from the Jewish version. Interesting dynamics of inner discussion—explicit in the excerpt "Maybe they made it [cholent] this way [with potatoes] some time ago"—shows the need for voicing another important claim: the one of separation between the two cultures.[19]

The dialectics of emphasizing the Jewish roots of ciulim while undermining them could signal the tension between the need to fit in with the public discourse (and political correctness) and the fear of being associated with Jewishness, strongly embedded in the antisemitism in Polish culture. Many locals have little knowledge about Jewish history and the Holocaust, superficial local or family memories of the prewar Jewish community in Lelów (often summarized in a short sentence as "the market square was Jewish") and limited access to the Hasidic community. Considering this, illuminating Jewishness through the origins of ciulim or folklorized difference proves to be insufficient. As the anthropologist Ewa Klekot argues in the context of Polish folklorism, "The folklorized people's culture allows [it] to dominate the dynamics of difference and differentiation: as a policy tool of multiethnic totalitarian states (USSR), and as a commodity on the shelves of a global supermarket of culture. Folklorism hides inequalities, showing them as differences—differences that are harmless, because they are reduced to the level of aesthetics."[20]

The cultural construction of ciulim and cholent in Lelów is a way of performing the imagined interethic and cross-cultural bonds as well as ethnic and cultural differences perceived and practiced by Lelowians. As food heritage, ciulim acts, on the one hand, as a mediator linking gentiles and Jews together and, on the other hand, as a referential touchstone for a group's self-identification that also represents the group to outsiders—both to the Hasidim (visiting the tomb of Rabbi Biderman) and to tourists and guests coming to Ciulim-Cholent Day. Within this framework, Jews are seen as alien; non-Polish; and ethnically, culturally, and religiously distant (which neatly fits within the popular antisemitic topos found in Polish culture).

The festival attracts inhabitants of Lelów and nearby villages as well as guests coming from other localities in the region, drawn in by the music program and culinary offerings. According to the organizers, the festival brings in around five thousand participants, predominantly non-Jewish Poles.[21] For the festival guests, the tasting of ciulim and cholent offered by the local cooks creates an opportunity to experience "the taste of Lelów" that is original and unique to the region. This culinary encounter involves the tasting of a locality packed with discourses of multiculturalism and with the imagined "Polish-Jewish heritage" of the town. Both perceived "Polishness" and "Jewishness" are represented at the festival through food, music, and dance. This simplified and folklorized way of representing communities or cultures constitutes a safe framework for experiencing otherness: the taste of ciulim or cholent, the melody of a song, or the dynamism of a performed dance may not appeal to the guests who experience them, but this does not entail any serious consequences. The use of multiculturalism as a label, which has inspired many other local festivals and similar activities in Poland, nods to the promotion of "unity in diversity" discourse, which is often employed in local development strategies and influenced by national and European identity politics.[22] As the anthropologist Agnieszka Pasieka points out, the tendency toward folklorization of minorities in contemporary Poland is a strategy of sustaining the existing hierarchies and reinforcing social distance and otherness. In this context, ethnic or religious diversity is perceived as attractive and positively valued, but only to the extent that they do not challenge existing hierarchies, as Pasieka demonstrates, drawing on her research in rural Poland.[23]

The organizers of the Lelów festival make sure that the Hasidim are represented on the festival stage every year. Their presence at the festival is an unquestionable attraction for the attendees. The Hasidic delegation draws people from outside Lelów, who want "to see a Jew," as some of the interviewed visitors explained to me. Their curiosity was also a factor in attracting local inhabitants to Rabbi Biderman's ohel during his yortsayt during the early years of the pilgrimage revival in the 1980s and 1990s. As an interviewee from Lelów clarifies, "The beginnings [of pilgrimages] were such that, when they came, then . . . then . . . people would flock here from the villages just to have a look, because those who remembered them from the past times, well, they knew what a Jew looked like, what their prayers looked like and so on, but these younger generations . . . they would come just out of curiosity."[24]

Observing the Hasidim is a practice of visitors who come to Lelów because of their interest in Hasidic pilgrimages. People from outside the village visit the festival not only for this purpose; like some locals, they drop by the ohel during the yortsayt celebrations to see this event. The yortsayt festivities also attract groups of photographers, mostly amateurs, who observe them through their cameras and document the experience according to their artistic visions or projects. Their motivations vary widely, from a deep need to understand Hasidic religious practices in the context of the Holocaust and the imagined "Polish-Jewish" history to a technical focus on the challenges of outdoor photography and a simple desire to experience something exotic without traveling abroad.

Photographs included in albums from the yortsayt in Lelów resemble those from other localities, published on photo blogs maintained by photographers who visited the yortsayt. Although there are projects that stand out (for example, the images captured by the photographer Agnieszka Traczewska that discover the intimate world of Hasidic families), the majority reiterate the most popular themes, such as prayer, dance, and the "revival of the shtetl." This way of perceiving and depicting the Hasidim corresponds to the iconography of controversial souvenirs that are offered by private sellers at the festival market. In addition to souvenirs that incorporate motifs such as the Star of David or a menorah, visitors can select from a wide range of figurines, paintings, and refrigerator magnets that represent Hasidim (see fig. 10.3). Such souvenirs often employ stereotypical imagery that has been recognized by scholars as antisemitic. The anthropologist Joanna Tokarska-Bakir presents an analysis of the image of "a Jew with a coin" used as a symbol of happiness and good luck in Poland. She explains how this phenomenon, interpreted by the author in terms of "return of the repressed" on the one hand and a grotesque on the other, is embedded in Polish culture.[25]

These kinds of artifacts are widely offered throughout Poland in the places where Jewish heritage attracts tourists and constitutes a part of popular imagery, described by Olga Goldberg-Mulkiewicz: "Today, under the influence of both the domestic and tourist market, the figure of the Jew has become conventionalized in its themes and iconography. Sculptors endlessly repeat the same pattern without innovation. Thus the stereotype of the Jew has become monolithic. The most popular forms are a supposedly Hasidic Jew in a prayer shawl, or a group of klezmer musicians."[26]

Although figurines inspired by the image of a Hasid are not an exclusively Polish phenomenon, Poland has a long tradition of carving and selling such artifacts, dating to the church fairs of the nineteenth century.[27] The Lelów festival, organized independently from the Catholic Church, reproduces several functional elements of the popular experience of church fairs with their atmosphere of a joyful and crowded picnic, accompanied by entertainment, food, music, and souvenirs (see a photo of an evening concert taking place during the festival in fig. 10.4).

The Lelów festival constitutes a platform for integrating local inhabitants with one another, an opportunity to spend time with family and neighbors as well as a space for performing "Lelówness" in front of outsiders. The Lelów festival internalizes and plays out the awareness of cultural difference experienced by Lelowians in their contact with the Hasidim. The presentation of cultural difference takes a fossilized form, mediated by the mechanisms of folklorization. As the anthropologists Jean and John Comaroff clarify, the processes of essentialization, objectification, and commoditization are often intertwined and interdependent.[28]

Figure 10.3 Figurines of a Hasid and a Catholic monk offered as souvenirs on a private stall during Ciulim-Cholent Day in Lelów. Photo by Urszula Borkowska, 2015. Photo made during fieldwork of the research team under supervision of the author.

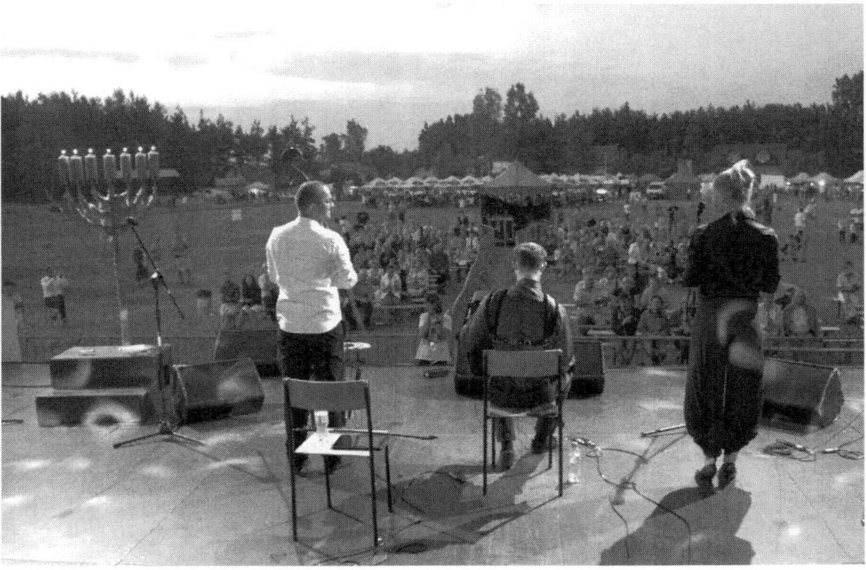

Figure 10.4 Evening concert during Ciulim-Cholent Day in Lelów. Photo by Urszula Borkowska, 2015. Photo made during fieldwork of the research team under supervision of the author.

These fossilized representations of perceived Jewishness and Polishness during the festival constitute only a superficial layer of performing imagined "Polish-Jewish heritage" by the local inhabitants in Lelów. The variety of undertakings, projects, and events organized in Lelów both formally and informally for local and wider audiences incorporate educational, artistic, and scholarly perspectives on the perceived "Polish-Jewish" past and present. The project of translating the texts of Rabbi Dovid Biderman into Polish, finalized in 2018, was initiated by the local activist and teacher Mirosław Skrzypczyk and pursued in cooperation with scholars of Judaic studies. It is an important example of profound work aimed at understanding and performing the perceived "Polish-Jewish" Lelów in a more open and inclusive way.[29] In recent years, there have been attempts to make the Polishness versus Jewishness binary of the festival more complex and multilayered during discussion sessions about films on Jewish or constructed "Polish-Jewish" topics that take place on Friday evening before the festival.

Conclusion

Creating an idealized image of the "Jewish-Polish" past through a narrative about the Jewish roots of non-Jewish regional food in the Polish countryside links gentiles and Jews in the local imaginary. In contrast, the cultural difference described by my interviewees in their interactions with Hasidim coming to Lelów is structured by ethnicity understood as a "process of creating and reproducing classificatory distinctions between in-groups and out-groups by people who perceive themselves as distinct from others."[30] Food mediates this process. For Lelowians, ciulim is a symbol of local identity—food associated with the home, holidays, family, and childhood. As a dish valued for its taste, it might serve as a kind of Lelowian "comfort food" and a local specialty that is served to guests as the flavor of Lelów. Additionally, ciulim carries another connotation. For many residents, it is tangible proof of historic gentile-Jewish cultural contacts in Lelów. This multidimensionality of ciulim inspired the creation of Ciulim-Cholent Day in the early 2000s. The festival celebrates the town, attracting local and regional audiences. It fits into the popular phenomenon of "towns' days"—local festivals built around food and entertainment. Ciulim-Cholent Day has a primarily popular character: for the residents of Lelów and the surrounding area, it is an opportunity to spend time together in a festive environment.

Imagined Jewishness appears at the festival mainly in the form of food (cholent) and klezmer music. Although for some Lelów residents, the festival's Jewish themes are of little or no importance (many of them simply skip the "Jewish day" of the event). But for some of my interviewees, the inclusion of Jewishness in the festival (albeit in such a limited way and using highly folklorized themes and stereotypes) is important. They see it as a step forward in educating the local community, whose knowledge of the history of Jews in Poland is perfunctory and separate from family memory and local history. Ciulim, as a dish grounded in the local identity of gentile Lelowians, establishes an imaginary link between gentile and Jewish cultures through a discourse on the Jewish genealogy of the dish.

The festival's function as a local holiday matches the popularity of towns' days and regional festivals that provide the opportunity for residents to perform their local identity. The manner of using simplified Jewish motifs during the event necessitates the reconsideration of the festival in the context of popular discourses of multiculturalism in Poland. On the local level, the multiculturalism of small towns in Poland is usually demonstrated in a folklorized and simplified way. In this sense, the initiators of the festival imitate a discourse about Jews in Poland that is well-established in local festivals. However, that discourse does not consider Jews at all—it concerns the local, gentile inhabitants' identity and culture; Jewish culture is instrumentalized as an additional cultural resource to distinguish this locality (at least a little) from the others. This approach has specific repercussions on the understanding of the historical inn as a phantasm in the contemporary Polish imaginary. Popular ways of presenting Jewish culture through the phantasmatic inn, incorporating klezmer music and food that is considered traditionally Jewish, materialize the danger hidden in the seeming openness to diversity, discussed by Sławomir Sikora in chapter 11. Referencing writings by Homi Bhabha, Sikora points out that such apparent openness to multiculturalism can be a covert form of domination and can conceal ethnocentric norms and prejudices as universalism, seemingly allowing diversity while making inequality and ethnocentric norms invisible. As Klekot points out, folklorism works in a similar way: because the relations of domination and inequality stay hidden, it provides a "safe" framework for juxtaposing different cultures on the grounds of aesthetics and taste.[31]

Magdalena Zatorska is a social researcher and an ethnographer. She works as a research fellow at the Faculty of Management at the University of Warsaw and simultaneously continues her PhD project at the Institute of Ethnology and Cultural Anthropology at the University of Warsaw.

Her scholarly interests include food studies, methodologies of participatory approaches and qualitative social research, Polish-Jewish-Ukrainian studies, and Hasidic pilgrimages to contemporary Poland and Ukraine. She recently published "The Tombs of the Righteous and Cosmic Energy in Ukraine" in *Etnografia Polska* (2023) and "Christian-Jewish Relations in Antagonistic Tolerance Model: From Religious Communities Towards Communities of Memory" in *Catholic Religious Minorities in Times of Transformation. Comparative Studies of Religious Culture: Poland/Ukraine* (2019).

Notes

This chapter is based on the research conducted as a part of the author's doctoral project and contains excerpts previously published in Polish in texts presenting the fieldwork in Lelów: Magdalena Zatorska, "Wstęp" and "Ciulim lelowski jako lokalne dziedzictwo jedzeniowe," in *Lelowianie, Polacy, Żydzi. Szkice etnograficzne o konstruowaniu lokalnego dziedzictwa*, ed. Magdalena Zatorska (Warsaw: Wydawnictwa Uniwersytetu Warszawskiego, 2018); Magdalena Zatorska, "Ciulim, czulent i konstruowanie polsko-żydowskiego dziedzictwa w Lelowie," in *Lelów: Miejsce, doświadczenie, pamięć*, ed. Mirosław Skrzypczyk (Lelów: Gmina Lelów and Lelowskie Stowarzyszenie Historyczno-Kulturalne im. Walentego Zwierkowskiego, 2016).

1. Dara Horn, *People Love Dead Jews: Reports from a Haunted Present* (New York: W. W. Norton, 2021).

2. Arjun Appadurai, "Gastro-Politics in Hindu South Asia," *American Ethnologist* 8, no. 3 (August 1981): 494.

3. Horn, *People Love Dead Jews*, 507.

4. A woman, ca. ninety years old (name of the interviewee has been anonymized).

5. As Raymond Sokolov argues, thinking of cholent as a dish made with specific ingredients is a misunderstanding. In his opinion, what defines this category of food is religious context: "Cholent is any hot food that satisfies the religious definition of a dish kosher for Shabbat" (see "A Simmering Sabbath Day Stew: The Worldwide Diaspora of a Culinary Concept," *Natural History* 97 [1988]: 88–91). Eric Mason explains that the "worldwide diaspora of cholent" described by Sokolov, understood as a certain culinary idea, is a result of cholent's religious significance (Eric Mason, "Cooking the Books: Jewish Cuisine and the Commodification of Difference," in *Edible Ideologies: Representing Food and Meaning*, ed. Kathleen LeBesco and Peter Naccarato [Albany: State University of New York Press, 2008], 105–25). The religious significance of the Sabbath meal is thus based not on the assumptions about the ingredients used to prepare it (although there are ingredients prohibited by the religious law). What the various versions of cholent have in common is that "all of them [are] hot and buried, cooked while you sleep and pray" (Sokolov, "Simmering Sabbath Day Stew," 91). By using the phrase "hot and buried," Sokolov is referring to the tradition according to which the Sabbath meal is prepared on Friday before sunset, placed in a warm place in a pot with a lid, and uncovered only on Saturday. This practice, according to Sokolov, has its source in the Talmud. On Jewish cookery and identity, see also Barbara Kirshenblatt-Gimblett, "The Kosher Gourmet in the Nineteenth-Century Kitchen: Three Jewish Cookbooks in Historical Perspective," *Journal of Gastronomy* 2, no. 4 (1986–87): 51–87. For a recipe with potatoes, see Claudia Roden, *The Book of Jewish Food: An Odyssey from Samarkand to New York with More than 800 Ashkenazi and Sephardi Recipes* (New York: Alfred A. Knopf, 2013), 146–51.

6. See also note 19, below.

7. Przemysław Zarubin, "Żydzi lelowscy w dobie staropolskiej," in *Żydzi lelowscy. Obecność i ślady*, ed. Michał Galas and Mirosław Skrzypczyk (Kraków: Wydawnictwo Austeria, 2006), 13.

8. Edyta Gawron, "Lelowscy Żydzi w XIX i XX wieku," in *Żydzi lelowscy. Obecność i ślady*, ed. Michał Galas and Mirosław Skrzypczyk (Kraków: Wydawnictwo Austeria, 2006), 29.

9. Gawron, "Lelowscy Żydzi w XIX i XX wieku," 35.

10. Gawron, "Lelowscy Żydzi w XIX i XX wieku," 30.

11. Gawron, "Lelowscy Żydzi w XIX i XX wieku," 37.

12. Mirosław Skrzypczyk, "Der kfices ha-derech—pielgrzymki chasydów do Lelowa," in *Wieża Dawida. Chasydzi lelowscy*, ed. Michał Galas and Mirosław Skrzypczyk (Kraków: Wydawnictwo Austeria, 2018), 45–46; Anna Walczyk, "Pamięć i upamiętnienie Żydów w Lelowie," in *Żydzi lelowscy. Obecność i ślady*, ed. Michał Galas and Mirosław Skrzypczyk (Kraków: Wydawnictwo Austeria, 2006), 80–83.

13. Skrzypczyk, "Der kfices ha-derech," 47–51.

14. Galas and Skrzypczyk, *Wieża Dawida*, 70; Walczyk, "Pamięć i upamiętnienie Żydów w Lelowie," 82.

15. Marcin Wodziński, *Historical Atlas of Hasidism* (Princeton, NJ: Princeton University Press, 2018), 198.

16. Michael A. Di Giovine and Ronda L. Brulotte, "Introduction: Food and Foodways as Cultural Heritage," in *Edible Identities: Food as Cultural Heritage*, ed. Ronda L. Brulotte and Michael A. Di Giovine (New York: Routledge, 2014), 16.

17. Di Giovine and Brulotte, "Food and Foodways," 5.

18. Woman, ca. forty-five years old (name of the interviewee has been anonymized).

19. When talking about Jews, the interviewee, as with the majority of Lelowians, refers to both Jews and Hasidim coming to Lelów. It does not necessarily mean that Lelowians do not differentiate between Hasidim and other Jews, but in the everyday discourse on Hasidim, both terms are used interchangeably, with the prevalence of "Jews."

20. Ewa Klekot, "Samofolkloryzacja. Współczesna sztuka ludowa z perspektywy krytyki postkolonialnej," *Kultura współczesna* 1 (2014): 98.

21. During the fieldwork in Lelów from 2014 to 2016, I met one family at the festival that identified themselves as Jews.

22. Joanna Kurczewska and Hanna Bojar, *Wyciskanie brukselki. O europeizacji społeczności lokalnych na pograniczach* (Warsaw: IFiS PAN, 2009).

23. Agnieszka Pasieka, *Hierarchy and Pluralism: Living Religious Difference in Catholic Poland* (New York: Palgrave Macmillan, 2015), 211–18.

24. Man, ca. fifty years old (name of the interviewee has been anonymized).

25. Joanna Tokarska-Bakir, "Żyd z pieniążkiem," in *PL: Tożsamość wyobrażona*, ed. Joanna Tokarska-Bakir (Warsaw: Wydawnictwo Czarna Owca, 2013), 8–31.

26. Olga Goldberg-Mulkiewicz, "The Changing Stereotype of the 'Other': The Jewish Figurine on the Polish Market," in *Na szczęście to Żyd. Polskie figurki Żydów / Lucky Jews: Poland's Jewish Figurines*, ed. Erica Lehrer (Kraków: Korporacja Ha!art, 2014), 215–16.

27. Shifra Epstein, "Imaging Hasidim in Wood and PVC: Hasidic Figurines Made Today in Poland, Ukraine and Israel," *Zutot* 6 (2009): 129–38.

28. Jean Comaroff and John L. Comaroff, *Ethnicity Inc.* (Chicago: University of Chicago Press, 2011): 22–59.

29. Skrzypczyk, "Der kfices ha-derech."

30. Di Giovine and Brulotte, "Food and Foodways," 3.

31. Klekot, "Samofolkloryzacja," 98.

11

Jewish Tavern, Jewish Places

Beyond Nostalgia

Sławomir Sikora

Translated by Aleksandra Rodzińska-Chojnowska

BRUNO SCHULZ, THE POLISH-JEWISH MAN of letters, an undisputed master of the Polish language, observed in his essay "Mythologization of Reality" (1936) that the myth is to be found in "elements as such." It is worth emphasizing that the very word *myth* used by Schulz possesses a strong ontological merit: it is more a synonym of "true reality" than of something false or artificial.[1] It is thus also close to the way in which the classics of contemporary anthropology envisage the myth.[2] Edmund Leach defined it as a true and significant story for those who tell it as well as those who listen to it.[3] This definition is both extensive and precise, but, above all, open. "Myth" would, therefore, signify "truth" and authenticity, the concept to be discussed further on. I would, however, like to additionally stress the word *elements*. This "past reality" does not exist and cannot exist in the form it possessed earlier, in its unchangeability, because of a radical break with tradition—probably in particular in Central and Eastern Europe and Poland itself due to the events that transpired here not only during World War II, but also during its aftermath. The consequence of those occurrences and the post-Shoah period is the residual presence of Jews in contemporary Poland.

One cannot envisage present-day taverns, pubs, and restaurants, which in various forms demonstrate their Jewishness, as a direct continuation of the "Jewish inn." The reason lies in their decidedly dissimilar social context: as a rule, not only the operators (i.e., lessees, owners, or managers—at least in Poland) but also the recipients—guests and habitués—are mostly different. "Jewish inn" is therefore treated here primarily as a metaphor and symbol for a new "Jewish space." Naturally, sometimes certain continuities can be traced, but they are not a rule. The phenomenon of the "Jewish inn," most often an inn leased by Jews, was very popular and hardly had a strictly standardized form, for it changed over time. It was strongly associated with the rural economy,[4] and the regulars were mainly (though, of course, not only) "locals," unless it was located by a tract. The anthropologist Kacper Pobłocki writes that inns often also served as shops (and a place of exchange).[5] The ethnographer and linguist Jan S. Bystroń, who writes of an inn, not necessarily a "Jewish inn," notes that there was often hardly anything to eat there, and travelers often carried provisions with them.[6] The ethnographer Józef Burszta also describes the "games" that the nobility sometimes arranged for themselves by getting the peasants drunk and observing their behavior.[7] Thus, the inn was a special "institution" in the countryside, and over time it also became mainly a place for the consumption of alcohol.[8] The "Jewish inn" was therefore not "Jewish" in the sense of serving kosher food and aimed at Jews only. It was a multiclass meeting place, although the different groups did not necessarily interact with one another. In this respect, I think it is difficult to speak of direct continuity here. I treat the revival and popularity, taking place not only in Poland, of the "Jewish tavern" as a step made by various actors, both Jews and non-Jews, toward the revival of Jewish culture, as the creation of a new Jewish place, aimed not only at Jews. I therefore treat it as a symbolic place; hence, I talk about Kazimierz (the Jewish district in Kraków) rather than individual premises. As a place directed toward the future (Diana Pinto, Erica Lehrer—see also below), and not just the past, which nevertheless often "plays" with "elements" (Schulz).[9] Taverns, restaurants, cafés, and pubs are places not so much of reconstruction of a certain past reality but rather of construction, places that give "signs" constructed of elements, symbolically and metaphorically making contact with the past. And these signs of Jewishness include both food (sometimes only nominally, through names of the dishes) and elements of decoration, names, and signboards. This does not alter the fact that the contemporary renascence of the Jewish inn can be recognized as an interesting and engrossing phenomenon.[10]

One of the most obvious associations with the phenomenon of the contemporary Jewish inn was and continues to be Kazimierz, described by Ruth Gruber as follows:

> The Kazimierz district, meanwhile, had evolved from being a desolate Jewish graveyard to a popular tourist and nightlife venue centered on what is the most extensive and important complex of Jewish sites in central Europe: synagogues, cemeteries, homes, marketplaces, and other buildings and monuments, almost all of which had been abandoned or in ruinous condition in 1990. Today's Jewish Kazimierz is built on this architectural skeleton, but—with its dozens of Jewish-style and other cafés, pubs, and clubs, its boutiques, its galleries, its restored synagogues, its constant tour groups—it bears little resemblance to the teeming district it was before World War II, when it was home to about sixty-five thousand Jews.[11]

Kazimierz is a district that, after World War II, succumbed to degradation; subsequently, for the past thirty years, it has undergone a sui generis renascence and revitalization: a gentrification associated with a return and references to Jewish culture or, more widely, with a certain attitude toward artistic and cultural life, as well as toward tourism (see figs. 11.1, 11.2, and 11.3). In this case, it is possible to speak of a specific cultural gentrification. The first Jewish Culture Festival took place here nearly forty years ago (1988). Obviously, restaurants, cafés, and bars referring to Jewishness can be encountered in many larger Polish towns and not only in Kazimierz.[12] Examples mentioned by Gruber concerned Poland and Central and Eastern Europe, while Agata Maksimowska wrote about Birobidzhan in the far east of Russia, Shelley Salamensky wrote about Birobidzhan, Poland, and Spain, and Erica Lehrer about Kazimierz.[13] The problem lies in the fact that the "genuine" Jewishness of those places is—often quite correctly—questioned. It is precisely Gruber, author of the significant *Virtually Jewish: Reinventing Jewish Culture in Europe* (2006), who can be recognized as one of the precursors of studies dealing with "Jewish places" in Poland and Europe. The titular term "virtually Jewish" was subsequently applied also by other authors, such as Lehrer, Murzyn-Kupisz, and Annamaria Orla-Bukowska.[14]

One may presume that the sentence cited at the beginning of this essay—that myth is to be found in elements as such—became even more topical after the war precisely due to the Holocaust and the disappearance of almost the entire prewar Jewish population, together with its culture. It is worth noting that Schulz's assertion—"the myth (that is, as I suggested earlier, true reality) is to be found in elements as such"—interestingly corresponds to concepts devised by Pierre Nora, author of "memory sites" (*lieux de mémoire*). Today, we speak so much about memory—Nora maintained—because it is absent. "If we were able to live within memory, we would not have needed to consecrate *lieux de mémoire* in its name. Each

Figure 11.1 Hamsa restobar, Kazimierz district in Kraków, 2018. Photo by the author.

gesture, down to the most everyday, would be experienced as the *ritual repetition of a timeless practice* in a primordial identification of act and meaning. With the appearance of the trace, of mediation, of distance, we are not in the realm of true memory but of history."[15] This "primordial" memory—in a somewhat idealized view of Nora—was alive (connected with life), repeated and practiced almost unreflectively. On the other hand, history intensely introduces an element of mediation but is also connected with the depersonalization of narration. "These *lieux de mémoire* are fundamentally *remains*, the ultimate embodiments of a memorial consciousness that has barely survived in a historical age that calls out for memory because it has abandoned it."[16] Nora proposed an expansive comprehension of memory places: starting with actual places (where, e.g., something worth remembering has happened) to firmly *constructed* and symbolic ones, such as museums. They could be places associated both with material and intangible heritage—*topoi*, that is, stratified places and themes, sometimes spreading in the manner of rhizomes.[17] Nora's project includes such entries as the "14th of July," "Joan of Arc," "the Marseillaise," and the "Battle of Verdun." These are symbolic places important for French history, and often important places and communal reference points for the history of the nation. Such a symbolic site is something often particular, which also has references to more general ideas. Sites of memory are a measure invented (devised) to counteract the fact that "environments of memory" (*milieux de mémoire*) have disintegrated.[18] A *milieu de mémoire* could be thus recognized as close to the somewhat dated term "collective memory" (*mémoire collective*) or "collective memory framework." According to Maurice Halbwachs, author of the latter concept, we remember thanks to the societies (communities) in which we live and which guarantee and supply the individual with memory frameworks and allow certain conceits to come into being and survive.[19] In an era of television and media, including those known as "social," this term must be reconsidered; nonetheless, it remains relevant. It could be said that the media grant a structure to and transform our cosmos in a transparent way.[20] The phenomenon of the Jewish inn, and precisely this book, I believe, can also be treated as a site of memory, created of efforts to reconstruct and interpret the history but also the contemporary layering and readings of this subject. (Virtually all chapters in this book are relevant here; see especially the chapters by Goldberg, Kurz, Lindskog, Rose, Shallcross, and Zatorska.)

This (former) environment of memory (*milieu de mémoire*) no longer exists in the Kazimierz district.[21] Both Gruber and Lehrer cited examples of gentile Poles (but not only those) who have engaged their emotions and strength in the re-creation (and creation) of the Jewish world. The two authors also highlighted that the initiators of the Jewish Culture Festival and those of other undertakings connected with Jewish culture and its promotion often have included non-Jews. This is a good example of creating precisely a "site of memory," in its metaphorical meaning, that is more performative than discursive.[22] The question is whether a "site of memory" can in time produce new "communities of memory" obviously already different from the original one?[23] This by no means rhetorical question is posed also in an interview held by Marek Bartosik with Janusz Makuch, director and initiator of the Jewish Culture Festival (2012):

> JM: Everyday Jewish life has returned to Kazimierz. [. . .]
>
> MB: What manifestations of this life do you observe?
>
> JM: Let's see . . . the Jewish community, functioning synagogues concentrating the Orthodox religious current, and the Jewish Community Centre in Miodowa Street, which attracts already more than three hundred young people proclaiming their Jewish roots. The Centre offers multiple opportunities for intensifying this affiliation. For years the Galicia Jewish Museum has been focusing on

Figure 11.2 Retro-style shops, Kazimierz district in Kraków, 2018. Photo by the author.

Figure 11.3 Jewish-style shop, Kazimierz district in Kraków, 2018. Photo by the author.

Reform Judaism. Then there is the Austeria Publishing House, the Stradom Dialogue Centre, and the Jewish Cultural Centre.

MB: These examples demonstrate that Kazimierz is a meeting place of local Jews. But is it also the site of their daily life?

JM: It varies. Some live here, while others reside in the city centre—just like before the war. Ostensibly, not much has changed with the exception of statistics describing the size of the Jewish community. There are two open synagogues (a third one is undergoing renovation) and two ritual bath houses—arranged not "with tourists in mind" but from the viewpoint of the daily life requirements of the Jews of Kraków and Kazimierz. Children living here attend a Jewish kindergarten, and there is even a theatre! You might say that this not the same as during the pre-war period. . . . What do you expect—a miracle?[24]

This attempt at transcending the aura of nostalgia is worth remembering. I would supplement this statement by Makuch and suggest that though different—Jewish and gentile—communities of memory are probably closest to one another in joint entertainment, practice, and engagement, nevertheless they should not be automatically equated. I agree with Diana Pinto that they should remain in dialogue and communication.

Memory, heritage, identity, and nostalgia are terms associated predominantly with the past. Jean-Claude Kaufmann wrote *expressis verbis* that identity is a "strange . . . and . . . annoying" concept. "The more one seeks to describe it with precision, the less, generally, one succeeds." Further on, he added that the fundamental error consists of the fact that we believe "that identity deals with history, our memory, and our roots. In fact, it is exactly the opposite." Identity is connected instead with the "production of meaning."[25] This is a strong and radical statement. It is worth, however, stressing that Kaufmann was by no means alone—recall the opinion of such a prominent author as Anthony Giddens.[26] "Identity is a project . . . a concept focused on the future."[27] It is worth mentioning that it is also built upon the basis of elements of the past, to evoke once again Schulz's essay. Even if we acknowledge that contemporary reality is a cultural supermarket,[28] in other words, connected with the situation of choosing one of many permissible diverse options, it is possible to say that we tend to select certain opinions/solutions/proposals and bypass others. Obviously, importance must be attached also to the sort of solutions we choose.[29] I use the plural for the sake of simplification, for it conceals the possibility of selecting assorted options.

The same emphasis on the future holds true for heritage, which Barbara Kirshenblatt-Gimblett defined as a "mode of cultural production that *produces something new*," while facing the threat of suffering a loss.[30] Sharon

Macdonald, another scholar dealing with heritage, wrote in the same spirit while simultaneously emphasizing the situation of making a choice: "Through heritage, selected memories are *inscribed* into public space"[31] and "that heritage turns the past into something visitable."[32] In both instances, tension between the past and the future (or the present) becomes clearly outlined. It is worth restating that inscribing (locating) heritage in space makes it visitable. After all, the same takes place in the case of memory linked with the materialization of the past in the present not only in the Proustian project. Heritage is not solely a contemporary manner of shaping identity and brand[33] but also a partially successful engagement with memory—in the case of Kazimierz and other former Jewish towns or districts in Poland, a memory greatly traumatic. Both Gruber and Lehrer wrote that for Jews visiting Poland, Kazimierz (Kraków) can be a short stopover on the way to the main destination—Auschwitz.[34]

As far as nostalgia is concerned, it was diagnosed as a disease by a Swiss doctor as early as the seventeenth century. In our times, however, it has transformed from a type of disease into an epochal syndrome. Svetlana Boym, one of the major researchers of various forms of nostalgia, noted, "The twentieth century began with a futuristic utopia and ended with nostalgia."[35] Boym distinguished two types of nostalgia, though they are far from ideal types, and the line between them seems blurred and porous: restorative nostalgia and reflective nostalgia. The former is closer to "a return to the original stasis." "The past for the restorative nostalgia is a value for the present; the past is not a duration but a perfect snapshot."[36] This is rather, she posited, a rebuilding of home and a return to it.[37] The latter, reflective nostalgia, seems more flexible, simultaneously meditative and reflective. Beyond longing, it emphasizes thinking, possible change, and transformation. It is, Boym asserted, "aware of the gap between identity and resemblance; the home is in ruins or, on the contrary, has been just renovated and gentrified beyond recognition. This defamiliarization and sense of distance drives them to tell their story, to narrate the *relationship between past, present and future*." This narration is "ironic, inconclusive and *fragmentary*." While restorative nostalgia spatializes time, the reflective nostalgia temporalizes space.[38]

While describing wartime New York City, Claude Lévi-Strauss drew attention to its multicultural nature and a simultaneous far-reaching disjunction of ethnic-cultural districts: Italian, Jewish, Polish, and Puerto Rican. New York City, he noticed, resembled Swiss cheese full of holes and enclaves, which did not necessarily maintain contact or communicate with one another.[39] In certain respects, such a vision of a town and districts does not veer from the one outlined by Pierre Mayol, who, while portraying a traditional working-class district of Lyon,[40] defined it as an area whose residents were essentially not compelled to leave because here they found everything indispensable for daily life; therefore, the district was, so to speak, a "self-sustainable organism." One could say that those somewhat "idealized" districts of the past were also *milieux de mémoire* as understood by Nora. Obviously, since then the cities and their quarters have undergone several essential changes. By way of example, Sharon Zukin described the significant transformations of Brooklyn during the pre–World War II period and particularly in its wake. These changes were sufficiently essential and holistic, and pertained to such a considerable extent to the so-called living tissue (from a working-class district, Brooklyn turned into an artists' quarter), for the researcher to regard the term *gentrification* as inadequate and lacking.[41] In this case, districts cease being enclosed "exotic enclaves." In Paris, the traditionally Jewish Le Marais quarter became also a gay neighborhood. Some changes and transformations taking place within a town and districts are both natural and normal.

Normal, but certainly not in all cases. Let us return to the example of Kazimierz as well as many other predominantly Jewish city quarters, small towns, and locations all over Poland. The example of Kazimierz is especially challenging considering that as a result of wartime and postwar history, almost of all its former residents vanished. We are thus dealing not so much with evolution as with dramatic severance. Here, the requirement of widely comprehended commemoration and remembrance carries a strong ethical component: one cannot disremember. Oblivion could be seen as a continuation of the evil that had taken place. Hence the extremely vivid element of nostalgia in numerous texts about Kazimierz and similar places.[42]

I mentioned above that for some time Kazimierz has been undergoing a renascence. Apart from the Jewish Culture Festival, it has witnessed the emergence of several restaurants and venues, which in assorted ways refer to Jewish culture, names, elements of interior design, music, and served dishes. Wojciech Ornat, the owner of the first café (Klezmer Hois), declared that he opened it "to counteract . . . the quarter's emptiness and sadness" (see fig. 11.4). The Ariel restaurant-café, established in 1990, "became the centre of all non-ceremonial Jewish activity in Kraków" (fig. 11.5).[43] The "genuine" Jewishness of numerous sites—as was mentioned earlier—is, however, questioned upon various occasions. Gruber recalled numerous examples of "fake" Jewishness: interior design, cuisine (names of dishes), the pseudo-Hasidic costume worn by a waiter in one of the Łódź restaurants.[44] She also cited the comical example of the "U Fryzjera" restaurant menu in Kazimierz Dolny on the Vistula, which alongside Jewish and non-Jewish dishes included the category of "non-Jewish, non-kosher, yet also recommended" ones.[45] Obviously, authenticity and its legitimization constitute an important motif apparent in the reflections of both earlier mentioned as well as nonmentioned authors. It is important to note that Jewishness often appears precisely in the elements that refer to a certain remembered but also often imagined whole that in some cases is not free of stereotyped Jewishness.[46]

We often think about authenticity as if it concerned an object that is not authentic, original, and genuine. For some time, the question of authenticity has been a significant topic of scholarly reflection due to, for example, research dealing with tourism, museums, historical reconstructions, and, obviously, heritage.[47] It is worth noticing that a certain essential shift has appeared: authenticity often has been understood in relative (subject–object) categories, and performativity and experience has been emphasized. Authenticity is "something which people can *do* and a feeling which is *experienced*. In this sense, authenticity is performed."[48] Such a subjective and relational treatment of authenticity permits a focus on the attitude, wishes, emotions, and affects of the interested subjects. It also makes it feasible to place stronger emphasis on assorted perspectives, including those within the range of what is customarily known in anthropology as the emic approach (i.e., from the viewpoint of social actors). Such a vantage point proved to be extremely essential in, for example, studies on historical reconstructions.[49] It also reveals different perspectives in reference to almost identical questions. A distant yet evocative example is the question of Holocaust monuments. Here, the intellectual historian Frank Ankersmit's interpretations of attitudes toward memory and monuments founded at Yad Vashem are thought-provoking.

Ankersmit drew attention to the multiplicity and diversity of remembrance and commemoration as well as the *nonhierarchic character* of such memory space. For the sake of his analysis, he selected two monuments from Yad Vashem: the Hall of Remembrance and the Children's Memorial.[50] In the Hall of Remembrance, on the ground level of the floor, there are engraved names (in Hebrew and national languages) of the sites of concentration camps set up by Nazis during World War II: the majority were located in the prewar Polish territory. The second monument is a more complex construction; one of its main elements is a showroom

Figure 11.4 Klezmer-Hois restaurant, Kazimierz district in Kraków, 2018. Photo by the author.

Figure 11.5 Ariel restaurant, Kazimierz district in Kraków, 2018. Photo by the author.

(an octagonal corridor encircling an octagonal central pillar), in which the flames of five memorial candles (*ner neshama*) are reflected and multiplied in mirrors behind Plexiglas covering both sides of the corridor, thus creating galaxies of stars, each of them symbolizing the soul of one of the children. Certain critics of the memorial described it as an example of kitsch. Kitsch is sometimes defined as an aesthetic phenomenon combined with an attempt at manipulating emotions or, more exactly, as a confusion of the order of ethics with aesthetics; this is the way it had been defined by the Austrian writer Hermann Broch.[51] Ankersmit embarked on an attempt at defending the idea of the monument: the first memorial, he argued, appeals predominantly to Holocaust survivors and those—one could add—connected with this event emotionally or through postmemory—to all those aware of the nature of the Holocaust. This is a space of reflections and contemplation, of discovering certain tropes in one's interior, thoughts, and emotions. The second monument, Ankersmit maintained, attracts rather those—and it must be added that they comprise a constantly growing group—who do not possess personal knowledge and know little about the nature of death camps and the Holocaust. In this case, the memorial appears to be trying to manipulate feelings, to "produce (create) them"; it does so—Ankersmit noticed—because it attempts to address visitors who, so to speak, "do not possess their own emotions" associated with this event from the past. This is an attempt at producing and stirring emotions, at creating an emotional link with the contemplated images, and at setting imagination into motion. Kitsch, as understood by Broch, is inauthentic art based on inauthentic emotions or, rather—as long as *our emotions are authentic* by their very nature precisely because they are ours—it is an attempt at manipulating emotions and imposing them on us; once again there emerges the question of a difference of perspectives. It is worth recalling that traumatic memory is the sort of memory that does not succumb to change, or does so with considerable resistance, and does not allow a reconstruction of the images and narratives constituting it. For this reason, it is very difficult to replace it with other (not one's own) emotions of the sort that could produce the impression of being inauthentic. This is exactly what the abovementioned Children's Memorial tries to do. For this reason, it is likely to give rise to critical opinions and evoke resistance from persons familiar from personal experience with the depicted reality, as if someone tried to replace his or her emotions with those of other people.[52] From this viewpoint, the second monument may be understood as kitsch. Nonetheless, if the Children's Memorial fulfills its task, and produces among some visitors emotions that become the emotions of concrete individuals, then those emotions should be regarded as authentic because such monuments simply appeal to different groups of people.

I believe that the two examples analyzed by Ankersmit indicate a departure from "objective," object-directed authenticity; in both cases, we are dealing with sui generis staging, although one of the memorials (the Hall of Remembrance) is based on "existing" knowledge: the names produce among the visitors a resonance and are synergistically linked with existing memory and emotions, while the second monument, in a manner of speaking, evokes (or rather produces) emotions as a "new experience." In both instances, we are dealing with different relations. Corporeality, emotions, and affects appear to be equally essential.

The examples analyzed by Ankersmit are particularly interesting since they demonstrate assorted approaches and ways of understanding the term *authenticity*. Nonetheless, they also firmly suggest that it is our emotions and affects more than our intellect that allow us to experience reality as authentic. After all, Nigel Thrift—one of the promoters of the nonrepresentative theory—called affectiveness a type of thinking.[53] Transferring these considerations back to the inn and Kazimierz (Kazimierz as a synecdoche for a contemporary inn as a meeting place), it can be argued that its different parts (the different restaurants and inns located there) are addressed to different customers (different visitors and tourists), and that in the emerging diversity there is a potential and an invigorating force. The move away from treating the category of kitsch as a (purely) aesthetic phenomenon brings it closer to the approach of Michael Meng, who in his book *Shattered Spaces* wrote: "Rather than arguing that tourism and nostalgia have simply produced kitschy, inauthentic spaces, I unearth the deeper political and cultural meanings of restoring the Jewish past in the urban environment."[54] Again, we are close to destroyed *milieux de mémoire* and the notion "*elements* of reality" as conceived by Schulz. Under the cloak of kitsch hide the "deeper political and cultural meanings of restoring the Jewish past." One can presume that the category of kitsch can be understood similarly in Ankersmit's approach to memory and the Children's Monument. Here, too, political and cultural meanings can be seen under the cloak of (produced) emotion.

Although the described "authenticities" differ, they should not be placed on an authentic–inauthentic axis (an "objective approach"), but one should rather speak about different kinds of authenticity: one directed toward the interior and the past (the retrospective turnabout) and a second, more prospective authenticity. In the latter case, we could speak about authenticity (but also identity) produced anew or conceived as a project albeit, obviously, also with references to the past. While discussing the question of the return of Jewish culture, Janusz Makuch implied in the earlier cited interview that we should not expect a miracle—that is, should not anticipate that the world that perished more than seventy years ago will be resurrected. Further on, Makuch noticed

> the festival became a *catalyst of an awareness* of that which Kazimierz was and is for Jews and Poles. . . . The festival changes endlessly! Kazimierz does not determine its shape. After many years it became apparent that its capacious and flexible formula makes it possible to reflect and, at the same time, concentrate phenomena, which according to our arbitrary conviction are most essential in contemporary Jewish culture. We never reduced this culture to the image of a fiddler playing on a roof, but showed, and continue to do so, the directions in which it develops. I assume that the festival program influences people's image of Kazimierz which, *after all, before the war was culturally pluralistic. This site is not so much a cemetery but a space of reborn life*. And it is in this sense that the festival tells the truth about Jewish life both here and all over the world.[55]

And if it nurtures nostalgia, it is closer to the reflective type.

A space of "reborn life," in reference to Homi Bhabha, is also a "third space."[56] Bhabha described it as a space of hybrid cultural practices. One could thus assume that this is a space devoted (dedicated) to multiculturalism. According to Bhabha, culture always possesses a spatial dimension. Since the original *milieu de mémoire* is no longer present—the space of Kazimierz became not so much a residential quarter but a tourist district (attraction)—it is difficult to speak in this case about authenticity comprehended as "auratic" (with clear reference to Benjamin's comprehension of the original).[57] As I have endeavored to present it, authenticity (with regard to the space of Yad Vashem) is connected more with (concrete) people than objects: with relations and practices. Those relations—we now return to Kazimierz—can vary depending on how often we deal with tourists. Bhabha preferred to speak about difference and not diversity, about hybridity and not multiculturalism. He treated the third space as that of openness directed toward the future.[58] This is perhaps how we should consider the space of Kazimierz and Jewish inns, if we were to transcend the climate of nostalgia. Neighborhoods, as described by Lévi-Strauss, have mostly gone, but there are also those like Kazimierz that, because of their history, require special care and attention. Therefore, I have paid attention to the future—the future as a project—in relation to identity, memory, and heritage. Beyond sites preserved from the past—that is, synagogues or cemeteries—there remain new places, sometimes based on a creative approach to the past, sometimes originating in a stereotype, that are *playing with elements* and occasionally attempting to produce (successfully or unsuccessfully) a "new authenticity"[59] addressed to assorted recipients. Cafés and inns are important elements of this space, as long as they *ex definitione* refer to corporeal presence and a person as a whole . . . as long as they provide food but also become food for thought.

It is difficult to "build" a genuine Jewish space without Jews. I believe, however, that the creation of an open space of diversity or, as Bhabha would say, hybridity ("third space") permits the emergence not only of a Jewish space but also of a Jewish-Jewish space.[60] This is why I treat this space of assorted bars and cafés, which *play with diverse elements* (even if often fictitious and artificial), as essentially positive; without such a backdrop, "truly authentic" elements (optimally: *milieux de mémoire*) that appeal to and are accepted by the Jews themselves would have a smaller chance to emerge. No doubt, the latter elements cannot be created by the gentiles. To avoid succumbing to excessive optimism, it is worth keeping in mind a certain danger—Bhabha, too, was aware of it—hidden in ostensible openness toward diversity and multiculturality. It could conceal ethnocentric norms and prejudices and be a hidden form of domination. "A transparent norm is constituted, a norm given by the host society or dominant culture, which says that 'these other cultures are fine, but we must be able to locate them within our own grid.' . . . This is because the *universalism that paradoxically permits diversity masks ethnocentric norms, values and interests.*"[61]

SŁAWOMIR SIKORA is an assistant professor at the Institute of Ethnology and Cultural Anthropology at the University of Warsaw. He holds a PhD in the arts and a habilitation degree in ethnology. His academic interests focus on visual anthropology, urban anthropology, and contemporary anthropology. He is author of *Photography: Between Document and Symbol* (in Polish) and *Film and the Paradoxes of Visuality: Practicing Anthropology* (in Polish), as well as numerous articles. He is author with Karolina Dudek of "Urban Walks: Footsteps, Narratives, and the Storied City," *Narrative Culture* 9, no. 2 (Fall 2022).

Notes

1. "The essence of reality is meaning. That which has no meaning is not real for us. Every fragment of reality lives due to the fact that it partakes of some sort of universal meaning. . . . But knowledge, too, is nothing more than the construction of myths about the world, *since myth resides in its very foundations* and we cannot escape beyond myth. . . . At present we consider the word to be merely a shadow of reality, its reflection. But the reverse would be more accurate: reality is but a shadow of the word." Bruno Schulz, "Mityzacja Rzeczywistości," trans. John M. Bates, last accessed January 2020, http://info-poland.icm.edu.pl/web/arts_culture/literature/fiction/schulz/reality.html. Emphasis mine—S.S. I am using the word *elements*—as it appears in the Polish original—because it is more ambiguous and polysemic than the one used in John Bates's translation (*foundations*).

2. Numerous Polish ethnologists and anthropologists (i.e., Joanna and Ryszard Tomicki, Czesław Robotycki, Stanisław Węglarz, and Ludwik Stomma) quoted this brief essay by Schulz starting from the late 1970s.

3. "In both cases (myth and history) they are stories which are believed to be true both by those who tell the stories and by those who listen to them in their original context. The peculiarity of myth is that it carries moral implication." Edmund Leach, "Masquerade: The Presentation of the Self in Holi–Day Life," *Visual Anthropology Review* 6, no. 2 (September 1990): 4, https://doi.org/10.1525/var.1990.6.2.2.

4. Cf. Józef Burszta, *Wieś i karczma—rola karczmy w życiu wsi pańszczyźnianej* (Warsaw: Ludowa Spółdzielnia Wydawnicza, 1950); and *Społeczeństwo i karczma. Propinacja, karczma i sprawa alkoholizmu w społeczeństwie polskim w XIX wieku* (Warsaw: Ludowa Spółdzielnia Wydawnicza, 1951). Kacper Pobłocki, Introduction to Józef Burszta, *Wieś i karczma—rola karczmy w życiu wsi pańszczyźnianej*, electronic re-edition of selected works of Józef Burszta (Poznań: Instytut im. Oskara Kolberga, 2014). http://cyfrowearchiwum.amu.edu.pl/archive/8644.

5. Kacper Pobłocki, *Chamstwo* (Wołowiec: Wydawnictwo Czarne, 2021).

6. Jan Stanisław Bystroń, *Dzieje obyczajów w dawnej Polsce, wiek XVI–XVIII* (Warsaw: PIW, 1960), 566–67.

7. Burszta, *Wieś i karczma*, 109.

8. Kacper Pobłocki, "Wódka—historia Polaków."

9. Play should not be understood here as amusement and a game but rather as an important cultural phenomenon. Cf. Hans-Georg Gadamer, *Truth and Method*, trans. Joel Weinsheimer and Donald G. Marshall (London: Continuum, 2006).

10. Cf. Eszter B. Gantner and Koby Oppenheim, "Jewish Space Reloaded: An Introduction," *Anthropological Journal of European Cultures* 23, no. 2 (2014): 1–10, https://doi.org/10.3167/ajec.2014.230201.

11. Ruth E. Gruber, "Beyond Virtually Jewish: New Authenticities and Real Imaginary Spaces in Europe," *Jewish Quarterly Review* 99, no. 4 (2009): 491–92.

12. Such restaurants (cafés) also functioned during the communist era—e.g., Menora (Menorah) in Warsaw (Grzybowski Square)—but they had a facade character and were rare. They were rather a top-down planned "obligation" and their reputation was not much different from the communist standard. The Charlotte Menorah restaurant, which now runs on the site, is garnering praise.

13. Gruber, "Beyond Virtually Jewish"; Agata Maksimowska, *Birobidżan. Ziemia, na której mieliśmy być szczęśliwi* (Wołowiec: Czarne, 2019); Shelley I. Salamensky, "'Jewface' and 'Jewfaçade' in Poland, Spain, and Birobidzhan," in *The Routledge Handbook of Contemporary Jewish Cultures*, ed. Nadia Valman and Laurence Roth (London: Routledge, 2015), 213–23; Erica Lehrer, "Jewish Heritage, Pluralism, and *Milieux de Mémoire*: The Case of Kraków's Kazimierz," in *Jewish Space in Contemporary Poland*, ed. Erica Lehrer and Michael Meng (Bloomington: Indiana University Press, 2015). My comments in some places

are close to Lehrer's observations (2015). I use, as she does, the important, though often criticized, notion of *lieux de mémoire* (Nora, see below). Her text, while aspiring to many theoretical findings, relies heavily on excellently selected and analyzed ethnographic micro-examples, taken both from observations and conversations with various actors involved in these changes.

14. Gruber wrote in a later article: "When I coined the phrase 'virtually Jewish' I also clearly wanted to relate the phenomenon to the cyberspace concept of virtual worlds and virtual communities existing today on the Internet. This is another new authenticity or real imaginary space that has developed rapidly in recent years. Second Life, for example, is now 'inhabited' by more than nine million 'residents' and maintains an active economy." Gruber, "Beyond Virtually Jewish," 491. The publisher of the Polish version of *Virtually Jewish* decided to change the title to *Odrodzenie kultury żydowskiej w Europie*, trans. Agnieszka Nowakowska (Sejny: Fundacja Pogranicze, 2004), possibly in connection with language issues; nonetheless, the change appears to possess a certain ideological dimension and decidedly alters the emphasis. The publisher's decision was arbitrary; personal communication with the book's translator Agnieszka Nowakowska (April 19, 2019).

15. Pierre Nora, "Between Memory and History: *Les Lieux de Mémoire*," trans. Marc Roudebush, *Representations* 26 (spring 1989): 8 (the second emphasis is mine—S.S.). Nora's ideas are used also by Lehrer, "Jewish Heritage."

16. Nora, "Between Memory," 12 (the second emphasis is mine—S.S.).

17. Cf. also Reinhard Bernbeck, Kerstin P. Hofmann, and Ulrike Sommer, "Mapping Memory, Space and Conflict," in *Between Memory Sites and Memory Networks: New Archaeological and Historical Perspectives*, ed. Reinhard Bernbeck, Kerstin P. Hofmann, and Ulrike Sommer (Berlin: Edition Topoi, 2017).

18. Nora, "Between Memory," 7.

19. Maurice Halbwachs, *Społeczne ramy pamięci*, trans. Marcin Król (Warsaw: PWN, 1968).

20. Roland Barthes noticed that each of us lives, in a manner of speaking, in a different cosmos: some in the world of the everyday press, others, like Barthes himself, in the world of Marcel Proust. See Roland Barthes, *Pleasure of the Text*, trans. Richard Howard (New York: Hill and Wang, 1975), 36. Cf. also Michael Herzfeld, *Anthropology: Theoretical Practice in Culture and Society* (Oxford: Blackwell, 2001), chapter 9 and footnote 1.

21. To recall the first quote from Gruber's book. Cf. also Izabela Suchojad, *Topografia żydowskiej pamięci: Obraz krakowskiego Kazimierza we współczesnej literaturze polskiej i polsko-żydowskiej* (Kraków: Universitas, 2010); and Monika Murzyn-Kupisz and Jacek Purchla, eds., *Przywracanie pamięci: Rewitalizacja zabytkowych dzielnic żydowskich w miastach Europy Środkowej* (Kraków: Międzynarodowe Centrum Kultury, 2008).

22. Nora's famous notion has received criticism, as well as various "national" implementations and different readings.

23. "According to [Robert] Bellah (1985: p. 154), people who grew up in 'communities of memory' know the stories of a community's past, share its ideal values, and understand what it means to participate in the ritual, aesthetic, and seasonal practices that defined the community as a way of life. However, such imagery can invoke intense nostalgia even among those who did not grow up in such communities through the construction of the parallel 'communities of imagination.'" Millie Creighton, "Anthropology of Nostalgia," in *International Encyclopedia of the Social & Behavioral Sciences*, 2nd ed., vol. 17 (2015), 35, http://dx.doi.org/10.1016/B978-0-08-097086-8.12118-X. Cf. also Michael Pickering and Emily Keightley, "Communities of Memory and the Problem of Transmission," *European Journal of Cultural Studies* 16, no. 1 (February 2013), https://doi.org/10.1177/1367549412457481.

24. "Kazimierz jak żydowski Disneyland? Marek Bartosik pyta, Janusz Makuch odpowiada," *Gazeta Wyborcza*, Kraków supplement, December 15, 2012, last accessed January 23, 2020,

https://gazetakrakowska.pl/kazimierz-jak-zydowski-disneyland-marek-bartosik-pyta-janusz-makuch-odpowiada/ar/720985.

25. Jean-Claude Kaufmann, "Identity and the New Nationalist Pronouncements," *International Review of Social Research* 1, no. 2 (June 2011), cited successively from p. 1, 2, and 3.

26. "The self is seen as a reflexive project, for which the individual is responsible." See Antony Giddens, *Modernity and Self-Identity: Self and Society in the Late Modern Age* (Cambridge: Polity, 1991), 76.

27. Obviously, this appears to be particularly topical in contemporary culture and in so-called postmodernism. One of the transsexual female protagonists in *All About My Mother*, the film directed by Pedro Almodóvar (1999), points to her silicone breast implants, saying, "You are more and more authentic the more you look like someone *you dreamed of being*," cited after Charles Lindholm, "The Rise of Expressive Authenticity," *Anthropological Quarterly* 86, no. 2 (Spring 2013): 371 (emphasis mine—S.S.).

28. Gordan Mathews, *Global Culture/Individual Identity: Searching for Home in the Cultural Supermarket* (London: Routledge, 2000).

29. In this context, it is worth recalling Adam Zucker's film *The Return* (2014) about conversions to Judaism among young gentile Polish women.

30. "I think that heritage is a mode of cultural production that produces something new that has recourse to the past." "The Making of Heritage: Barbara Kirshenblatt-Gimblett Talks to Karolina J. Dudek and Sławomir Sikora," in *Images of Cultural Diversity and Heritage NAFA Film Festival 2015*, ed. Karolina J. Dudek and Sławomir Sikora (Warsaw: Institute of Ethnology and Cultural Anthropology University of Warsaw, 2015), 100 (emphasis mine—S.S.).

31. Sharon Macdonald, "Unsettling Memories: Intervention and Controversy over Difficult Public Heritage," in *Heritage and Identity: Engagement and Demission in the Contemporary World*, ed. Marta Anico and Elsa Peralta (London: Routledge, 2009), 93 (emphasis mine—S.S.).

32. Sharon Macdonald, *Memorylands: Heritage and Identity in Europe Today* (London: Routledge, 2013), 18.

33. Anne-Britt Gran, "Staging Places as Brands: Visiting Illusions, Images and Imaginations," in *Re-Investing Authenticity: Tourism, Place and Emotions*, ed. Britta Timm Knudsen and Anne Marit Waade (Bristol: Channel View, 2010), 22–37.

34. Ruth E. Gruber, *Poza wirtualną żydowskością . . . Próba osiągnięcia równowagi pomiędzy miejscami rzeczywistymi, surrealnymi i naprawdę wyimaginowanymi*, trans. Monika Myszkiewicz, in *Przywracanie pamięci: Rewitalizacja zabytkowych dzielnic żydowskich w miastach Europy Środkowej*, ed. Monika Murzyn-Kupisz and Jacek Purchla (Kraków: Międzynarodowe Centrum Kultury, 2008), 65; Lehrer, "Jewish Heritage," 178.

35. Svetlana Boym, *The Future of Nostalgia* (New York: Basic, 2001), "Introduction."

36. Boym, *Future of Nostalgia*, chap. 5.

37. Silke Arnold-de Simine: "By essentializing . . . past [nostalgia] comes to embody an 'imagined community' (Benedict Anderson) based on an uncritically affirmative self-image." Arnold-de Simine, *Mediating Memory in the Museum: Trauma, Empathy, Nostalgia* (London: Palgrave Macmillan, 2013), 55.

38. Boym, *Future of Nostalgia*, chap. 5 (emphasis mine—S.S.).

39. Claude Lévi-Strauss, "Nowy Jork post- I prefiguratywny," trans. Wincenty Grajewski, in *Spojrzenie z oddali* (Warsaw: PIW, 1993).

40. Pierre Mayol, "Mieszkać," in *Wynaleźć codzienność. 2. Mieszkać, gotować*, by Michel de Certeau, Luce Giard, Pierre Mayol, trans. Katarzyna Thiel-Jańczuk (Kraków: WUJ, 2011).

41. Sharon Zukin, "How Brooklyn Became Cool," in *Naked City: The Death and Life of Authentic Urban Places* (Oxford: Oxford University Press, 2010).

42. Murzyn-Kupisz and Purchla, *Przywracanie pamięci.*

43. Eva Jochnowitz, cited after Lehrer, "Jewish Heritage," 179 and 180.

44. Gruber, "Beyond Virtually Jewish," 493–95.

45. Gruber, "Beyond Virtually Jewish," 493.

46. It is probably worth remembering here both *Imagined Communities: Reflections on the Origin and Spread of Nationalism* by Benedict Anderson (London: Verso, 2006) and *Modern Social Imaginaries* by Charles Taylor (Durham, NC: Duke University Press, 2004). See also the below example of the two approaches to memory described after Frank Ankersmit. Regarding the question of authenticity in the present volume, see Magdalena Zatorska's discussion of heritage and contemporary food-related practices in chap. 10.

47. Of course, the question of authenticity—the original, aura—was discussed much earlier by, among others, Walter Benjamin, "The Work of Art in the Age of Its Technological Reproducibility (Third Version)," in *Selected Writings*, vol. 4, ed. Howard Eiland and Michael W. Jennings, trans. Edmund Jephcott and others (Cambridge, MA: Belknap, 2003), 251–83.

48. Britta Timm Knudsen and Anne Marit Waade, "Performative Authenticity in Tourism and Spatial Experience: Rethinking the Relations between Travel, Place and Emotion," in *Re-Investing Authenticity: Tourism, Place and Emotions*, ed. Britta Timm Knudsen and Anne Marit Waade (Bristol: Channel View, 2010), 1.

49. On the question of authenticity, Kamila Baraniecka-Olszewska wrote: "An instrument appearing from the body of the actor and merged with him makes it possible for him to experience his own immersion in recreated history and History without losing identity and the necessity of transforming into someone else." *Reko-rekonesans: Praktyka autentyczności* (Kęty: Wyd. Marek Derewiecki, 2018), 214.

50. Frank Ankersmit, "Pamiętając Holocaust: żałoba i melancholia," trans. Andrzej Ajschtet et al., in *Narracja, reprezentacja, doświadczenie: Studia z teorii historiografii*, by Frank Ankersmit, ed. Ewa Domańska (Kraków: Universitas, 2004).

51. Hermann Broch, "Kilka uwag o kiczu," in *Kilka uwag o kiczu i inne eseje*, trans. Danuta Borkowska (Warsaw: Czytelnik, 1998).

52. The evidence of camp inmate Jean Améry, pertaining to the trauma of torture, says this unambiguously; as he claims, "*Whoever was tortured, stays tortured.*" Jean Améry, *At the Mind's Limits: Contemplations by a Survivor of Auschwitz and Its Realities*, trans. Sidney Rosenfeld and Stella P. Rosenfeld (Bloomington: Indiana University Press, 1980), 34.

53. Knudsen and Waade, "Performative Authenticity," 13.

54. Michael Meng, *Shattered Spaces: Encountering Jewish Ruins in Postwar Germany and Poland* (Cambridge, MA: Harvard University Press, 2011), 12–13.

55. "Kazimierz jak żydowski Disneyland" (emphasis mine—S.S.).

56. Homi Bhabha, "Interview with Homi Bhabha: The Third Space," in *Identity: Community, Culture, Difference*, ed. Jonathan Rutherford (London: Lawrence & Wishart, 1990), 207–21.

57. In this context, however, it is worth remembering Benjamin's comprehension of the term *translation* to which contemporary researchers, among others Homi Bhabha, refer quite often. It is also relevant to recall here how Bhabha understands the original: "The 'original' is never finished or complete in itself. The 'originary' is always open to translation. . . . What this really means is that cultures are only constituted in relation to that otherness internal to their own symbol-forming activity which makes them decentred structures." "Interview with Homi Bhabha," 210.

58. "The present of the world that appears through the breakdown of temporality, signifies a historical *intermediacy*, familiar to the psychoanalytic concept of *Nachtraglichkeit* (deferred action): 'a transferential function, whereby the past dissolves in the present, so that the future becomes (once again) an open question, instead of being specified by the fixity of the past?' The iterative 'time' of the future as *a becoming 'once again open.'*" Homi Bhabha, *The Location of Culture* (London: Routledge, 1994), 219.

59. Reference to this term was made by Gruber ("Poza wirtualną żydowskością" 65), but it was also discussed by Zukin, who wonders how easy it is to create new authenticity. See Zukin, "How Brooklyn."

60. Diana Pinto, "Epilogue: Jewish Spaces and Their Future," in *Jewish Space in Contemporary Poland*, ed. Erica Lehrer and Michael Meng (Bloomington: Indiana University Press, 2015), 280–86.

61. Bhabha, "Interview with Homi Bhabha," 208 (emphasis mine—S.S.).

BIBLIOGRAPHY

Archives Consulted

Archiwum Artystyczne i Biblioteka Teatru im. Juliusza Słowackiego. Kraków, Poland.

Archiwum Główne Akt Dawnych, Archiwum Skarbu Koronnego. Warsaw, Poland.

Archiwum Narodowe w Krakowie. Kraków, Poland.

Biblioteka i Fototeka Instytutu Muzykologii, Uniwersytet Jagielloński w Krakowie. Kraków, Poland.

Biblioteka Jagiellońska, Uniwersytet Jagielloński w Krakowie. Kraków, Poland.

Biblioteka Narodowa. Warsaw, Poland. Biblioteka Politechniki Wrocławskiej. Wrocław, Poland.

Digital Collections of the National Museum in Warsaw. Warsaw, Poland.

The Israel Museum. Jerusalem, Israel.

Lower Silesian Digital Library. Wrocław, Poland.

Mazowiecka Biblioteka Cyfrowa. Warsaw, Poland.

Muzeum Narodowe w Krakowie, Zbiory Czartoryskich. Kraków, Poland.

Muzeum Narodowe w Warszawie. Warsaw, Poland.

Muzeum Teatralne. Warsaw, Poland.

The National Digital Library Polona. Warsaw, Poland.

Национальный Исторический Архив Беларуси [Natsional'nyĭ Istoricheskiĭ Arkhiv Belarusi]. Minsk, Belarus.

Центральний Державний Історичний Архів України м. Київ [Tsentral'nyĭ Derzhavnyĭ Istorychnyĭ Arkhiv Ukraïny m. Kyïv]. Kyiv, Ukraine.

Центральний Державний Історичний Архів України м. Львів [Tsentral'nyĭ Derzhavnyĭ Istorychnyĭ Arkhiv Ukraïny m. L'viv]. Lviv, Ukraine.

YIVO Institute for Jewish Research. New York, New York.

Primary Sources (including pre–Second World War printed sources in original and later editions; literature, film, and other media)

Aftermath (Pol. *Pokłosie*). Directed by Władysław Pasikowski. Apple Film Productions, 2012.
Aleichem, Sholem. *My First Jewish Novel, Stempenyu*. Translated by Daniel Kennedy. 2016. http://www.yiddishbookcenter.org/language-literature-culture/yiddish-translation/my-first-jewish-novel-stempenyu.
Austeria (Eng. *The Inn*). Directed by Jerzy Kawalerowicz. Zespół Filmowy "Kadr," 1982.
Batowski, Zygmunt. *Wystawa dzieł Jana Piotra Norblina (1745–1830)*. Warsaw: Towarzystwo Zachęty Sztuk Pięknych w Król. Pol., 1910.
Biegeleisen, Henryk. "Pan Tadeusz" Adama Mickiewicza: Studyum estetyczno-literackie. Warsaw: T. Paprocki, 1884.
Brzozowski, Stanisław. *Legenda Młodej Polski. Studya o strukturze duszy kulturalnej*. Lwów: Nakładem Księgarni Polskiej Bernarda Połonieckiego, 1910.
Calori, Wergiliusz. *Pan Twardowski*. Warsaw: Druk i Nakład Drukarni Teatrów Warszawskich "Jan Cotty" 1874.
Czas: dodatek miesięczny. October–December 1857. June 1897.
Der Moment. "A skandal in groysn teater." No. 234. October 13, 1921.
Döblin, Alfred. *Journey to Poland*. Edited by Heinz Graber. Translated by Joachim Neugroschel. London: I. B. Tauris, 1991.
Галант, Илья [Galant, Il'ya]. "Арендовали ли евреи православные церкви на Украине?" [Arendovali li evrei pravoslavnye na Ukraine?] *Еврейская старина* [Evreĭskaya starina], 1909.
Gloger, Zygmunt. *Budownictwo drzewne i wyroby z drzewa w dawnej Polsce*. Vols. 1–2. Warsaw: Wł. Łazarski, 1907–9.
Gołębiowski, Łukasz. *Gry i zabawy różnych stanów w kraju całym* . . . Warsaw: Nakładem autora, 1831.
Grabowski, Michał. *Pamiętniki domowe*. Vol. 1. Warsaw: Nakładem S. Orgelbranda, 1845.
Haur, Jakub Kazimierz. *Oekonomika ziemiańska generalna*. Kraków: Drukarnia Dziedzica Krzysztofa Schedla, 1675.
Hi Tereska (Pol. *Cześć Tereska*). Directed by Robert Gliński. Telewizja Polska, Propaganda Film, 2001.
Izraelita. Vol. 6, 1871. Vol. 10, 1875. Vol. 11, 1876. Vol. 12, 1877.
J. R. "Teatr Wielki." *Robotnik*. May 12, 1921.
Kamiński, Jan Nepomucen. *Zabobon, czyli Krakowiacy i Górale: Zabawka dramatyczna ze śpiewkami w 3 aktach*. Lwów: K. B. Pfaff, 1821.
Kolberg, Oskar. *Lud*, ser. 5, *Krakowskie*, pt. 1. Kraków: Drukarnia Uniwersytetu Jagiellońskiego, 1871.
Kowalski, Franciszek. *Wspomnienia (1819–1823)*. Kijów: Nakładem Idzikowskiego, 1850.
Kraszewski, Józef Ignacy. *Wspomnienia Wołynia, Polesia i Litwy*. Vol. 1. Wilno: Teofil Glucksberg, 1840.
Kurier poranny. Review of *Karczma*. Vol. 44, no. 278. 1921.
Kurjer Warszawski: wydanie poranne. Review of *Karczma*. Vol. 101, no. 283. 1921.
Lerue, Adam. *Album Lubelskie*. Warsaw: Adolf Pecq, 1857.
Löw, Chaim. "Rodowód Jankiela. W stulecie *Pana Tadeusza*." *Muzykalia* 6, *Judaica* 3 (2019). Originally published in *Miesięcznik żydowski*, no. 5 (1934): 385–401. http://demusica.edu.pl/wp-content/uploads/2019/07/low_muzykalia_11_judaica31.pdf.

Maimon, Solomon. *An Autobiography*. Introduction by Michael Shapiro. Translated by J. Clark Murray. Urbana-Chicago: University of Illinois Press, 2001.

Makosińska, Jadwiga. *Etnografja Polski w nauczaniu geografji objaśniona na fryzach ludowych Pillatiego*. Lwów-Warsaw: Książnica-Atlas, 1931.

Marx, Karl. "Economic and Philosophical Manuscripts of 1844." In *Karl Marx-Frederick Engels Collected Works, Volume 3, 1843–1844*. London: Lawrence & Wishart, 1975.

Mickiewicz, Adam. *Pan Tadeusz czyli ostatni zajazd na Litwie*. Edited by Leon Płoszewski. Warsaw: Spółdzielnia Wydawnicza Czytelnik, 1948.

———. *Pan Tadeusz, or, the Last Foray in Lithuania*. Translated by Bill Johnston. Brooklyn: Archipelago, 2018.

Norwid, Cyprian. "Letter to Włodzimierz Cybulski." In *Pisma wszystkie*. Vol. 9, *Letters, 1862–1872*, edited by Wiktor J. Gomulicki. Warsaw: Państwowy Instytut Wydawniczy, 1971.

Peretz, Y. L. "In My Little Corner." *Haynt*, no. 210 (November 1, 1912).

Piątkowski, Henryk. "Norwid o *Panu Tadeuszu*. Trzy listy poety z r. 1866." *Wiadomości Literackie* (1925).

Reymont, Władysław. *Chłopi*. 2 vols. Wrocław: Zakład Narodowy im. Ossolińskich, 1999.

Ruch muzyczny. 1862: 52, 828.

Schulz, Bruno. "Mityzacja Rzeczywistości." Translated by John M. Bates. Last accessed January 2020. http://info-poland.icm.edu.pl/web/arts_culture/literature/fiction/schulz/reality.html.

Шабад, Яков Б. [Shabad, Yakov B.]. "Минская губерния" [Minskaya guberniya]. *Еврейская энциклопедия* [Evreĭskaya ėntsiklediya], ред. Авраам Гаркави, Лев Каценельсон [red. Avraam Garkavi, Lev Katsenel'son]. Vol. 11. С-Петербург [Saint Petersburg]: Брокгауз-Ефрон [Brokgauė-Efron], 1908–13.

Słomka, Jan. *Pamiętnik włościanina: od pańszczyzny do dni dzisiejszych*. Kraków: Krakowska Drukarnia Nakładowa, 1912.

Stryjkowski, Julian. *Austeria*. Warsaw: Czytelnik, 1966.

———. *Bieg do Fragalà*. Warsaw: Czytelnik, 1951.

———. *Echo*. Warsaw: Czytelnik, 1988.

———. *Głosy w ciemności*. Warsaw: Czytelnik, 1956.

———. *The Inn*. Translated by Celina Wieniewska. New York: Harcourt Brace Jovanovich, 1972.

———. *Sen Azrila*. Warsaw: Czytelnik, 1975.

Syrokomla, Władysław. *Wycieczki po Litwie w promieniach od Wilna*. Vol. 2. Wilno: Nakładem A. Assa, 1860.

Szewc, Piotr. *Annihilation*. Translated by Ewa Hryniewicz-Yarbrough. Normal, IL: Dalkey Archive Press, 1993.

———. *Zagłada*. Warsaw: Czytelnik, 1987.

Szymanowski, Wacław. "Ostatni cymbalista warszawski." *Tygodnik Illustrowany* 16, no. 407 (July 13, 1867): 16.

Thomas, William I., and Florian Znaniecki. *The Polish Peasant in Europe and America*. 5 vols. Boston: Richard G. Badger, 1918–20.

Tuwim, Julian. "We the Polish Jews . . ." Translated by Madeline G. Levine. *Polish Review* 17, no. 4 (1972): 82–89.

Ulanowski, Bolesław, ed. *Księgi sądowe wiejskie*, 2 vols. Starodawne prawa polskiego pomniki, XI–XII. Kraków: Nakładem Polskiej Akademii Umiejętności, 1921.

Vautrin, Hubert. *L'observateur en Pologne*. Paris: Giguet et Michaud, 1807.

Wesele w Ojcowie: balet układu P. Maurice Pion. Vilnius: n.p., [c. 1840].

Wischnitzer, Mark, ed. *Zikhronot Rabi Dov mi-Boliḥov (5483–5565)*. Berlin: Kelal, 1922.

Wyspiański, Stanisław. *The Wedding*. Translated by Noel Clark. London: Oberon, 1998.
———. *Wesele*. Kraków: Zakład Narodowy im. Ossolińskich, 1977.
Zbiór krakowiaków z baletów Wesele w Ojcowie *i* Stach i Zośka. Warsaw: Klukowski, [1842].

Secondary Sources

Abramowicz, Hirsz. *Profiles of a Lost World: Memoirs of East European Jewish Life before World War II*. Edited by Dina Abramowicz and Jeffrey Shandler. Translated by Eva Zeitlin Dobkin. Detroit: Wayne State University Press, 1999.
Abrams, M. H. *The Mirror and the Lamp: Romantic Theory and the Critical Tradition*. New York: Oxford University Press, 1971.
Améry, Jean. *At the Mind's Limits: Contemplations by a Survivor of Auschwitz and Its Realities*. Translated by Sidney Rosenfeld and Stella P. Rosenfeld. Bloomington: Indiana University Press, 1980.
Anderson, Benedict. *Imagined Communities: Reflections on the Origin and Spread of Nationalism*. London: Verso, 2006.
Ankersmit, Frank. *Narracja, reprezentacja, doświadczenie. Studia z teorii historiografii*. Edited by Ewa Domańska. Kraków: Universitas, 2004.
Appadurai, Arjun. "Gastro-Politics in Hindu South Asia." *American Ethnologist* 8, no. 3 (August 1981): 494–511.
Arkin, Lisa C., and Marian Smith. "National Dance in the Romantic Ballet." In *Rethinking the Sylph: New Perspectives on the Romantic Ballet*, edited by Lynn Garafola. Hanover and London: Wesleyan University Press, 1997.
Arnold-de Simine, Silke. *Mediating Memory in the Museum: Trauma, Empathy, Nostalgia*. London: Palgrave Macmillan, 2013.
Auerbach, Karen. "Bibliography: Jewish Women in Eastern Europe." In *Polin: Studies in Polish Jewry*. Vol. 18, *Jewish Women in Eastern Europe*, edited by Chaeran Freeze, Paula Hyman, and Antony Polonsky, 273–306. Littman Library of Jewish Civilization, 2005.
Bachelard, Gaston. *The Poetics of Space*. Translated by Maria Jolas. Boston: Beacon, 1994.
Bacon, Gershon. "Woman? Youth? Jew? The Search for Identity of Jewish Young Women in Interwar Poland." In *Gender, Place and Memory in the Modern Jewish Experience: Re-placing Ourselves*, edited by Judith Tydor Baumel and Tova Cohen, 3–28. London: Vallentine Mitchell, 2003.
Banach, Jerzy. *Tematy muzyczne w plastyce polskiej*. Vol. 2. Kraków: Polskie Wydawnictwo Muzyczne, 1960.
Baraniecka-Olszewska, Kamila. *Reko-rekonesans. Praktyka autentyczności*. Kęty: Wyd. Marek Derewiecki, 2018.
Bartal, Israel, and Magdalena Opalski. *Pleasure of the Text*. Translated by Richard Howard. New York: Hill and Wang, 1975.
———. *Poles and Jews: A Failed Brotherhood*. Hanover, NH: University Press of New England, 1992.
Bartana, Yael. *Nightmares* (Pol. *Mary Koszmary*). 2008. Last accessed May 17, 2020. https://artmuseum.pl/en/filmoteka/praca/bartana-yael-mary-koszmary-2.
Barthes, Roland. *Mythologies*. Translated by Annette Lavers. Hill and Wang: New York, 1972.
Bauer, Dominique. "Interior Spaces as Traces in Balzac's *La Comédie Humaine*." *Palgrave Communications* 3, no. 17043 (2017). doi:10.1057/palcomms.2017.43.
Benjamin, Walter. "On the Concept of History." In *Selected Writings, Vol. 4, 1938–1940*, edited by Howard Eiland, Michael W. Jennings, and Smith, Gary, translated by Edmund Jephcott, 389–411. Cambridge, MA: Belknap, 1996.

———. "The Work of Art in the Age of Its Technological Reproducibility (Third Version)." In *Selected Writings, Vol. 4, 1938–1940*, edited by Howard Eiland, Michael W. Jennings, and Smith, Gary, translated by Edmund Jephcott, 251–83. Cambridge, MA: Belknap, 2003.

Beregovski, Moshe. *Old Jewish Folk Music: The Collections and Writings of Moshe Beregovski*. Edited and translated by Mark Slobin. Syracuse, NY: Syracuse University Press, 2000.

Bernbeck, Reinhard, Kerstin P. Hofmann, and Ulrike Sommer. "Mapping Memory, Space and Conflict." In *Between Memory Sites and Memory Networks: New Archaeological and Historical Perspectives*, edited by Reinhard Bernbeck, Kerstin P. Hofmann, and Ulrike Sommer, 9–32. Berlin: Edition Topoi, 2017.

Bhabha, Homi. "Interview with Homi Bhabha: The Third Space." In *Identity: Community, Culture, Difference*, edited by Jonathan Rutherford, 207–21. London: Lawrence & Wishart, 1990.

———. *The Location of Culture*. London: Routledge, 1994.

Biale, David, David Assaf, Benjamin Brown, Uriel Gellman, Samuel C. Heilman, Murray Jay Rosman, Gad Sagiv, and Marcin Wodziński. *Hasidism: A New History*. Princeton, NJ, Princeton University Press, 2018.

"Bibliografia przedmiotowa." Schulz Forum. Last accessed June 15, 2019. https://schulzforum.pl/pl/bibliografia/przedmiotowa.

Boni, Michał. "Przed dniem ostatnim." *Kino*, no. 193, April 1983.

Borkowska, Grażyna. "The Homelessness of the Other: The Homosexual Experience in the Prose of Julian Stryjkowski." In *Framing the Polish Home: Postwar Cultural Constructions of Hearth, Nation, and Self*, edited by Bożena Shallcross, 54–67. Athens: Ohio University Press, 2002.

Boym, Svetlana. *The Future of Nostalgia*. New York: Basic, 2001.

Boy-Żeleński, Tadeusz. "Plotka o *Weselu*." In *Tadeusz Boy-Żeleński, O Wyspiańskim*, edited by Stanisław Witold Balicki. Kraków: Wydawnictwo Literackie, 1973.

———. "Plotka o *Weselu* Wyspiańskiego." In *Ludzie żywi*. Warsaw: Państwowy Instytut Wydawniczy, 1956.

Brandstaetter, Roman. *Ja jestem Żyd z "Wesela."* Poznań: Wydawnictwo Poznańskie, 1972.

Broch, Hermann. *Kilka uwag o kiczu i inne eseje*. Translated by Danuta Borkowska. Warsaw: Czytelnik, 1998.

Burszta, Józef. *Społeczeństwo i karczma. Propinacja, karczma i sprawa alkoholizmu w społeczeństwie polskim w XIX wieku*. Warsaw: Ludowa Spółdzielnia Wydawnicza, 1951.

———. *Wieś i karczma—rola karczmy w życiu wsi pańszczyźnianej*. Warsaw: Ludowa Spółdzielnia Wydawnicza, 1950.

Bystroń, Jan Stanisław. *Dzieje obyczajów w dawnej Polsce, wiek XVI–XVIII*. Warsaw: PIW, 1960.

Cała, Alina. "The Social Consciousness of Young Jews in Interwar Poland." In *Polin: Studies in Polish Jewry*. Vol. 8, *Jews in Independent Poland, 1918–1939*, edited by Antony Polonsky, Ezra Mendelsohn, and Jerzy Tomaszewski, 42–65. Littman Library of Jewish Civilization, 1994.

Carroll, Robert P. *Jeremiah: A Commentary*. Philadelphia: Westminster, 1986.

Chaniecki, Zbigniew. *Organizacje zawodowe muzyków na ziemiach polskich do końca XVIII w*. Kraków: Polskie Wydawnictwo Muzyczne, 1980.

Cichopek-Gajraj, Anna, and Glenn Dynner. "Pogroms in Modern Poland, 1918–20 and 1935–7." In *Pogroms: A Documentary History*, edited by Elissa Bemporad and Eugene Avrutin, 193–218. New York: Oxford University Press, 2021.

Coates, Paul. "Revolutionary Spirits: *The Wedding* of Wajda and Wyspiański." *Literature/Film Quarterly* 20, no. 2 (1992): 127–32.

Comaroff, Jean, and John L. Comaroff. *Ethnicity Inc*. Chicago: University of Chicago Press, 2011.

Creighton, Millie. "Anthropology of Nostalgia." In *International Encyclopedia of the Social & Behavioral Sciences*. 2nd ed. Vol. 17. 2015. http://dx.doi.org/10.1016/B978-0-08-097086-8.12118-X.

Czapliński, Przemysław. "Shifting Sands: History of Polish Prose 1945–2015." In *Being Poland: A New History of Polish Literature and Culture since 1918*, edited by Tamara Trojanowska, Joanna Niżyńska, and Przemysław Czapliński, with the assistance of Agnieszka Polakowska, 373–80. Toronto: University of Toronto Press, 2018.

Dąbrowska, Grażyna W. *Taniec w polskiej tradycji. Leksykon*. Warsaw: Muza S. A., 2006.

Daszyński, Ignacy. *Pamiętniki*. Warsaw: Partia Razem, 2016.

Di Giovine, Michael A., and Ronda L. Brulotte, eds. *Edible Identities: Food as Cultural Heritage*. New York: Routledge, 2014.

Dmochowska, Jadwiga Waydel. *Jeszcze o dawnej Warszawie: Wspomnienia*. Warsaw: Państwowy Instytut Wydawniczy, 1960.

Dondziłło, Czesław. "Austeria." *Trybuna Ludu*, May 5, 1983.

Doniger, Wendy. *The Bedtrick: Tales of Sex and Masquerade*. Chicago: University of Chicago Press, 2000.

Dudek, Karolina J., and Sławomir Sikora, eds. *Images of Cultural Diversity and Heritage NAFA Film Festival 2015*. Warsaw: Institute of Ethnology and Cultural Anthropology University of Warsaw, 2015.

Duker, Abraham G. "The Mystery of the Jews in Mickiewicz's Towianist Lectures on Slavic Literatures." *Polish Review* 7, no. 3 (Spring 1962): 40–66.

Dworak, Tadeusz. "Analiza porównań w *Panu Tadeuszu*." *Pamiętnik Literacki* 38 (1948): 265–97.

Dynner, Glenn. "Those Who Stayed: Women and Jewish Traditionalism in East Central Europe." In *New Directions in the History of the Jews in the Polish Lands*, edited by Antony Polonsky, Hanna Węgrzynek, and Andrzej Żbikowski, 295–312. Boston: Academic Studies Press, 2018.

———. *Yankel's Tavern: Jews, Liquor, & Life in the Kingdom of Poland*. Oxford: Oxford University Press, 2014.

Ellis, Markman. *The Coffee House: A Cultural History*. London: Orion, 2004.

Encyklopedia Teatru Polskiego. "Jan Szer." 2016. Accessed December 30, 2019. http://encyklopediateatru.pl/osoby/70238/jan-szer.

———. "Stanisław Zaborski." 2016. Accessed December 30, 2019. http://encyklopediateatru.pl/osoby/82114/stanislaw-zaborski.

———. "Wesele w Ojcowie." 2016. Accessed December 30, 2019. https://encyklopediateatru.pl/sztuki/8099/wesele-w-ojcowie

Engel, Barbara Alpern. "Gesia Gelfman: A Jewish Woman on the Left in Imperial Russia." In *Jews and Leftist Politics: Judaism, Israel, Antisemitism, and Gender*, edited by Jack Jacobs, 183–99. Cambridge: Cambridge University Press, 2017.

Epstein, Shifra. "Imaging Hasidim in Wood and PVC: Hasidic Figurines Made Today in Poland, Ukraine and Israel." *Zutot* 6 (2009): 129–38.

Evans, Dylan. *An Introductory Dictionary to Lacanian Psychoanalysis*. London: Routledge, 1996.

Fater, Isachar. *Muzyka żydowska w okresie międzywojennym*. Warsaw: Rytm, 1997.

Feldman, Walter Zev. *Klezmer: Music, History, and Memory*. New York: Oxford University Press, 2016.

Fiećko, Jerzy. "Co robi Żyd w narodowej epopei?" In *Pan Tadeusz: Poemat, Postacie, Recepcja*, edited by Andrzej Fabianowski and Ewa Hoffman-Piotrowska. Warsaw: Wydawnictwa Uniwersytetu Warszawskiego, 2017.

Foucault, Michel. "Of Other Spaces: Utopias and Heterotopias." Translated by Jay Miskowiec. *Architecture /Mouvement/ Continuité*, October 1984, 164–71.

Freeze, ChaeRan Y. *Jewish Marriage and Divorce in Imperial Russia*. Hanover, NH: Brandeis University Press, 2001.

Fuks, Marian. *Muzyka ocalona: judaica polskie*. Warsaw: Wydawnictwa Radia i Telewizji, 1989.

Gadamer, Hans-Georg. *Truth and Method*. Translated by Joel Weinsheimer and Donald G. Marshall. London: Continuum, 2006.

Galas, Michał, and Mirosław Skrzypczyk, eds. *Żydzi lelowscy. Obecność i ślady*. Mirosław Skrzypczyk. Kraków: Wydawnictwo Austeria, 2006.

Galewski, Józef, and Ludwik B. Grzeniewski. *Warszawa zapamiętana. Ostatnie lata XIX stulecia*. Warsaw: Państwowy Instytut Wydawniczy, 1961.

Gantner, Eszter B., and Koby Oppenheim. "Jewish Space Reloaded: An Introduction." *Anthropological Journal of European Cultures* 23, no. 2 (2014): 1–10. https://doi.org/10.3167/ajec.2014.230201.

Gawron, Edyta. "Lelowscy Żydzi w XIX i XX wieku." In *Żydzi lelowscy. Obecność i ślady*, edited by Michał Galas and Mirosław Skrzypczyk. Kraków: Wydawnictwo Austeria, 2006.

Giddens, Antony. *Modernity and Self-Identity. Self and Society in the Late Modern Age*. Cambridge: Polity, 1991.

Girard, René. "The Goodness of Mimetic Desire." In *The Girard Reader*, edited by James G. Williams, 62–65. New York: Crossroad, 2000.

———. "Triangular Desire." In *The Girard Reader*, edited by James G. Williams, 33–44. New York: Crossroad, 2000.

Goldberg-Mulkiewicz, Olga. "The Changing Stereotype of the 'Other': The Jewish Figurine on the Polish Market." In *Na szczęście to Żyd. Polskie figurki Żydów / Lucky Jews: Poland's Jewish Figurines*, edited by Erica Lehrer. Kraków: Korporacja Ha!art, 2014.

Goldfarb, David. Introduction to *The Street of Crocodiles and Other Stories*, by Bruno Schulz. Translated by Celina Wieniewska. New York: Penguin, 2008.

Gollance, Sonia. "Dance as a Tool of Pleasure and Humiliation in I. J. Singer's *The Brothers Ashkenazi*." *Prooftexts* 39, no. 3 (2022): 422–53.

———. *It Could Lead to Dancing: Mixed-Sex Dancing and Jewish Modernity*. Stanford, CA: Stanford University Press, 2021.

Gossett, Philip. "Writing the History of Opera." In *The Oxford Handbook of Opera*, edited by Helen M. Greenwald, 1032–46. New York: Oxford University Press, 2014.

Got, Jerzy. *Repertuar teatru w Krakowie 1781–1843*. Warsaw: Instytut Sztuki Polskiej, 1969.

Graczyk, Ewa. "Szczęście *Pana Tadeusza*." In *Balsam i trucizna: 13 tekstów o Mickiewiczu*, edited by Ewa Graczyk and Zbigniew Majchrowski. Gdańsk: Wydawnictwo ATEXT, 1993.

Gran, Anne-Britt. "Staging Places as Brands: Visiting Illusions, Images and Imaginations." In *Re-Investing Authenticity: Tourism, Place and Emotions*, edited by Britta Timm Knudsen and Anne Marit Waade, 22–37. Bristol: Channel View, 2010.

Greenwald, Helen M., ed. *The Oxford Handbook of Opera*. New York: Oxford University Press, 2014.

Gross, Jan Tomasz. *Neighbors: The Destruction of the Jewish Community in Jedwabne, Poland*. New York: Penguin, 2002.

Gruber, Ruth E. "Beyond Virtually Jewish: New Authenticities and Real Imaginary Spaces in Europe." *Jewish Quarterly Review* 99, no. 4 (2009): 487–504.

Guesnet, François, Benjamin Matis, and Antony Polonsky, eds. *Polin: Studies in Polish Jewry*. Vol. 32, *Jews and Music-Making in the Polish Lands*. Library of Jewish Civilization, 2020.

Hagen, William W. *Anti-Jewish Violence in Poland, 1914–1920*. Cambridge: Cambridge University Press, 2018.

Halbwachs, Maurice. *Społeczne ramy pamięci*. Translated by Marcin Król. Warsaw: PWN, 1968.

Harbison, Robert. *The Built, the Unbuilt and the Unbuildable: In Pursuit of Architectural Meaning.* Cambridge, MA: MIT Press, 1992.

Hen, Józef. *Nowolipie Street.* Translated by Krystyna Boron. Bethesda, MD: DL, 2012.

Herbaczyński, Wojciech. *W dawnych cukierniach i kawiarniach warszawskich.* Warsaw: Państwowy Instytut Wydawniczy, 1988.

Hertz, Aleksander. *The Jews in Polish Culture.* Evanston, IL: Northwestern University Press, 1988.

Hertz, Benedykt. *Na taśmie 70-lecia.* Edited by Ludwik B. Grzeniewski. Warsaw: Państwowy Instytut Wydawniczy, 1966.

Herzfeld, Michael. *Anthropology: Theoretical Practice in Culture and Society.* Oxford: Blackwell, 2001.

Holmgren, Beth. "Cabaret Nation: The Jewish Foundations of the Polish-Language Literary Cabaret." In *Polin: Studies in Polish Jewry.* Vol. 31, *Poland and Hungary: Jewish Realities Compared.* Littman Library of Jewish Civilization, 2019.

Horn, Dana. *People Love Dead Jews: Reports from a Haunted Present.* New York: W. W. Norton, 2021.

Horowitz, Brian. "A Jewish Russifier in Despair: Lev Levanda's Polish Question." In *Polin: Studies in Polish Jewry.* Vol. 17, *The Shtetl: Myth and Reality,* edited by Antony Polonsky, 279–98. Littman Library of Jewish Civilization, 2004.

Hyman, Paula. *Gender and Assimilation in Modern Jewish History.* Seattle: University of Washington Press, 1995.

Idelsohn, Abraham Zevi. *Jewish Music in Its Historical Development.* 3rd ed. New York: Schocken, 1975.

Jankowski, Tomasz. "Ludność żydowska Piotrkowa Trybunalskiego, 1808–1870." PhD diss., University of Warsaw, 2014.

Jędrzejek, Stanisław. "O rabinie Jakubie i Świętej Pani z Zagórza." *Wspomnienie o Stanisławie Jędrzejku.* Katowice: Infograf, 2005.

Kalik, Judith. "The Inn as a Focal Point for Jewish Relations with the Catholic Church in the Polish-Lithuanian Commonwealth." In *Jews and Slavs,* vol. 21, edited by Wolf Moskovich and Irena Fijałkowska-Janiak. Jerusalem and Gdańsk, 2008.

———. "An Interaction of the Rural Jews with Different Social Strata in the 16th–18th Centuries Polish-Lithuanian Village." *Jewish History Quarterly* 273 (2020): 49–68.

———. "Jewish Leaseholders (Arendarze) in 18th-Century Crown Poland." *Jahrbücher für Geschichte Osteuropas* 54 (2006): 229–40.

———. *Movable Inn: The Rural Jewish Population of Minsk Guberniya from 1793 to 1914.* Warsaw /Berlin: De Gruyter, 2018.

———. "The Orthodox Church and the Jews in the Polish-Lithuanian Commonwealth." *Jewish History* 17 (2003): 229–37.

Kalish, Ita. *Etmoli.* Israel: Ha-kibbutz ha-meyuhad, 1970.

Kalwat, Wojciech. "Staropolskie karczmy. Brud, paskudne jedzenie, niewygodne posłania . . . i jedne z najważniejszych miejsc w dawnej Rzeczypospolitej." CiekawostkiHistoryczne.pl, last modified February 25, 2023, https://ciekawostkihistoryczne.pl/2023/02/25/staropolskie-karczmy/.

Kaniecki, Przemysław. "Z archiwum KC PZPRR." In *Adaptacje, adaptacje,* edited by Sławomir Bobowski, 203–10. Wrocław: Wydawnictwo Uniwersytetu Wrocławskiego, 2009.

Kaufmann, Jean-Claude. "Identity and the New Nationalist Pronouncements." *International Review of Social Research* 1, no. 2 (June 2011): 1–13.

Kawalerowicz, Jerzy. "Austeria (1982)." In *Więcej niż kino,* edited by Seweryn Kuśmierczyk and Stanisław Zawiśliński. Warsaw: Skorpion, 2001.

"Kazimierz jak żydowski Disneyland? Marek Bartosik pyta, Janusz Makuch odpowiada." *Gazeta Wyborcza*. Kraków supplement. December 15, 2012. Last accessed January 23, 2020. https://gazetakrakowska.pl/kazimierz-jak-zydowski-disneyland-marek-bartosik-pyta-janusz-makuch-odpowiada/ar/720985.

Kedourie, Elie, ed. *The Jewish World: Revelation, Prophecy and History*. London: Thames and Hudson, 1979.

Kępiński, Zdzisław. *Mickiewicz hermetyczny*. Warsaw: Państwowy Instytut Wydawniczy, 1980.

Kirshenblatt-Gimblett, Barbara. "The Kosher Gourmet in the Nineteenth-Century Kitchen: Three Jewish Cookbooks in Historical Perspective." *Journal of Gastronomy* 2, no. 4 (1986–87): 51–87.

Klekot, Ewa. "Samofolkloryzacja. Współczesna sztuka ludowa z perspektywy krytyki postkolonialnej." *Kultura współczesna* 1 (2014).

Klezmer Pioneers: European & American Recordings, 1905–1952. Rounder Records 1089, compact disc, overview. 1993.

Knichowiecki, Bogdan. "Tuż przed chwilą zagłady." *Trybuna Robotnicza*, March 12, 1983.

Knudsen, Britta Timm, and Anne Marit Waade. "Performative Authenticity in Tourism and Spatial Experience: Rethinking the Relations between Travel, Place and Emotion." In *Re-Investing Authenticity: Tourism, Place and Emotions*, edited by Britta Timm Knudsen and Anne Marit Waade, 1–21. Bristol: Channel View, 2010.

Konwicki, Tadeusz. *Dolina Issy*. Directed by Tadeusz Konwicki. 1982.

———. *Jak daleko stąd, jak blisko*. Directed by Tadeusz Konwicki. 1971.

———. *Kronika wypadków miłosnych*. Directed by Andrzej Wajda. 1985.

Kopaliński, Władysław. Słownik mitów i tradycji kultury. 4th ed. Kraków: Państwowy Instytut Wydawniczy, 1993.

Kornacka-Sareło, Katarzyna. "Where Is the World of Ours? Assimilation, Acculturation, and Emancipation Process of the Galician Jews in the Prose by Julian Stryjkowski (Pesach Jakob Stark)." In *Jews in Eastern Europe*, edited by Waldemar Szerbiński and Katarzyna Kornacka-Sareło. Newcastle upon Tyne: Cambridge Scholars, 2016.

Koropeckyj, Roman. *Mickiewicz: The Life of a Romantic*. Ithaca, NY: Cornell University Press, 2008.

Kowalski, Piotr. *Theatrum świata wszystkiego i poćciwy gospodarz: o wizji świata pewnego siedemnastowiecznego pisarza ziemiańskiego*. Kraków: Wydawnictwo Uniwersytetu Jagiellońskiego, 2000.

Kozakiewiczowa, Helena, and Stefan Kozakiewicz. *Renesans w Polsce*. Warsaw: Arkady, 1976.

Kożuszek, Radosław. "Kuczki." *Wiedza i życie*, no. 6 (June 1, 2019).

Kukla, Adam Tomasz. "Kwestia autorstwa muzyki do baletu na przykładzie *Wesela w Ojcowie*." *Muzyka* 64, no. 4 (2019): 37–64.

Kurczewska, Joanna, and Hanna Bojar. *Wyciskanie brukselki. O europeizacji społeczności lokalnych na pograniczach*. Warsaw: IFiS PAN, 2009.

Kurz, Iwona. "'This Picture Is a Bit Horrifying.' The Story of a Film or the Polish Nation Face to Face with the Jew." *Holocaust Studies and Materials* (2010): 422–38.

Lacan, Jacques. *The Psychoses: The Seminar of Jacques Lacan, Book III*. Translated by Russell Grigg. New York: W. W. Norton, 1993.

———. *The Sinthome: The Seminar of Jacques Lacan, Book XXIII*. Translated by A. R. Price. Cambridge: Polity, 2016.

Lang, Berel. *Holocaust Representation: Art within the Limits of History and Ethics*. Baltimore: Johns Hopkins University Press, 2000.

Leach, Edmund. "Masquerade: The Presentation of the Self in Holi-Day Life." *Visual Anthropology Review* 6, no. 2 (September 1990): 2–13. https://doi.org/10.1525/var.1990.6.2.2.

Leder, Andrzej. *Prześniona rewolucja*. Warsaw: Wydawnictwo Krytyki Politycznej, 2013.

Lehmann, Rosa. "Jewish Patrons and Polish Clients: Patronage in a Small Galician Town." In *Polin: Studies in Polish Jewry*. Vol. 17, *The Shtetl: Myth and Reality*, edited by Antony Polonsky, 153–69. Littman Library of Jewish Civilization, 2004.

Lehrer, Erica T. "Jewish Heritage, Pluralism, and *Milieux de Mémoire*: The Case of Kraków's Kazimierz." In *Jewish Space in Contemporary Poland*, edited by Erica Lehrer and Michael Meng, 170–92. Bloomington: Indiana University Press, 2015.

———. *Jewish Poland Revisited: Heritage Tourism in Unquiet Places*. Bloomington: Indiana University Press, 2013.

Lévi-Strauss, Claude. "Nowy Jork post- i prefiguratywny." Translated by Wincenty Grajewski. In *Spojrzenie z oddali*. Warsaw: PIW, 1993.

Lindholm, Charles. "The Rise of Expressive Authenticity." *Anthropological Quarterly* 86, no. 2 (Spring 2013): 361–95.

Lisek, Joanna. "'To Write? What's This Torture For?': Bronia Baum's Manuscripts as a Testimony of the Formation of a Writer, Activist, Journalist." *Jewish History* 33, no. 1/2 (March 2020).

Łupienko, Aleksander. *Kamienice czynszowe Warszawy*. Warsaw: Polska Akademia Nauk, 2015.

———. "Mikroświat kamienicy czynszowej doby zaborów. Funkcjonowanie i życie w warszawskich kamienicach w źródłach z lat 1864–1914." *Journal of Urban Ethnology* 11 (2013): 117–34.

Lyotard, Jean-François. *The Postmodern Condition: A Report on Knowledge*. Translated by Geoff Bennington. Minneapolis: University of Minnesota Press, 1984.

Macdonald, Sharon. *Memorylands: Heritage and Identity in Europe Today*. London: Routledge, 2013.

———. "Unsettling Memories: Intervention and Controversy over Difficult Public Heritage." In *Heritage and Identity: Engagement and Demission in the Contemporary World*, edited by Marta Anico and Elsa Peralta, 93–104. London: Routledge, 2009.

Magnes, Shulamit. "Sins of Youth, Guilt of a Grandmother: M. L. Lilienblum, Pauline Wengeroff, and the Telling of Jewish Modernity in Eastern Europe." In *Polin: Studies in Polish Jewry*. Vol. 18, *Jewish Women in Eastern Europe*, edited by Chaeran Freeze, Paula Hyman, and Antony Polonsky, 87–120. Littman Library of Jewish Civilization, 2005.

Majewski, Jerzy S. *Warszawa nieodbudowana: Muranów i okolice*. Warsaw: Agora, 2012.

Maksimowska, Agata. *Birobidżan. Ziemia, na której mieliśmy być szczęśliwi*. Wołowiec: Czarne, 2019.

Manekin, Rachel. "The *Lost Generation*: Education and Female Conversion in Fin-de-Siècle Cracow." In *Polin: Studies in Polish Jewry*. Vol. 18, *Jewish Women in Eastern Europe*, edited by Chaeran Freeze, Paula Hyman, and Antony Polonsky, 189–219. Littman Library of Jewish Civilization, 2005.

Markiewicz, Henryk. "Perypetie Jankiela." In *W ogrodzie świata: profesorowi Aleksandrowi Fiutowi w siedemdziesiąte urodziny*, edited by Tischner Łukasz and Józef Wróbel. Kraków: Wydawnictwo Uniwersytetu Jagiellońskiego, 2015.

Maroszek, Józef. "Żydzi wiejscy na Podlasiu w XVII i XVIII wieku w świetle przemian struktury rynku wewnętrzego." *Studia Podlaskie* 2 (1986): 56–71.

Mason, Eric. "Cooking the Books: Jewish Cuisine and the Commodification of Difference." In *Edible Ideologies: Representing Food and Meaning*, edited by Kathleen LeBesco and Peter Naccarato, 105–25. Albany: State University of New York Press, 2008.

Mathews, Gordon. *Global Culture/Individual Identity: Searching for Home in the Cultural Supermarket*. London: Routledge, 2000.

Mayol, Pierre. "Mieszkać." In *Wynaleźć codzienność. 2. Mieszkać, gotować*, by Michel de Certeau, Luce Giard, Pierre Mayol, translated by Katarzyna Thiel-Jańczuk. Kraków: WUJ, 2011.

Mazur, Daria. "Paradoks i topika judajska. *Austeria* Jerzego Kawalerowicza." In *Gefilte film. Wątki żydowskie w kinie*, edited by Joanna Preizner. Kraków: Szolem Alejchem, 2008.

Mazurkiewicz, Filip. "Męskość dziewiętnastowieczna—prolegomena." *Teksty Drugie*, no. 2 (2015): 30–52.

McQuillen, Colleen. "Sanctity or Sanctimony in Stanisław Wyspiański's *Akropolis*. On Boundary Oppositions, Subverted Expectations, and Irony." *Sarmatian Review* 29, no. 2 (2009): 1468–75.

Meng, Michael. *Shattered Spaces: Encountering Jewish Ruins in Postwar Germany and Poland*. Cambridge, MA: Harvard University Press, 2011.

Merwin, Ted. "Jew-Face: Non-Jews Playing Jews on the American Stage." *Cultural and Social History* 4, no. 2 (2007): 215–33.

Molisak, Alina. "Figures of Memory: Polish Holocaust Literature of the 'Second Generation.'" In *Imaginary Neighbors: Mediating Polish-Jewish Relations after the Holocaust*, edited by Dorota Głowacka and Joanna Żylinska, 205–22. Lincoln: University of Nebraska Press, 2010.

Moseley, Marcus. *Being for Myself Alone: Origins of Jewish Autobiography*. Stanford, CA: Stanford University Press, 2005.

Moskalówna, Ewa. "Austeria." *Głos Wybrzeża*, February 7, 1983.

Murav, Harriet. *David Bergelson's Strange New World: Untimeliness and Futurity*. Bloomington: Indiana University Press, 2019.

Murzyn-Kupisz, Monika, and Jacek Purchla, eds. *Przywracanie pamięci. Rewitalizacja zabytkowych dzielnic żydowskich w miastach Europy Środkowej*. Kraków: Międzynarodowe Centrum Kultury, 2008.

Nora, Pierre. "Between Memory and History: *Les Lieux de Mémoire*." Translated by Marc Roudebush. *Representations* 26 (Spring 1989): 7–24.

Norberg, Jakob. "No Coffee." *Eurozine*. Last modified August 8, 2007. Last accessed July 6, 2020. https://www.eurozine.com/authors/jakob-norberg/.

Oytsres-Treasures, Klezmer Music 1908–1996. Wergo LC 06356, compact disc, overview. 1999.

Pacewicz, Piotr. "Płonie stodoła." *Gazeta Wyborcza: Duży Format*. Last modified May 22, 2010. Last accessed June 15, 2019. http://wyborcza.pl/1,76842,7899683,Plonie_stodola.html?as=1&startsz=x.

Parkitna, Anna. "Opera in Warsaw, 1765–1830: Operatic Migration, Adaptation, and Reception in the Enlightenment." PhD diss., Stony Brook, 2020.

Parush, Iris. *Reading Jewish Women: Marginality and Modernization in Nineteenth-Century Eastern European Jewish Society*. Waltham, MA: Brandeis University Press, 2004.

Pasieka, Agnieszka. *Hierarchy and Pluralism: Living Religious Difference in Catholic Poland*. New York: Palgrave Macmillan, 2015.

Petrovsky-Shtern, Yohanan. *The Golden Age Shtetl: A New History of Jewish Life in East Europe*. Princeton, NJ: Princeton University Press, 2015.

Pickering, Michael, and Emily Keightley. "Communities of Memory and the Problem of Transmission." *European Journal of Cultural Studies* 16, no. 1 (February 2013): 115–31. https://doi.org/10.1177/1367549412457481.

Piekarski, Ireneusz. *Z ciemności: O twórczości Juliana Stryjkowskiego*. Wrocław: Wydawnictwo Uniwersytetu Wrocławskiego, 2010.

Pinsker, Shachar M. *A Rich Brew: How Cafés Created Modern Jewish Culture*. New York: New York University Press, 2018.

Pinto, Diane. "Epilogue: Jewish Spaces and Their Future." In *Jewish Space in Contemporary Poland,* edited by Erica Lehrer and Michael Meng, 280–86. Bloomington: Indiana University Press, 2015.

———. "A New Jewish Identity for Post-1989 Europe." *Institute for Jewish Policy Research,* no. 1 (June 1996). Accessed September 1, 2021. https://www.jpr.org.uk/reports/new-jewish-identity-post-1989-europe.

Piwińska, Marta. "Staropolska 'nauka budownicza' w *Panu Tadeuszu.*" *Rocznik Towarzystwa Literackiego imienia Adama Mickiewicza* 25 (1990): 109–22.

Pizem-Karczag, Ida. "The 'Jewish' Trilogy of Julian Stryjkowski." *Polish Review* 28, no. 4 (1983): 89–97.

Plach, Eva. "'Botticelli Woman': Rachel Singer and the Jewish Theme in Stanisław Wyspiański's *The Wedding.*" *Polish Review* 41, no. 3 (1996): 309–27.

Pobłocki, Kacper. *Chamstwo.* Wołowiec: Wydawnictwo Czarne, 2021.

———. "Wódka—historia Polaków." Introduction to Józef Burszta, *Wieś i karczma—rola karczmy w życiu wsi pańszczyźnianej,* electronic re-edition of selected works of Józef Burszta. Poznań: Instytut im. Oskara Kolberga 2014. http://cyfrowearchiwum.amu.edu.pl/archive/8644.

Prussak, Maria. "Demonstracje żydowskich studentów (1903)." In *Teatr żydowski w Polsce,* edited by Anna Kuligowska-Korzeniewska and Małgorzata Leyko, 98–105. Łódź: Wydawnictwo Uniwersytetu Łódzkiego, 1998.

Pudelek, Janina, and Jadwiga Kosicka. "The Warsaw Ballet under the Directorships of Maurice Pion and Filippo Taglioni, 1832–1853." *Dance Chronicle* 11, no. 2 (1988): 219–73.

Rakovsky, Puah. *My Life as a Radical Jewish Woman.* Edited by Paula E. Hyman. Translated by Barbara Harshav with Paula E. Hyman. Bloomington: Indiana University Press, 2002.

Roden, Claudia. *The Book of Jewish Food: An Odyssey from Samarkand to New York with More Than 800 Ashkenazi and Sephardi Recipes.* New York: Alfred A. Knopf, 2013.

Roderick, Noah. *The Being of Analogy.* London: Open Humanities, 2015.

Rodziewicz, Joanna. "Rola karczmy w życiu dawnej wsi polskiej." *Rolniczy Magazyn Elektroniczny* 54 (2019). Accessed January 12, 2025. https://rme.cbr.net.pl/index.php/archiwum-rme/377-marzec-kwiecie-nr-54/kultura-i-tradycje-ludowe40-7681/339-rola-karczmy-w-yciu-dawnej-wsi-polskiejRadziewicz.

Rosenthal, Harold. "Labia, Maria." In *Grove Music Online,* edited by Deane Root. January 20, 2001. Accessed December 30, 2019. https://doi.org/10.1093/gmo/9781561592630.article.15755.

Rosman, Murray Jay. *Lords' Jews: Magnate-Jewish Relations in the Polish-Lithuanian Commonwealth during the Eighteenth Century.* Cambridge, MA: Harvard University Press, 1990.

Rossen, Rebecca. "Dancing Jews and Jewesses: Jewishness, Ethnicity, and Exoticism in American Dance." In *The Oxford Handbook of Dance and Ethnicity,* edited by Anthony Shay and Barbara Sellers-Young, 66–90. New York and London: Oxford University Press, 2016.

Salamensky, Shelley I. "'Jewface' and 'Jewfaçade' in Poland, Spain, and Birobidzhan." In *The Routledge Handbook of Contemporary Jewish Cultures,* edited by Nadia Valman and Laurence Roth, 213–23. London: Routledge, 2015.

Sapoznik, Henry. *The Compleat Klezmer.* New York: Tara, 1988.

———. *Klezmer! Jewish Music from Old World to Our World.* Yazoo CD 7017, compact disc, overview. 2000.

———. "Overview." In *Klezmer Music 1910–1942.* Folkways Records. FW34021, FSS 3402. 1981, 5, compact disc.

Schainker, Ellie R. *Confessions of the Shtetl: Converts from Judaism in Imperial Russia, 1817–1906.* Stanford, CA: Stanford University Press, 2017.

Scharfstein, Tzvi. "Mehayei aheinu be- Galiẓiyah: Hinukh habanot." *Ha'olam*. September 29, 1910.
Seidman, Naomi. *The Marriage Plot: Or, How Jews Fell in Love with Love, and with Literature*. Stanford, CA: Stanford University Press, 2016.
———. *Sarah Schenirer and the Bais Yaakov Movement: A Revolution in the Name of Tradition*. Liverpool: Liverpool University Press, 2019.
Сергачев, Сергей. [Sergachev, Sergeĭ]. "Архитектура корчмы в Белоруссии" [Arkhitektura korchmy v Belorussii]. *Архитектурное наследство* [Arkhitekturnoye nasledstvo] 3 (1985): 148–56.
Shallcross, Bożena. "'The Wondrous Fire': Adam Mickiewicz's *Pan Tadeusz* and the Romantic Improvisation." *East European Politics and Societies* 9, no. 3 (1995): 523–33.
Shandler, Jeffrey, ed. "Esther." In *Awakening Lives: Autobiographies of Jewish Youth in Poland before the Holocaust*. New Haven, CT: Yale University Press, 2002.
Sheppard, W. Anthony. *Extreme Exoticism: Japan in the American Musical Imagination*. New York: Oxford University Press, 2019.
Shmeruk, Chone. "*Mayufes*: A Window on Polish-Jewish Relation." In *Polin: Studies in Polish Jewry*. Volume 10: *Jews in Early Modern Poland*, edited by Gershon David Hundert, 273–86. Littman Library of Jewish Civilization. Liverpool: Liverpool University Press, 1997.
Singer, Bernard. *Moje Nalewki*. Edited by Eugeniusz Szrojt. Warsaw: Czytelnik, 1959.
Singer, Isaac Bashevis. *A Day of Pleasure: Stories of a Boy Growing Up in Warsaw*, with photos by Roman Vishniac. New York: Farrar, Straus and Giroux, 1969.
———. "The Suicide." In *In My Father's Court*, 74–80. New York: Farrar, Straus and Giroux, 1966.
Skrzypczyk, Mirosław. "Der kfices ha-derech—pielgrzymki chasydów do Lelowa." In *Wieża Dawida. Chasydzi lelowscy*, edited by Michał Galas and Mirosław Skrzypczyk. Kraków: Syrakuzy: Wydawnictwo Austeria, 2018.
Slezkine, Yuri. *The Jewish Century*. Princeton, NJ: Princeton University Press, 2004.
Słonimski, Antoni. *Wspomnienia warszawskie*. Warsaw: Czytelnik, 1957.
Smith, Ayana O. *Inclusive Music Histories: Leading Change through Research and Pedagogy*. New York: Routledge, 2023.
Sobański, Oskar. "Karczma na polskich rozstajach." *Film*, no. 22 (1983).
Sokolov, Raymond. "A Simmering Sabbath Day Stew: The Worldwide Diaspora of a Culinary Concept." *Natural History* 97 (1988): 88–91.
Sokolow, Florian. *Avi, Nahum Sokolov*. Jerusalem: Hasefriyah haẓiyonit, 1970.
Solski, Ludwik. *Wspomnienia 1855–1893*. Kraków: Wydawnictwo Literackie, 1955.
Sowa, Jan. *Fantomowe ciało króla. Peryferyjne zmagania z nowoczesną formą*. Kraków: Universitas, 2011.
———. "Spectres of Sarmatism." In *Being Poland: A New History of Polish Literature and Culture since 1918*, edited by Tamara Trojanowska, Joanna Niżyńska, and Przemysław Czapliński, with the assistance of Agnieszka Polakowska, 30–47. Toronto: University of Toronto Press, 2018.
Śrutowski, Tomasz. "Pech Żyda Taga." *Gazeta Olsztyńska*, August 21, 1983.
Stampfer, Shaul. "Gender Differentiation and the Education of the Jewish Woman in Nineteenth-Century Eastern Europe." *Polin: Studies in Polish Jewry*. Vol. 7, *Jewish Life in Nazi-Occupied Warsaw*, edited by Antony Polonsky, 53–85. Littman Library of Jewish Civilization, 1992.
Stein, Louise K. "How Opera Travelled." In *The Oxford Handbook of Opera*, edited by Helen M. Greenwald, 843–61. New York: Oxford University Press, 2014.

Steinlauf, Michael. "Polish-Jewish Theater: The Case of Mark Arnshteyn, a Study of the Interplay among Yiddish, Polish and Polish-Language Jewish Culture in the Modern Period." PhD diss., Brandeis University, 1988.
Stola, Dariusz. "Jewish Emigration from Communist Poland: The Decline of Polish Jewry in the Aftermath of the Holocaust." *East European Jewish Affairs* 47, nos. 2–3 (2017): 169–88.
Suchojad, Izabela. *Topografia żydowskiej pamięci. Obraz krakowskiego Kazimierza we współczesnej literaturze polskiej i polsko-żydowskiej.* Kraków: Universitas, 2010.
Swack, Jeanne. "Anti-Semitism at the Opera: The Portrayal of Jews in the Singspiels of Reinhard Keiser." *Musical Quarterly* 84 (2000): 389–416.
Sztyma, Tamara, and Magdalena Prokopowicz, eds. *Szafa grająca! Żydowskie stulecie na szelaku i winylu.* Warsaw: POLIN Museum of the History of Polish Jews, 2017.
Taylor, Charles. *Modern Social Imaginaries.* Durham, NC: Duke University Press, 2004.
Teller, Adam. "Ḥakhira kelalit veḥokher kelali be'aḥuzot beit Radziwiłł bame'a ha-18." In *Yazamut yehudit be'et haḥadashah. Mizraḥ Eiropa ve'ereẓ Yisra'el,* edited by Ran Aaronsohn and Shaul Stampfer, 48–78. Jerusalem: Magnes, 2000.
Termer, Janusz. "Glosy do *Austerii* Kawalerowicza." *Film,* no. 21 (1983).
T. G. "Austeria." *Nowiny,* April 26, 1983.
Thompson, Ewa. "Sarmatism, or the Secrets of Polish Essentialism." In *Being Poland: A New History of Polish Literature and Culture since 1918,* edited by Tamara Trojanowska, Joanna Niżyńska, and Przemysław Czapliński, with the assistance of Agnieszka Polakowska, 3–29. Toronto: University of Toronto Press, 2018.
Tokarska-Bakir, Joanna. "Żyd z pieniążkiem." In *PL: Tożsamość wyobrażona,* edited by Joanna Tokarska-Bakir, 8–31. Warsaw: Wydawnictwo Czarna Owca, 2013.
Tomaszewska, Grażyna B. "*Pan Tadeusz* a pochwała niedoskonałości." In *Pan Tadeusz: Poemat, Postacie, Recepcja,* edited by Andrzej Fabianowski and Ewa Hoffman-Piotrowska. Warsaw: Wydawnictwa Uniwersytetu Warszawskiego, 2017.
Tomaszewski, Wojciech. Kronika życia muzycznego na prowincji Królestwa Polskiego w latach 1815–1862. Warsaw: Biblioteka Narodowa, 2007.
Topolski, Jerzy. "Uwagi o strukturze gospodarsko-społecznej Wielkopolski, czyli dlaczego na jej terenie nie było żydowskich karczmarzy." In *Żydzi w Wielkopolsce na przestrzeni dziejów,* edited by Jerzy Topolski and KrzysztofModelski. Poznań: Wydawnictwo Poznańskie, 1995.
Turska, Irena. *Przewodnik Baletowy.* Kraków: PWM, 1997.
Twardowska, Emilia. "Rzecz o kuczkach." *Miastol.* Last modified October 11, 2015. Last accessed July 6, 2020. http://miastol.pl/rzecz-o-kuczkach/.
Ury, Scott. *Barricades and Banners: The Revolution of 1905 and the Transformation of Warsaw Jewry.* Stanford, CA: Stanford University Press, 2012.
Veselská, Dana. "Svatební obřady aškenázských Židů – historie a současnost." *Folia Ethnographica* 40, Supplementum ad Acta Musei Moraviae (2006).
Vogel, Beniamin. *Der Einfluss des professionellen auf den nicht professionellen Instrumentenbau in Polen.* In *Studia instrumentorum musicae popularis* VI. Stockholm: Musikhistoriska museet, 1979.
———. "Klezmerzy Księstwa Warszawskiego." *Studia Musicologica Stetinensis* 2 (2010).
———. "'Na wierzbach zawiesiliśmy nasze . . . skrzypce.' Rzecz o dawnych instrumentach, macewach, synagogach i klezmerach." *Muzyka* 52, no. 2 (2007).
———. "'There on the Willows We Hung Our' . . . Violins: On Old Macewas, Synagogues and Klezmorim." *Muzykalia* 7/*Judaica* 2 (2009). http://demusica.edu.pl/wp-content/uploads/2019/07/vogel_muzykalia_7_judaica22.pdf.

Walczyk, Anna. "Pamięć i upamiętnienie Żydów w Lelowie." In *Żydzi lelowscy. Obecność i ślady*, edited by Michał Galas and Mirosław Skrzypczyk. Kraków: Wydawnictwo Austeria, 2006.

Walden, Joshua S. "The 'Yidishe Paganini': Sholem Aleichem's Stempenyu, the Music of Yiddish Theatre and the Character of the Shtetl Fiddler." *Journal of the Royal Musical Association* 139, no. 1 (2014): 89–139.

Watt, Ian. *The Rise of the Novel: Studies in Defoe, Richardson and Fielding*. London: Chatto and Windus, 1957.

Werb, Bret. "Majufes: A Vestige of Jewish Traditional Song in Polish Popular Entertainments." *Polish Music Journal* 6, no. 1 (2003). https://polishmusic.usc.edu/research/publications/polish-music-journal/vol6no1/majufes/

———. "Musical Afterthoughts on Shmeruk's 'Mayufes.'" In *Polin: Studies in Polish Jewry, Volume 32: Jews and Music-Making in the Polish Lands*, edited by François Guesnet, Benjamin Matis, and Antony Polonsky, 63–82. Littman Library of Jewish Civilization. Liverpool: Liverpool University Press, 2020.

WIK. "Karczma i austeria." *Tak i Nie*, no. 23, September 1983.

Witkowska, Matylda. "Historia i obyczaje: Wiszące szałasy Łodzi." *Dziennik Łódzki*. Last modified October 2, 2007. Last accessed July 6, 2020. https://dzienniklodzki.pl/historia-i-obyczaje-wiszace-szalasy-lodzi/ar/168844.

Włodarczyk, Wojciech. "Powiślańscy Żydzi w dawnych wiekach." *Powiśle Lubelskie* 56, no. 6 (2013): 2–6. https://rtpwilkow.files.wordpress.com/2013/11/pow-lub-6-2013.pdf.

Wodziński, Marcin. *Historical Atlas of Hasidism*. Princeton, NJ: Princeton University Press, 2018.

Wolff, Larry. "Dynastic Conservatism and Poetic Violence in Fin-de-Siècle Cracow: The Habsburg Matrix of Polish Modernism." *American Historical Review* 106, no. 3 (June 2001): 735–64.

Zarubin, Przemysław. "Żydzi lelowscy w dobie staropolskiej." In *Żydzi lelowscy. Obecność i ślady*, edited by Michał Galas and Mirosław Skrzypczyk. Kraków: Wydawnictwo Austeria, 2006.

Zatorska, Magdalena. "Ciulim, czulent i konstruowanie polsko-żydowskiego dziedzictwa w Lelowie." In *Lelów: Miejsce, doświadczenie, pamięć*, edited by Mirosław Skrzypczyk. Lelów: Gmina Lelów and Lelowskie Stowarzyszenie Historyczno-Kulturalne im. Walentego Zwierkowskiego, 2016.

———. "Ciulim lelowski jako lokalne dziedzictwo jedzeniowe." In *Lelowianie, Polacy, Żydzi. Szkice etnograficzne o konstruowaniu lokalnego dziedzictwa*, edited by Magdalena Zatorska. Warsaw: Wydawnictwa Uniwersytetu Warszawskiego, 2018.

———. "Wstęp." In *Lelowianie, Polacy, Żydzi. Szkice etnograficzne o konstruowaniu lokalnego dziedzictwa*, edited by Magdalena Zatorska. Warsaw: Wydawnictwa Uniwersytetu Warszawskiego, 2018.

Zieniewicz, Andrzej. "The Already-Non-Existence as a Category of Autobiographical Memory: Galician Places of Timelessness in the Prose of Bruno Schulz, Artur Sandauer, and Julian Stryjkowski." In *Galician Polyphony: Places and Voices*, edited by Alina Molisak and Jagoda Wierzejska, 81–91. Warsaw: Dom Wydawniczy ELIPSA, 2015.

Zubrzycki, Geneviève. "Nationalism, 'Philosemitism,' and Symbolic Boundary-Making in Contemporary Poland." *Comparative Studies in Society and History* 58, no. 1 (January 2016): 66–98.

———. *Resurrecting the Jew: Nationalism, Philosemitism, and Poland's Jewish Revival*. Princeton, NJ: Princeton University Press, 2022.

Zukin, Sharon. *Naked City: The Death and Life of Authentic Urban Places*. Oxford: Oxford University Press, 2010.

INDEX

Figures and tables are indicated by page numbers in italics. All locations are in Poland unless otherwise indicated.

For Indiana University Press
Tony Brewer, Artist and Book Designer
Dan Crissman, Editorial Director and Acquisitions Editor
Gary Dunham, Director and Acquisitions Editor
Anna Francis, Assistant Acquisitions Editor
Anna Garnai, Editorial Assistant
Katie Huggins, Production Manager
Dave Hulsey, Marketing Director
Nancy Lightfoot, Project Manager/Editor
Alyssa Nicole Lucas, Marketing and Publicity Manager
Dan Pyle, Online Publishing Manager
Michael Regoli, Director of Publishing Operations
Leyla Salamova, Senior Artist and Book Designer